A
BEEKEEPER'S
PROGRESS

John Phipps

First published by Merlin Unwin Books, 2013
Text © John Phipps 2013

Merlin Unwin Books Limited
Palmers' House, 7 Corve Street,
Ludlow, Shropshire, SY8 1DB

www.merlinunwin.co.uk

The right of John Phipps to be identified as
author of this work has been asserted by him in accordance with the
Copyright, Designs and Patents Act 1988.

A CIP record of this book is available from the British Library.

Designed by Merlin Unwin

Printed and bound by Jellyfish Print Solutions

ISBN 978-1-906122-56-0

A
BEEKEEPER'S
PROGRESS

John Phipps

MERLIN UNWIN BOOKS

Therefore it is necessary, in order to manage bees, whether on the old principles or the new, that one should know how to stay 'the beginning of strife', to subdue them to his will, and to bring them completely under control. Firmness, without aggression; gentleness, without fear; and a knowledge of their habits, tastes and fancies, are all required to constitute a master of bees. With such qualifications one can do with them as one pleases; can revolutionise their kingdom; depose their queen; regulate their enterprise; intercept their swarms; order the manner of their industry; deprive them of their stores; and, without provoking their anger, turn them again to peaceful labour. It is not a charm that may be worked by a privileged few. It is the application of knowledge to which all may attain readily.'

From *A Manual of Modern Beekeeping – Irish Bee Guide*, Revd Digges, first published in 1904.

> *Honey spread on brown, brown bread*
> *Nothing else I'll have instead*
> *Supper comes at nine*
> *I will have for mine*
> *Honey spread on brown, brown bread.*
>
> *When I'm led away to bed*
> *Beneath my counterpane of red*
> *I shall dream of bees and of yellow seas*
> *Honey spread on brown, brown bread*

– a song I was taught at my junior school from the radio programme *Time and Tune* and sung by me as a lullaby to our children.

Contents

The Beekeeper's Year

MONTH	TASKS	FORAGE
Sep	Treat colonies with two applications of Apiguard for varroa control. Feed colonies strong syrup solution. Ensure colony has fertile queen.	
Oct	Continue feeding. Ensure hives are weather-proof and in sheltered position. Fit mouseguards and plastic skirts around hives in woodpecker districts.	Ivy
Nov Dec Jan	Check apiaries for storm damage, vandalism or theft. Heft hives to assess the amount of stores. Feed blocks of candy if the colonies feel light. Check mouseguard isn't blocked by dead bees. Clear snow from roof. If sun is bright slope boards in front of the hive to deter bees from flying as they will fall in the snow and perish. Tidy apiary. Melt solid combs of oil seed rape honey. Make candles, wax polish, etc.	Snowdrops
Feb	On mild days bees should be flying – check that pollen is being carried into the hive as this is a good sign that the queen is present and laying. At end of month start feeding small amounts of syrup regularly to stimulate growth.	Heliotrope Winter aconite Crocus Willows
Mar	Provide bees with water – but not too close to the hive – replenish until the end of summer. Check food supply and feed syrup if needed. Many bees die of starvation at this time of year. Prepare equipment for new season. Review last season's record cards. Survey area for crops being grown.	Mahonia j. Daphne Fl. currant Hazel Celandine
Apr	First brief examinations can be made if temperature is over 15°C, to see all is OK. Rape will soon be flowering in fields nearby; add supers well in advance. Inform farmers of colony locations and request timing of spraying.	Oil seed rape Dandelion Soft fruit Blackthorn
May	Swarming from now until July. Start 9-day inspections for queen cells. Fit Snelgrove boards to colonies which show signs of swarming. Have equipment for collecting swarms ready— skep, sack, secateurs, small saw. Start extracting oil seed rape honey. Have bait hives in place (completely dark, narrow entrance and at least 3-4 metres above ground).	Top fruit Sycamore Deadnettles Horse chestnuts Holly Field beans
Jun	Make nucleus colonies from queens reared above the Snelgrove board and move to a new site. Give collected swarms and the nucleus colonies frames with new sheets of wax foundation and feed with syrup. Finish extracting rape honey. Store, or leave on hives combs with solid honey.	Hawthorn Wild clover Dog rose
Jul	If colonies are to be moved to the heather, unite a nucleus colony (nuc) to a colony with an old queen. Put out wasp traps.	Lime Blackberry
Aug	Move colonies to the heather by the middle of the month with plenty of food in the brood box. Fit supers with thin sheets of wax so that comb honey can be produced. All colonies (apart from those going to the heather) should have any surplus honey harvested by now. Unite colonies if no increase is desired or to fortify a colony with a new queen. Spray with Certan combs which are emptied of honey to prevent wax moth damage and store with a queen excluder at top and bottom of the stacks to prevent mice and rats getting at the combs.	Willowherb Water balsam Buddleia globosa

Introduction

It's a quiet time. The crickets have finished their night-time chirping and the cicadas will not begin their monotonous chorus until the sun rises over the ridges of the Taygetos Mountains, high above my garden apiary. Already though, the foraging bees are zipping in and out of their hives, making the most of the nectar flow from the compact bushes of rose-pink thyme which adorn the mountainsides and carpet the upland plateau. On the hive walls bees too young to leave their home are fanning their wings, the draught helping to remove the excess moisture from the nectar already stored in the honeycombs, the perfume of the thyme honey wafting through the warm air. Other bees, just three weeks old, their lives already half over, are tentatively leaving their nest for the first time. After polishing their antennae, the bees rise from the hive and fly in tight circles, spiralling upwards and, in excitement as their confidence grows, the circles continuously increase until they have fixed in their minds the location of their home.

It is over forty years since I first watched the dawning of a colony's new day and even now it gives me the same thrill as when I established the first hive in my Bedfordshire garden all that time ago.

Over the ensuing four decades my life has been dominated by these fascinating insects, and the pleasure that they have given me is immeasurable. Each time a hive is opened there is always the chance of learning something new so, year by year, experience and knowledge are gained through handling the bees themselves and observing their behaviour.

I have had the good fortune to meet like-minded beekeepers from many diverse backgrounds and in different countries – several of whom have been excellent mentors – without whose help and encouragement my beekeeping would have been a less rich experience. In turn, I have used my experience to introduce many people to the craft, including students from abroad, and it has given me immense pleasure to learn of their subsequent success in this rural activity.

However, the bees themselves, the weather and the state of the environment are all variables with which they have to contend, so it is nature itself which ultimately becomes the best teacher.

The demise of millions of colonies of bees over the last decade brought about by pests, diseases, agrochemicals, pollution and loss of native flora, has resulted in a groundswell of interest in beekeeping, for people are anxious to do all that they can to help repopulate the country with these valuable pollinating insects. The membership of beekeeping associations has doubled and many would-be beekeepers are sensibly on the waiting lists for courses, before they obtain their own colonies.

To those starting out on the road to beekeeping I would emphasise that they must have a true love of nature, a responsible and humane approach to husbandry and be of an optimistic disposition. I hope that those joining the craft will come into contact with those who work in the countryside, as I have done; farmers, foresters, conservationists and gamekeepers, and in doing so will gain a good understanding of the bees' role both in agriculture and the environment.

John Phipps
July 2013

Acknowledgements

I am indebted to a large number of people who have contributed to my progress in beekeeping: Beowulf Cooper, of all beekeepers he changed my way of thinking about bees; Jeremy and Ruth Burbidge who had confidence in me to produce beekeeping journals of world standing (which have served as an excellent aide-memoire for some of the material in this book); and, subsequently, of course, to the many contributors to the *Beekeepers' Quarterly* who have for many years informed us of beekeeping developments in their own countries and inspired us with new ideas and innovations. Furthermore, many of these writers have welcomed us into their homes and apiaries so we could experience for ourselves how beekeeping is an important adjunct to their lives.

All photographs are by the author, reproduced where necessary by kind permission of Northern Bee Books - publishers of *The Beekeepers' Annual* and *Beekeepers' Quarterly* (www.beekeepers.peacockmagazines. com) except for the Smith Hives on page 17 which was provided by the Robson family.

CHAPTER ONE

Starting Out

IN the small lecture room the scent of freshly-cut cedar and pine and warm beeswax drifted from the adjoining workshops. Accompanied by the drone and buzz of the planes and saws, the factory manager welcomed us to the year's first course and briefly outlined our programme for the next three days. There were about a dozen of us, all wishing to learn about bees and beekeeping, at one of England's oldest and most well-respected beekeeping firms, E. H. Taylor, of Welwyn, Hertfordshire which was established in 1880. Conveniently located adjacent to the main LNER railway line, Taylor's had been able to despatch its hives and live bees both quickly and safely to their destinations for nearly a century. Travellers on the Great North Road to London would have seen the company's hives, immaculate, white painted, telescopic and double-walled, carefully spaced in neat rows on a gently sloping hillside.

Why was I here and what had attracted me to beekeeping? I had no knowledge of the craft and none of my family had been beekeepers. The only scenes I recall to do with bees are the presence of two white hives with gable roofs under an almond tree in our grammar school quadrangle and the brief glimpse of senior boys filling squat jars with a golden stream of honey from a tank in the chemistry preparation room, accompanied by the rich heavy smell of beeswax. Whilst the chance discovery of honey bottling was enough to make me plead with my parents for 3/6d to buy a jar of school honey, further interest in bees wasn't aroused for many years – and even then it was just by chance.

It happened in the small market town of Biggleswade, in Bedfordshire. I was three years out of Culham College where I had qualified as a teacher of Rural Studies and Divinity. My first teaching post was at Potton County Primary school just a few miles from the Biggleswade home where I lived with Val, my wife. In the town's market place was one of those old ironmonger's stores, the sort that had a long wooden, well-worn counter, inlaid in various places with brass, the kind of shop that sold everything you would need as a householder, gardener or farmer, with screws, nails, seeds and animal feed all sold loose, by weight. As always there were the delicious country scents of creosote, tarred rope and musty hessian sacking.

Old Mr Fisher the proprietor was, as usual, in his grey warehouse coat standing behind the counter. He was unwrapping fresh, bright yellow sheets of beeswax embossed with hexagonal cells, the aroma of which drowned the usual shop scents, and was weighing them out on the cast-iron scales for a customer. There was a small stack of beekeeping catalogues on the counter from one of which Mr Fisher sought the price of the wax. When the customer had left, I asked him if I could have a copy and, of course, he was happy to oblige.

I perused the catalogue all weekend, and back in school the following Monday I found amongst the school library books Alexander Dean's *The Beekeeper's Encyclopaedia*, a book which didn't seem to have been opened since the date of its publication in 1949. Its contents fascinated me and, with the catalogue by my side, I began to consider which items I would need to buy and how much it would cost to start up in the craft. This wasn't easy as many types of hives were described, as well as the frames to put inside them and several expensive pieces of equipment for harvesting honey.

There was also the price of the bees to be considered. My salary wasn't enough to give me much spare money, especially since our first child was expected in the following spring, the time I wanted to begin with bees.

However, good fortune arrived in two unexpected ways. First of all, a parent of one of the schoolboys, Jim Parker, had a smallholding on which he grew crops of lettuce, tomatoes, peppers and celery, the majority of them under glass or in polythene tunnels. Jim and I became good friends and I sometimes helped him out. Jim offered me some old beehives and a honey extractor which had been left behind by a previous tenant. 'Clean them up and they're yours until you can afford to replace them,' he said.

My next piece of luck was equally unexpected. In the beekeeping catalogue was a brochure advertising two three-day courses at Taylor's factory in Welwyn. I would have loved to have been able to attend one of them, but sadly they were both mid-week and in term time.

The head of the school at which I taught, Mr Pierce, was a genial man: ex-army, a stickler for doing the right thing and proud of his position in the community. He was not far off retiring age, with combed-back grey hair, a prominent military moustache, always smartly dressed in a black blazer and regimental tie. Pupils moving between the school, the dining hall and playing field, were trooped along the pavements in tidy columns, each pair of children an arm's length apart; outward appearances were particularly important in the small town. At the end of the school day he was always at his most relaxed and I found him as usual in his office, hand-rolling a cigarette.

'We have a small orchard in the school garden....' I said to him.

'Yes,' he replied, tapping the end of his cigarette on the Will's tobacco tin, 'But it's been neglected for many years.'

'Maybe it would be good to put some beehives in there....' I suggested.

'Bees?' he asked raising his eyebrows. 'Ah, bees,' he repeated, smiling thoughtfully this time, and lighting his cigarette. 'The mayor is a beekeeper, and he's one of the school's governors.' Enough said!

After this short conversation all was settled – I had an apiary site and I could attend the beekeeping course in spring with the headmaster willing to cover my classes so that I wouldn't lose my pay.

From January onwards, whenever I had any spare time, I was in Jim's barn cleaning up the old-fashioned garden hives, those with gabled roofs and splayed telescopic 'lifts', the outer covers which protected the inner boxes that the bees used for their brood nest and for honey storage. Although decorative and giving good shelter for the colonies, the doubled-walled WBC hives (named after their inventor William Broughton Carr) were cumbersome, heavy and needed regular painting. Renovating the lifts was straightforward enough; it was just a matter of sanding them down and repainting the outer sides a couple of times. The inner boxes needed more careful attention but were a pleasure to work on. They had to be scraped free of wax, propolis (the resinous gum that bees use to cement the frames in place) and old wax moth cocoons, then thoroughly scorched with a blow lamp to kill off any disease spores. The smell of the wax, propolis and cedarwood when I scraped and scorched away was like incense, and, as I was working in winter, the wax and propolis were very brittle and broke away from the wood easily. The pile of old used frames, which Jim and I decided not to use, came in useful for kindling for making fires, the wax and propolis making fire lighting very easy.

My first type of bee hive – a renovated WBC.

In May, with my hive already set up and with an elementary knowledge of both honeybee colony life and beekeeping practice, thanks to my winter's studying of *The Beekeeper's Encyclopedia*, I was well-prepared for the course at Taylor's factory. For three days we learned how to use all the necessary equipment, and to weigh up the hive types available and their particular advantages and disadvantages. Most importantly, we were familiarised with the life of a honeybee colony, its seasonal pattern and the roles played by each of the castes. Without this background knowledge, it would be difficult for a beekeeper to understand the tasks which needed to be accomplished during a beekeeping year.

The final session, which I had been greatly looking forward to, was learning how to open a hive and handle bees. We were taken to one of Taylor's apiaries in a small field deep in the Hertfordshire countryside, the high hedges which sheltered the site frothy-white with May blossom.

I'll never forget the day that I first looked into a hive: after a little smoking at the entrance, the roof and inner cover of the hive were removed allowing us to see the shallow box, the super, which contained frames with combs that the bees were filling with nectar, the ripened honey already sealed in the cells with beautiful white wax cappings. This box was removed gently so that we could explore the deep brood chamber in which the bees reared their family.

The bees, almost Welsh gold in colour, remained quite still on the comb when a frame was removed from the hive, and I can still recall the smell of the wax and the floral-scented honey which mingled with the smoke being used to pacify the colony. We saw with our own eyes the intimate life of the bees as each frame was carefully removed, every new comb revealing a page in the story of the colony's life: the stores of honey, the multi-coloured bands of pollen, the pearly white larvae, the dark-coloured pupal cells, the bigger drones with huge black eyes, and even the long golden body of the queen as she bent her abdomen into a cell to lay an egg, surrounded by her group of workers. How wonderful it was to see the colony carrying on with its daily work, unperturbed, in the hands of a gentle beekeeper. Fortunately, the weather had been reasonably good for the beginning of May, the early rain had moved on by midday and despite a stiff breeze the bees were well-behaved, dispelling any fear of bees in even the most timid of the course members.

Not surprisingly, at the end of the afternoon I put in my order for a 'nucleus' colony – six frames of bees with a queen, to be securely packed in a ventilated travelling box, for collection the following week.

With the renovated hive set up in the school garden and with a gallon of syrup mixed up ready to feed the bees, after school Val and I set off to Welwyn to bring the small colony home. Val was pleased to be driving again after giving birth to our daughter, Catherine, who was just one month old. Catherine's carry cot filled the whole of the back seat of our VW Beetle so, having collected the bees, I had the travelling box between my legs in the front of the car.

The bees buzzed quietly on the journey, though a sudden bump in the road or the braking of the car elicited a momentary roar before they settled down again. Through the mesh screen which provided the bees with ventilation came the delightful honey and wax aroma, a scent which has given me continued pleasure throughout my life.

In the school garden, following the course instructions, I dismantled the WBC hive, leaving only the floorboard in place on to which I put the travelling box. On top of this was put the hive roof and then, having covered my head with a flimsy black veil, I opened the entrance to the travelling box. I expected the bees to rush out madly, but this was not the case. Two or three bees crawled out, followed by just a few more. They took to the air slowly, making exploratory flights around the new hive to fix its location in their memory. The way the bees came out of the hive reminded me of what someone said about choosing a puppy:

'Don't go for the one which rushes to greet you and makes a fuss of you. Wait for the one which carefully and slowly emerges from the kennel and takes stock of what is going on before making any approaches!'

I waited for a while to ensure that plenty of bees were flying and then left them to it: I had to return later anyway to transfer the bees into the brood chamber of the hive and to feed them.

Those who have not transferred a small colony of bees to their new home for the first time, when given the opportunity will, like me, find the whole experience an exciting milestone in the craft. There is at the back of one's mind a feeling of apprehension: will everything go according to plan? Will the bees be as well-behaved as those we saw in Taylor's apiary? Or an even more serious thought: had the queen been squashed during the journey if the frames had been jolted?

Jim and his son Nicholas came to help me with the transfer a couple of hours later. Our net veils were tucked into our shirts and with smoker alight we approached the bees. We gave them a touch of smoke at the entrance in the box, to which the bees responded with a short hiss. We waited for a couple of minutes to give the bees the chance to imbibe some honey, which would make them docile and easy to handle, and then moved the box to one side so that we could rebuild the bottom section of the WBC hive.

Fortunately the weather had changed in the last couple of hours.

Instead of a strong WSW wind and showers, the sun was shining brightly. Thus, on a memorable early summer evening, we carefully transferred my first colony of bees, frame by frame, to the brood box of my borrowed hive. Whilst doing so, we quickly scanned each face of the combs and saw all we needed to see: plenty of bees, good stores of honey and pollen, and the queen surrounded by her usual retinue of workers. The bees were quiet on the combs and the transfer took place easily, so any anxiety on our part was soon put to rest. Using just a touch of smoke again, enough for it to drift across the frame tops, the bees moved down, allowing us to put a calico quilt over the top of the box. In the centre of the quilt was a small opening over which we placed a tin feeder filled with a strong solution of sugar syrup which would help the bees to produce wax and build comb on the four extra frames we had given them, each of which had been fitted with sheets of beeswax foundation.

The first task was completed successfully, much to our satisfaction; no stings, no crushed bees – just one small mishap – Nicholas managed both to spill and sit in a pool of sticky sugar syrup. I was just thankful he wasn't travelling home in my car!

One of the most frustrating things about first having bees is that there is always the temptation to open the hive to see what is happening; to repeat the sheer pleasure of handling bees; to indulge oneself in the delightful aroma which rises from between the combs; to witness the intense activities of the worker bees; and to watch the newly-developed bees bite their way out of their cells and emerge with their grey damp-looking covering of fine hair. Unfortunately, any disruption to a colony is not conducive to its well-being. The inside of the hive has its own micro-climate and within seconds of taking off the roof, the temperature and humidity are rapidly reduced and it can take many hours for the colony to be restored to its former state. My patience was sorely tried in those first few months. I was forever waiting for the time when I could make my next inspection. I adhered strictly to examining the hives at nine-day intervals, the normal practice amongst beekeepers who have strong colonies and who wish to prevent their bees from swarming. I knew, though, that this was unlikely to happen in my new colony as it was headed by a young queen, it hadn't as yet built up to its full size, and it had both sufficient stores of food and storage space.

Whenever I had some spare time during the school lunch hour, I would go to the school garden, usually taking some pupils with me, so that we could watch the activities of the bees on the alighting board below the hive entrance. I was able to point out the worker bees returning to the hives and speculate on the type of flowers on which the bees may have been foraging by looking at the colour of the pollen loads on their legs. The children could see the guard bees patrolling the hive entrance and, as it was the middle of the day, watch the departure and return of the noisy drones.

On very hot days, worker bees could be observed in large numbers on the alighting board, their heads down and abdomens pointed upwards as they beat their wings to send cooling air into the hive. Occasionally, on a hot muggy evening when the lime trees were in flower, I would stand by the hive and not only watch the fanning bees which were still hard at work, but smell the moist lime-scented air being expelled

Drones fly out on sunny days to find the drone assembly areas in which queens will be mated

by the bees as they reduced the water content of the gathered nectar, giving the promise of honey which could soon be harvested.

Threatened swarm

When I next looked inside the hive, the promise was being realised. Comb building was well advanced in the 'super' – the shallow box I had added a few weeks before with ten new frames and wax foundation – and there were nearly five combs of sealed honey. However, when I removed the queen excluder which prevents the queen from laying eggs where only honey is to be stored, and examined the brood frames, I was alarmed to

find open queen cells containing fat larvae. Two of the cells were at the bottom of a comb – the usual place for the swarm cells if the bees intended to swarm – the other on the face of the comb usually signified that the bees were dissatisfied with the queen and wished to supersede her.

When this occurs, the bees rear a new queen and once she is mated she may be laying eggs alongside the older queen until her demise. According to the books, the bees should not have been constructing queen cells as the hive was not congested and the young Italian queen would be secreting enough pheromones to deter the worker bees

Regardless of the hive being opened, the Italian queen carried on examining cells before laying eggs

from producing them. Additionally, the colony certainly hadn't been disturbed too often, nor was I heavy-handed during inspections, possible reasons why the bees would want to replace the queen.

Whatever factors had led to this event, I had a problem which needed to be dealt with quickly. Once one of those cells was sealed, possibly in a couple of days, the colony would swarm and I could lose not only most of the bees and the queen, but also a sizeable amount of the honey, for the bees gorge on it prior to swarming so that they have full crops of honey to convert into wax combs for their new nest. I decided to seek advice. Immediately.

It was old Mr Whitfield who helped me out. He was a well-respected beekeeper with many years of experience and the grandfather of one of my pupils. Small in size, but tough despite his age, he came to the school garden dressed in a brown warehouse coat and carrying an old net veil. As soon as he reached the hive, he bent down and began to pull away at the weeds in front of the alighting board, muttering 'This won't do; the bees need a clear flight path to their hive.' My miserable attempt to light my smoker didn't go well. 'Give it to me,' he sighed, 'This is the way to do it'.

Once the hive was opened and the honey super had been taken away, he looked down on the brood frames, sighing again. 'You have the frames in line with the front of the hive, that's no good. Any debris from the frames or dead bees in winter could block the hive entrance. We need to turn the box around so that the frames are at right angles to the entrance'. And this he did immediately. Three reprimands in three minutes! My confidence was slipping and I was grateful that no one else had been there to witness my embarrassment. I am sure that Mr Whitfield meant to give helpful advice, but the manner in which it was given seemed more like a scolding.

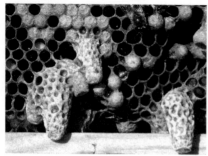

Swarm cells are numerous and usually at the edges and bottoms of the comb in the brood nest

Supersedure cells are normally found on the face of the comb and usually very few are constructed

Fortunately, the rest of the examination proceeded with no more criticism. Each frame was thoroughly examined and two queen cells were destroyed leaving the plumpest larva in an open cell which could, if I wanted, develop into a new queen. The original queen was soon spotted and Mr Whitfield deftly picked it up by its thorax and with nail scissors clipped off part of the queen's right wing. 'The swarm might leave the hive,' he explained, 'But as the queen won't be able to fly, the bees will return. You will lose the queen, but that is better than losing most of the bees. Anyway – they can replace her from the queen cell we have left.'

There was another option, he announced before he left. I could put the frame with the queen cell and a couple more frames in a small nucleus hive and take her to a new site. That way, if all turned out well, I would have two colonies.

I decided to go for the two colony option and that night made a roof for the travelling box in which my bees had come so that I would have a temporary home for the small colony.

The following evening I was back at the orchard accompanied by a couple of pupils and their parents. They, like Jim, were interested in having bees on their plots of land and for them it was their first glimpse inside a beehive. Although one boy was stung (he was quite nonchalant about it even though it must have hurt) we found the queen easily and I gave the frame she was on to a parent to hold whilst I transferred the one with the queen cell plus two additional ones to make up the nucleus that I was taking home to my Biggleswade garden. All I had to do now was to provide the nucleus with food and leave it undisturbed for a couple of weeks to allow the queen to develop, get mated and begin her role as mother of the new colony. The original queen stayed in the orchard hive and a later inspection showed that the bees had no intention of building any more queen cells.

Gathering a swarm

Thanks to the help of Mr Whitfield, my colony's attempt to swarm was thwarted. Not so, unfortunately, for Jim Parker's bees. On the hottest day so far that summer, Jim came to my classroom after school had finished to tell me that a huge swarm from one of his hives had settled on the corner of one of his greenhouses, about seven feet from the ground. One of Bedfordshire's bee disease officers had already visited his apiary earlier in the day and during inspection of his hives, many queen cells were found – both sealed and unsealed. Mr Kent, the bee officer, was a very quiet, helpful and gentle man, the sort of beekeeper who was never critical and gave positive and friendly advice. Although well past retiring age, he enjoyed this seasonal work for the Ministry of Agriculture and travelled around Bedfordshire in an old estate car, packed to the roof with all sorts of beekeeping equipment – and many bees which flew up and down the windows. He told Jim that although the queen cells had been cut out, it might have been too late for the bees to change their mind about swarming – and a swarm could possibly emerge that afternoon.

Whilst I had read about dealing with swarms, I had no practical experience of catching them, so Jim and I decided to seek advice from another of the town's beekeepers, Mr Brown, a retired wheelwright. To get to Mr Brown's back door we had to walk down a narrow passage which led to a small yard shaded by workshops and high walls. It was here in this almost sunless place that Mr Brown kept his many hives of bees. He was only too willing to help us and went to collect the things he needed. Whilst waiting for him we took a closer look at his bees.

There was only one problem with this – we had to make a direct approach to the front of the hives. Within seconds I realised that this was a bad idea, for without warning a bee struck then stung me on the face between my eye and the bridge of my nose. The pain was intense, enough to make my eyes water, and if this wasn't bad enough the strong smell of vaporising venom guided other bees to the spot. I retreated quickly, covering my face with my hands. Mrs Brown looked at me unsympathetically, matter-of-factly removed the sting, and applied some honey to the affected part. Without further ado we set off to deal with Jim's swarm.

Mr Brown looked at the huge swarm which was still on the corner of the greenhouse. Without any fuss, he quietly put an old hessian sack on the ground beneath it and tucked the open end of the veil underneath the collar of his brown warehouse coat. Placing a straw skep under the cluster of bees and using a hearth brush, he deftly swept the bees into the skep. Before the bees could realise what was happening, the skep was upturned on to the sack and propped up with a small stone to allow the bees which were flying around to join their nest mates. The bees milled around for a while but, guided by the scent of those at the entrance to the skep, within a few minutes all were safely inside.

At dusk, we carried the skep to a hive already prepared and shook the bees on top of the new frames. Once they were down we gave the bees a good feed of syrup to help them to build new honeycombs.

This turned out to be a day of firsts for me: my first sting, though I wish it could have been somewhere less painful; my first lesson in how to take, and hive, a swarm; and my first meeting with Mr Brown, whom I visited on many occasions afterwards and learnt about his early life.

Mr Brown and I had two things in common: our interest in bees and the fact that we were both born (albeit sixty years apart) in north Lincolnshire. I had spent the first eighteen years of my life in the steel town of Scunthorpe, whilst Mr Brown's childhood home was just a few miles to the north and rather unique. He lived on Read's Island, a small stretch of land in the River Humber. It is believed that Read's Island was formed by sand collecting around a sunken French vessel in the middle of the 19th century and augmented later by the scuttling of a naval ship to help stabilise the north Lincolnshire coastline around Barton on Humber. Though only two miles across and very narrow, the island was originally used for grazing sheep, but eventually a farmhouse was built in which Mr Brown's family lived. As a child, he would be rowed across the fifty yard channel to the school in South Ferriby each day. Mr Brown once showed me an unusual photograph. It was of the farmhouse packed round with sandbags and looking as if it was floating in the Humber.

There had been a big problem, he explained, with rats. All attempts to exterminate them had failed, so a unique plan was put into operation. Channels were cut through the island in readiness for the high Neap Tide. This tide, a huge bore – or 'eagre' as it is known locally – rushes along the Humber and River Trent as far as Gainsborough each spring and, as hoped, the huge swell swept all rat life away.

As nature abhors a vacuum, other creatures have dominated the island since Mr Brown's days. Voles breed in profusion making it an ideal habitat for short-eared owls, and in winter the island is one of the largest feeding places for pink-footed geese. No one lives there permanently any more: it is a nature reserve managed by the RSPB.

When August came, both hives were doing well and the queen in the nucleus had produced plenty of brood, but still needed feeding. The colony in the orchard, despite losing three frames of bees, was gradually filling the super with honey, the foragers working relentlessly on blackberry flowers. Jim and I decided we would extract our honey on St Bartholomew's Day, 24th August, which is the traditional day for honey harvesting. There is some sense in choosing this date, for we would only take the honey in the supers and leave for the bees any that they had stored in the brood box below which mean that, as the queen reduced her egg laying, the colony could fill the empty brood cells with nectar and pollen from the late summer and autumn flowers.

The day before we were to harvest the honey, Jim and I went to our hives to make the necessary preparations. The weather was the best that summer could offer; a still, clear day with the temperature in the upper 70°F. Using the minimum amount of smoke, we lifted the honey supers clear of the brood boxes and inserted boards with bee escapes between them. The two pairs of copper springs in the escapes allowed the bees to move down into the main part of the hive but not move up again. As expected, on the following day we found that the bees had left the boxes except for a few stragglers which we cleared from the surface of the combs with a handful of grass. Most of the combs were covered with pure white beeswax cappings and, pleasantly surprised by the heaviness of the boxes, we speculated on the possible weight of our honey harvest.

Fortunately, amongst the beekeeping things left by the previous tenant were an old honey extractor and storage tank with sieve-like filters. Externally, there were patches of rust on the extractor and tank, but on their inside, the tinplate coating was almost perfect as liquid paraffin had been smeared over the surface to prevent the metal from corroding. Val, and Jim's wife, Ann, had the messy job of removing the wax cappings from the surface of the combs with serrated kitchen knives, whilst Nicholas, Jim and myself took turns at cranking the handle of the extractor to spin the honey out of the combs.

The extractor rumbled noisily, as I imagined a tumbril might, and the centrifugal force threw threads and globules of honey against the inner wall and filled the air with the scent of the fields, trees and flowers where the bees had worked. It was a joyous experience at the end of the evening to see the honey glistening in the tank and to know that we had accomplished what we had set out to do just a few months ago. The next day Jim brought us twenty-five pounds of our own honey, bottled in the same type of squat jars with gold lacquered tops and oval 'county' labels that I had seen in my grammar school many years before. The honey itself was a good light amber colour, sweet, but with a slightly sharp aftertaste, probably due to the many lime trees in the area, and not at all like the clover honey I remembered from the 1950s.

A freshly-sealed comb of honey with metal spacers on the frame lugs

Now that the honey had been harvested, the two colonies needed to be prepared for winter.

But first of all I decided to move the hive from the school orchard to our garden where I would be able to keep a careful watch on it over the winter months. Looking back at the event, I can't believe that the moving of the hive was done with so little real forethought and with such disregard for both the safety of the bees or people driving along the road. The WBC hive is one that is best kept on a permanent site and not moved about. It is heavy and has too many parts which could become detached from each other. At dusk in early September, Graham, the husband of a fellow teacher, came to help me with the move. He was an ex-rugby player who was capable of lifting the whole hive without any assistance from me. We closed up the entrance and tied school skipping ropes around the hive, making them as tight as we could.

As we lifted the hive, Graham picked it up by one of the outer boxes, not from beneath the floor, and at a very steep angle. The box inside which contained the bees became dislodged and the bees began to pour out from a small gap between the outer boxes. We had to put the hive down, open up the entrance and then coax the bees back into the hive, encouraging them with a little smoke.

By the time the bees chew through the paper they will unite peacefully.

Once we had tightened the ropes again, we had the most difficult task ahead of us: we had to lift the hive on to the roof-rack of my VW Beetle. This fortunately wasn't quite as difficult as we imagined and once in place, the hive sat proudly on top of the car like a pagoda. We made use of more of the school skipping ropes to tie the hive to the roof rack, for the tough elastic expanders I had planned to use were lost in the darkness of the orchard. At a very slow speed I drove the four miles home with Graham following me in his Vauxhall Viva – it was his task to keep his eyes fixed on the hive and flash his car's lights if it looked in danger of toppling.

Our slow speed caused a bit of a tail-back and when we stopped a couple of times, the overtaking drivers rubbernecked us to see what on earth was going on. There was nothing to give us any concern – the hive had just slid a couple of inches one way or another after some tricky bends had been negotiated. Needless to say, we were relieved when the hive had completed its journey and was standing a couple of yards away from the other hive in my garden.

Preparing hives for winter

It had been impressed upon me at Taylor's that autumn is not the end of the beekeeping season, but the beginning of the beekeeper's new year. Whatever preparations are made (or not made) in autumn will have an enormous effect on the bees the following spring.

One decision I had to make was whether or not to keep the two colonies or to unite them, thus making a stronger overwintering population. It wasn't too difficult a decision as I had only one beehive that would stand up to the winter weather. Also, as the bees had shown dissatisfaction with the original queen, it would be better to replace her with the queen raised in the nucleus colony. So I opened up the WBC colony one afternoon and found the queen. Picking her up gently, I crushed her thorax between my finger and thumb, an unenviable task and one which I have never come to terms with even today. With the old queen out of the way, I placed a box with the combs from the nucleus hive on top of the original colony, separating them with a sheet of newspaper punched with a few small holes through which, I was told, the bees would chew after a time and unite peacefully.

Later, I placed the wet combs from which we had extracted the honey into the hive for the bees to clean up and, following the standard practice of that time, removed the box when the combs were dry and wrapped it tightly in newspaper, having first sprinkled some crystals of it on top of the frames to protect the valuable combs from wax moth damage. Since then I have learnt that the use of PDB crystals is no longer recommended or even legal in some countries, as it is a carcinogen which is absorbed by the wax combs and can leave residues of the chemical in honey. Only a few years ago two of Greece's major honey suppliers to supermarkets had to recall thousands of jars of honey which had been contaminated with PDB, as beekeepers persisted in using the crystals for wax moth control.

To complete my autumn work, I made sure that the bees had enough food for winter by giving them a good feed of strong syrup, and reduced the entrance to the hive so that mice would not be able to gain access to the bees' stores of honey once they were in their winter cluster.

First year summary

My accounts for my first beekeeping season of 1972 make interesting reading. I had spent a total of £32.12 on the bees, equipment, honey jars and sugar and had harvested 25lbs of honey which had a retail value of about £16 – but most of it was given away to friends and family and we kept the rest for ourselves. Additionally, on the plus side, I had, hopefully, a strong colony ready for the next spring, though I would have to buy my own beehive.

Whilst an expected pattern of beekeeping didn't occur (and, as I have found since, it often doesn't), with the new colony making swarm preparations, I was given the opportunity to receive some much-appreciated extra help and instruction from local experts in the craft. The beekeeping course I had attended had certainly provided me with an overview of beekeeping, but not in any great detail, and I looked forward to having time through the winter to read more about bees and the many ways in which they could be managed. As is always the case, I had learned a lot about handling bees by the mistakes I had made, the bees themselves in no uncertain way letting me know if I had been too heavy-handed or clumsy. Although I was unlikely to need to open the hive again during the winter, it was good to have the bees near the house so that on fine winter days I would be able to enjoy watching their activities on the alighting board.

Certainly, the bees had given me all the pleasure that I thought they would – and equally important, it was good to be able to share my passion with pupils and their parents. I also enjoyed the company of other beekeepers who patiently answered my questions and allowed me into their apiaries as well as their homes. What I didn't realise at the time was the effect that bees, those fascinating insects, were to have on shaping the rest of my life. Val, jokingly, still says that it is no coincidence that my beekeeping activities began at the time Catherine was born, as 'important' and 'urgent' work in the apiary often called me away from mundane domestic duties or aspects of family life in which she was sure that I didn't really want to be involved.

One thing I was sure of, though, at the end of this first season. I was going to have to replace the awkward, out-dated WBC hive with one that was more modern and easier to work with. But with so many types in the beekeeping catalogues, which was I to choose?

CHAPTER TWO

Moving On

THERE were several possible contenders for replacing my WBC hive, for Britain, unlike many other countries, caters for the individual rather than the mass of beekeepers. Modified National, British Commercial, Smith, Langstroth and Dadant hives were all featured in the manufacturers' catalogues. They are all single walled, seven-eighths of an inch in thickness, in pine or cedar, either rectangular or square in cross section, and with flat metal-covered roofs. The Dadant, Langstroth and British Commercial hives are all very large, but the Smith, and the most popular hive in Britain, the Modified National, both had frames of the same size as those in my WBC, so really, my choice was reduced to two. I eventually selected the Smith, a Scottish hive, manufactured by Steele and Brodie at their Wormit factory in Fife.

There were three main reasons for my choice: it had the simplest construction, each box being made with just four boards so it was easy to replicate (working drawings were printed in Dean's book); it was very cheap compared with other cedar hives (even cheaper if I opted for the 'seconds'); it had the smallest profile and weighed less than other types. For decades the Smith hive has found popularity amongst beekeepers in Scotland and the northern counties of England, and even today the Robson family of Northumberland has over a thousand of them in their commercial apiaries.

In late winter, I sent an order to Scotland for three flat-packed Smith hives and spent a couple of weekends putting the hives together. The 'seconds' quality parts needed little more than a bit of planing or sanding here or there so I got the hives at a bargain price. I was very impressed with the sheradised nails which were sent to fix the hive parts together. I had not come across this type of nail before. They are much smoother than the usual galvanised nails, the difference being that the coating given to the iron or steel to prevent corrosion is applied as a dust rather than their being dipped in molten zinc.

The reasons why the Smith hive has never achieved the status of the National Hive, particularly in England, are probably two-fold. Firstly, many beekeepers don't like the short lugs by which the frames are suspended and secondly, instead of the tops of the frames being flush with the tops of the boxes, there is a ³⁄₁₆ inch space above the frames in the Smith hive which means that the queen excluder can sag, causing the bees to build wax in the space.

One of the fundamental rules of modern beekeeping is that, for a hive to be managed successfully, the 'bee-space' must be maintained at all times. This means, in practise, that a space – no less, nor higher, than the height of a honeybee – should exist between the external walls of the hive and the frames, and the frames themselves should be twice that distance apart, so that bees can work comfortably, back-to-back on the faces of the combs. If that space is too small – or too large – it becomes bridged with wax or propolis making it difficult to remove the frames or other hive parts during examinations – and in turn causes unnecessary disturbance to the bees. The long-lugged frames that I was currently using allowed tin spacers to be fixed to them so that the frames could be kept the correct distance apart and, as far as I was concerned,

The Smith hive is simple and economical and still used by the Robsons in Northumberland

they were an abomination. I had to remove them from the frames when I was extracting honey, a tedious job that wasn't always easy as the bees stuck them to the lugs with propolis, and prising them off often meant that I ended up being cut by the sharp metal, and without due care my blood would have been flowing over the honey combs.

The most usual method for spacing the frames in the Smith hive at that time was to use castellated strips of metal which were fixed along the rebates in the hive. I tried them for a while, but found them to be unsatisfactory. When I examine a colony, I like to remove a frame from the side wall of the hive and lean it against the outside of the hive. Then, using my hive tool I lever, sideways, the next frame away from another – but applying forward pressure on the frame to prevent it from jarring. This means that when I lift the frame out I am not brushing the bees against each other which could agitate them or even crush them.

I gradually changed all my frames for the more expensive Hoffman self-spacing frames that had wide 'shoulders' – flat one side, and tapered on the other so they made little contact when they were placed next to each other. The problem with the queen excluder was easily solved; I just put some ³⁄₁₆ inch laths around its perimeter and a couple across its length.

I continued my visits to Mr Brown throughout the winter. With little work to do with the bees, he was either in his workshop or out with the Cambridgeshire Hunt. We invited him and the Parker family to our house one evening to watch a couple of films on beekeeping. At school, I was in charge of all the audio/visual aids, so I had access to a Bell and Howell 16mm film projector. I had a love/hate relationship with that machine. It could let me down when I least expected, so I was always on edge when showing films to classes or parent/teacher meetings. Whilst my father, and particularly my grandfather, were adept at cine photography, I have always preferred taking stills and learned to develop my own pictures when I was just twelve years old. Even today I have never used a video camera. My grandfather lived for his Thursday mornings. It was the day that Exchange & Mart came out. He was always buying and selling movie cameras and projectors. If he were alive today, he would be checking out similar items on ebay all the time.

During the showing of the bee film, everything went smoothly; there was none of the clickity clack when the film jumped the sprockets which, without quick action on my part, would lead to a huge pile of cellulose coils on the floor. Not long ago in our next village here in Greece, we had an outdoor film show. It was a beautifully clear night with a full moon and, just as in Cinema Paradiso, when the cinema had burnt down, the film 'Goodbye Lenin' was being projected onto an outside wall. To my horror, there was the same old Bell and Howell with its huge spools ready to roll. The old sensations came back. I couldn't relax. Then suddenly, everything went black. Using a torch, the projectionist played around with the machine for a while and realised that the fuse had gone. Of course, there was no spare one, so he proceeded to do what we had done as students; he collected pieces of silver paper from cigarette packets to bridge the contacts. Three quarters of the way through, the film jumped its sprockets . . . . how relieved I was that the responsibility wasn't mine!

Spring approached slowly, very slowly, and I had to resign myself to the fact that it would be some time before shirt-sleeve temperatures would allow me to open up the hives again. On mild winter days the bees worked the flowers not far from the hive and collected water from the edge of the fish pond. Occasionally a bee would emerge from the hive carrying the carcase of her sister. She would fly a yard or so from the hive with all six of her legs grasping the body, then fall to the ground before relinquishing her grip. The orange loads of pollen which the bees had gathered from the crocuses, though, were a sure sign that the queen was alive and laying.

In May, when the dandelions and apple blossom were in full flower, I transferred the bees to their new Smith hive. The bees were not as good tempered as the year before and didn't take kindly to my shortening of the lugs with a pair of secateurs, a job which was not easy to accomplish without jolting the frames. I took a few stings, but got off lightly considering the upheaval that was taking place. Later in the season I bought another six-frame nucleus, and, when queen cells appeared in the older hive, I made up two other small colonies.

One summer evening we had a couple of guests join us for supper. After darkness had fallen and half-way through the meal, a bee flew through the open window and buzzed around the light bulb. I couldn't think why a bee should be out at that time of night. I learned the answer the following morning: a hedgehog was lying dead a few yards from the hive. As it had been very warm the night before, some of the bees had undoubtedly clustered outside the entrance to the hive.

Unfortunately, the foraging hedgehog's attraction to what promised to be a nourishing meal was fatal. Whilst a hedgehog would ordinarily seem to have adequate protection, against dozens of attacking bees it would have needed to have been very quick to defend its vulnerable parts – its face and underbelly. Clearly, this hedgehog had failed, for its body lay on its side, unrolled. Honeybees have one advantage over creatures larger than themselves: they act in unison when their colony is at risk. When a bee stings, the sting itself becomes detached from the last segment of the abdomen, and the sharp lancets, controlled by a nerve, continue to plunge into their victim. At the same time an alarm pheromone is released which brings more bees homing in to the same spot, thus incapacitating one area of an animal's body and being much more effective than placing an odd sting here and there.

Coping with a bee attack

I became very aware of this during the summer of my second season with bees when I needed to look inside one of the hives to ensure that no more queen cells were being built. It was July, late in the afternoon and the weather was hot and humid. The lime trees along the roadside near our house gave off their heavy perfume and dripped sticky deposits of honeydew onto the cars below them. The sky was leaden, but as yet it was not raining though already the distant rumble of thunder could be heard. As the bees were flying well, despite the impending storm, I lit my smoker and carefully removed the hive roof. Before I could examine the brood frames for queen cells, I had to remove the super with honey combs. No problem there, so this was put on to the upturned roof beside the hive. As usual, I removed the first brood comb from the side of the hive, checked that the queen wasn't on it, then leant it against the side of the hive.

As I reached in for the next comb, all hell broke loose. Angry bees with their high-pitched buzzing rocketed upwards trying to sting me through the net veil, then many dived down to my feet and homed in on my unprotected ankles. Time after time I felt the sharp pain as one bee after another lunged its sting home. I pumped the bellows of my smoker furiously so that the smoke would drive the bees away from around my shoes but unfortunately this only made them more angry. I tried swatting the bees around the ankles with the soles of my shoes, but it was just like the scene in the Sorcerer's Apprentice with the broomsticks; the more bees I knocked down, the more their numbers seemed to double. Just then there was a huge crack of thunder and the rain hurled down, making the wet lower part of my trousers easier for the bees to sting through.

What had happened, of course, was that the bees out foraging had quickly returned to the hive to escape the storm and, alerted by the other bees, had joined in the attack. With my bare hands thrust deep in my pocket for protection, I left the hive, open as it was, and ran as fast I could for the shelter of the house, fifty yards away, with scores of bees in chase.

Val helped me to remove dozens of bee stings that were still embedded around my ankles – which by now were swelling enormously, burning and itching and very hard to the touch. The whole of my body was covered in nettle rash and I felt far from well. As it was a few minutes before seven, we knew that the doctor's surgery, luckily just a few hundred yards away, would still be open, so I was bundled into our car to seek treatment. The adrenalin shot the doctor immediately jabbed into my arm worked quickly and despite the pain I was soon feeling less woozy.

'Did you have to run away from the bees?' the doctor enquired.

Somewhat surprised at his question I answered, 'Yes, of course.' After all, who wouldn't, I thought to myself, given the circumstances.

'Ah,' he said, 'The heart is a very good pump; the faster it beats the more quickly the poison can spread round your body. You have been very lucky.'

I certainly didn't feel lucky an hour or so later when I had to hobble back painfully to the hive to rebuild it. A light rain was still falling so putting on as much protective clothing as I could find, including gloves, and using just a little smoke, I was able to reassemble the hive without obtaining any more stings. I stumbled around for many days on swollen legs, Val having to drive me everywhere. But what troubled me most was: what would happen when I was stung again? Would I have another bad reaction which might mean that I would have to give up beekeeping? I sincerely hoped not.

Fortunately, subsequent stings, often numerous, have not resulted in further allergic reactions. Though always painful, they are easily forgotten and are just one of the things I have come to accept as part of beekeeping. I always wear a veil of some sort, as I consider protection for the face, especially the eyes, is extremely important. And, in forty years of beekeeping, although I have had to handle some bees which can only be described as having been downright nasty, I have had the sense to stop the examination, close up the hive and hope that on a subsequent visit they might be more amenable.

After four years of teaching at Potton, both Val and I resigned from our posts. We had been living in a small flat on the top floor of her adopted parents' house and needed our own home with more space as our daughter Catherine was now fifteen months old. Buying a house in Bedfordshire was beyond our means, and on our visits to north Lincolnshire, where my parents lived, we had found a very cheap property in their small village. The house, a double-fronted Georgian farmhouse, set in a third of an acre with an old orchard and many outbuildings, needed complete renovation. This was achieved with the help of a very friendly bank manager and county council improvement grants. The bank manager gave us an open cheque book to get all the work completed and once we had been reimbursed by the council, he helped us to get a competitive mortgage to cover the outstanding debt.

We were sad to leave Potton School. By this time Val was in charge of a unit on a separate campus and I had built up a small animal unit which was used as a resource by the whole school. Children whose parents didn't allow them to have pets, were able to have them for short spells, either at weekends or during the school holidays. Friday afternoons saw rabbits, gerbils, rats, mice and guinea pigs being loaded into cars or transported around the small town on trolleys made from pram wheels. Children often brought us butterflies, moths and flowers to identify and on one occasion we were presented with a very young leveret. The child in all innocence believed it had been deserted by its mother, not knowing that the doe hides each of its young in different parts of a field and then goes round to feed them at regular intervals. However, it was our responsibility to fend for it now as it would be unlikely that the mother would accept it, even if its original location could have been found. We reared it on dilute milk using a baby doll's banana-shaped feeding bottle and transported it to school and back each day. At night it would run around our flat or sit on my shoulder when I was reading and undoubtedly it was one of the most beautiful creatures I have ever encountered. To get it ready for its eventual release into the wild I wired off a huge section of the garden, where it lived for many weeks. It was a very sad day when we took it to the RSPB's nature reserve at nearby Sandy to let it go. For a while it shuffled around our feet until we clapped our hands, yelling and stamping our feet to scare it. The hare, nearly fully grown now, gave us a last, startled, look and ran off in a straight line, its black-fringed ears raised to the sky. We never saw it again.

Having worked in a very small rural community we had made many friends (a bus load of pupils had attended our wedding in Biggleswade) and had empathy with the hardworking market gardeners. We were often on one small-holding or another to hear that the price of a skip of tomatoes had dropped dramatically or that American Green celery was no longer wanted, meaning that a whole strip of the crop would have to be ploughed up. Val was no stranger to this; her adopted father was a market gardener and she used to spend many a morning during her childhood working alongside him before school, the best time of her day. She had often seen him pull up the shire horses when the plough faced the main A1 road where the returning Covent Garden lorry was dumping all the produce he had loaded on the previous evening. Solemn, quiet, withdrawn and uncomplaining, he accepted that a glut in the market, or some other cause, would leave him out of pocket that week. Indeed, he often had to work a night shift as a boilerman in the local workhouse to supplement his income, going straight out onto the land when his shift ended at 6am.

Relocating bees

Our journey to our new home in Lincolnshire took longer than expected for it was on one of the days of the East of England show, held near Peterborough. There was a long tailback of traffic approaching the roundabout on the A1 at Norman Cross. I wasn't too worried about the four hives of bees in the removal van which was following us. The tops of the hives had been covered with mesh screens so they had plenty of ventilation for the three hour journey. Just to be sure that the bees wouldn't become overheated I had sprayed water over the screens – but I doubt if this was really necessary as it was dark in the huge van and it was a cool, grey and typically wet summer's day.

The removal men showed no concern about transporting the hives; they were just pleased that their previous trip a couple of days before was finished. They had travelled all the way from Bedford to south Devon with an elderly couple in the cab, members of the Salvation Army, who sang snatches of hymns and choruses for the entire journey, driving them crazy.

It was raining steadily by the time we reached our house and one of my first tasks was to put up a temporary stand in the old orchard, which was waist high with weeds. A stand is easily achieved by placing a ladder horizontally above the ground with each of its ends supported by a couple of empty bee boxes. I have used this method on many occasions and a beekeeper would do well to look out for ladders at farm sales and auctions as they are very useful for raising the bees above the damp earth and make it easy to cut the grass below the hives.

Despite being confined since the night before, only a few bees poked their heads out through the entrance and made short flights before being driven back inside by the rain. The village church diagonally across the road from our garden had a row of lime trees in full flower so once the weather improved I knew that there would be forage for the bees – well, at least in the short term.

When I looked into the hives after a few days – having given them time to settle down – I found that one of the colonies was not only without a queen, but there was no sign of the bees replacing her. I could easily have taken a frame or two with eggs from one of the other hives, but I was quite interested to see what the local bees were like. I was introduced to a beekeeper in the next village who very kindly brought me a couple of frames to add to the queenless hive. I had an empty box and some newspaper ready so that I could unite the bees in the usual way, a technique which I always found successful.

'Don't do it that way,' said Barry, 'If the frames are isolated for some time in the box above the newspaper, the developing young larvae will get chilled and die before the bees chew their way through to them.'

He took out an ordinary aerosol of air freshener, and once a space had been made for the two frames in the brood box, he sprayed the bees, especially the ones on each side of the empty space. The two frames which were to be introduced to the colony were sprayed on each side and then inserted into the middle of the colony.

'They'll produce their own queen now,' Barry assured me, 'But if I were you, I'd leave the bees completely alone until the queen has emerged and mated. There are still some drones about; they're not usually kicked out of the hive here until the middle of August.'

Despite this rather unconventional method of uniting bees (which I have never used since), everything went as planned and my bees reared a new queen from one of the young larvae in the comb that Barry had provided for me. The queen, when mature, mated with local drones and soon headed the colony.

During the first few days in my new home, I began to explore the immediate area to see what forage there might be for the bees throughout the year. The surrounding countryside, though flat, was completely different from Bedfordshire. Instead of small fields for market gardens and the water meadows along the River Ivel, the land was divided into large arable fields in which cereals, sugar beet, field beans and potatoes were grown.

What remained in the way of hedgerows were cut back to less than two or three feet high with many gaps along their length. The occasional trees which had escaped the flail were mainly ash, and, as the land was cultivated almost to the very edges of the fields, there was an absence of headlands and verges which would have been a refuge for wild flowers. Apart from what my bees might collect from the willow scrub which grew on the banks of a wide stream, the roadside verges, one small paddock in which a couple of milch cows were kept which was fortunately enclosed by blackthorn and hawthorn hedges, and village gardens, the prospects for beekeeping in the immediate vicinity of my apiary seemed to be far from good.

A couple of miles from the village was a huge area of low-lying land consisting of blown sand, which had been driven from the coast several centuries ago. In the 19th century hemp had been grown in this region, the harvested crop being retted in the numerous shallow ponds. The retting, or soaking, process would last for several weeks, the water partly rotting the stems so that the fibres could be more easily removed from the woody tissue.

When the Forestry Commission was set up after the First World War, the majority of the poorer sandy land was drained and turned into huge plantations of Scots and Corsican Pines, the trees planted about five feet apart. In the darkness below the trees there was no ground flora, just carpets of dead pine needles or clumps of bracken. Alongside the forest was a tract of land, a nature reserve, with mature and scrub silver birch, some scattered young pines, gorse and some small patches of heather.

My garden, a third of an acre corner plot, was sheltered by tall outbuildings, a high hawthorn hedge and the badly-neglected orchard. The boundary between our property and the next, though, had just a low wire fence. To make sure that my bees' flight path was lifted well over our neighbours' heads when they were in their garden, I erected a six foot high larchlap fence along its length. To my dismay, on one mild but windy autumn morning when the bees were foraging on the abundant ivy encircling roadside trees, our neighbour was stung whilst reaching upwards to remove some washing from her line.

Although I removed the sting and she suffered no side effects, her comment – which was supported by her husband's later on was – 'You shouldn't be keeping bees in the village!' I had always been careful not to open the hives when they were busy in the garden, I told them, but that wasn't good enough: they wanted the bees to be taken away. When the weather cooled down in November, and the bees hadn't flown for a few days, I moved the four hives across to the bottom of my parents long garden which backed onto open fields. None of the bees returned to their former site although the distance was only a few hundred yards.

Normally (for I have found that this certainly isn't always the case) bees need to be moved only a couple of yards or over three miles, for when they make their first flights the hive's position is fixed in their memory. If bees are subsequently moved to a new location nearby then they fly back to the original site of their home. However, if the move is extended beyond their usual foraging range the bees make orientation flights when released and thereafter return to the new position of their hive.

During the few years we spent in our new home, the village became a dormitory for white collar, higher earners from the nearby steel town. Many of them liked the status of having a home in the countryside, but rural life was alien to them. Several of the incomers became members of various local committees and were sympathetic to those who disliked cockerels crowing, church bells ringing, cow pats along the lane from the farmer's paddock to his milking shed, and, of course, noisy tractors and combine harvesters being moved through the village in the evenings and on Sundays.

I didn't realise until nearly the end of winter that my mother enjoyed having the bees in the garden. She would coax chilled bees into jam jars, warm them up in the kitchen, and just before nightfall empty them out onto the alighting board of one of the hives. As there would be no guards on duty, the bees could crawl safely into the hive. Her activities reminded me of Hazel Underwood, the heroine of Mary Webb's *Gone to Earth*. Hazel's father was a coffin maker and a beekeeper and whenever someone ordered a coffin, Hazel would go and 'Tell the Bees' who had died. Abel told his daughter it wasn't necessary – the bees only needed to be told when someone in their own house was dead – a simple ceremony he carried out himself when his wife died; 'Maray's jead,' he solemnly announced to the bees on that 'vivid June day.' After Hazel was abducted by Jack Reddin, she collected chilled bees and kept them in a box by the fire so that they would have a good life before they died. Hearing the buzzing, Reddin picked up the bees and threw them in the fire. In order to placate Hazel who refused to speak to him, Reddin obtained some bees in a box from his servant Vessons and presented them to her saying that she could be civil again. 'But these be hive-bees!' said Hazel, 'and they was comforble to begin with! I dunna want that sort! I wanted miserable uns!'. *Gone to Earth*, a tragic tale, is one of Mary Webb's classic stories of Shropshire country life, reminiscent of times gone by when bees had few of the problems they have to put up with today.

Unforthcoming local beekeepers' association

During the quiet winter months I studied as many books on beekeeping and bees as I could get from the library but the choice was limited. I also joined the local beekeepers' association. The meetings were held in a doctor's surgery each month, and, on my first visit, the doctor approached me and inquired:

'And what type of hive do you favour, young man?'

'I have four Smith hives,' I replied.

'Do you, indeed,' he went on, 'For myself, I prefer the traditional WBCs. Maybe you noticed them in the garden?' and he walked away.

And that was it. No one else showed any interest in the newcomer in their midst and the meeting proceeded with discussions on whether frames in the hive were best at right angles to the hive entrance or parallel, and if bees should be given through ventilation in the hive during winter. The dozen or so beekeepers present, all of them elderly, were so set in their ways that they stubbornly defended their own methods and were derisory about anyone else's opinions. I was pleased to slink away at the end of the meeting and never returned.

However, all was not a waste of time that evening for I was able to pick up a free duplicated newsletter written by a Mr Bernhard Mobus, the beekeeping advisor of the North of Scotland College of Agriculture, a man who subsequently contributed enormously to my beekeeping education. Additionally, I had learnt about an old beekeeper who no longer went to the meetings but lived near my new school. I intended to visit him one lunchtime.

I had left Bedfordshire without securing a permanent teaching post so for the first year in Lincolnshire I worked as a supply teacher in two very small rural primary schools, teaching all age groups including a reception class. By the end of the school year I had been appointed to the staff of a primary school in Scunthorpe, my home town, which I had left nearly ten years before. I had never expected to return to the steel town and it had changed enormously over the decade. My father was a steel worker having moved north from the Welsh coalfields where he had been employed as a pit safety officer. Generations of his family had been engineers. Originating from the tin mines of Cornwall, they had installed the first pithead gear in the Rhondda and Rhymney Valleys, so that deep seams of coal could be mined.

As a student, I spent all my holidays on one of the steel plants, to supplement my grant. Like most students I was part of the general labour pool, and each morning we would gather outside the mess where we would learn our fate for the day. The foreman, in a black shiny suit, formerly his Sunday best, would stand with his clipboard, and mumble through his half-closed mouth, a corner of which held a hand-rolled cigarette, and say:

'Parsons, Richards, Phipps and Overy, go wi' Al.'

We would then go to the stores with our chargehand and collect the tools needed for our work and make our slow wheelbarrow-walk to the site. If we were unlucky, as we often were, it would mean a day of floating on a pallet twenty feet below a cooling tower filling buckets with sludge whilst someone else hauled them up, or cleaning the scale from the inside of five foot wide flue pipes. These were nevertheless interesting and exciting times for us students, especially when we were working in the coke ovens, the rolling mill, or the blast furnaces and the melting shop. The variety of jobs that we were given in different parts of the plant enabled us to gain a lot of knowledge and experience of the industry very quickly. This was the time when restrictive practices were in force; each tradesman could only carry out his own skill. Because of this, when I was working with a mechanic on a big Aveling Barford truck which transported the iron ore from the mines, we had to wait for several hours for an electrician to come to disconnect the battery. In those days each craftsman also had a mate and an apprentice to help him, but all this disappeared during Margaret Thatcher's time. My brother joined my father in the steelworks with a full seven-year apprenticeship. Pre-Thatcher, he travelled around the country making a small fortune as a contract worker extending and modernising steel plants; post-Thatcher he made an equal amount of money when they were decommissioned.

I think it is extremely important to have some knowledge of the industry in which one's pupils' parents are involved, even though in my particular school most of the parents weren't working on the shop floor. The families that lived in the school catchment area had moved there purposely, because they knew that when their children were ready for secondary education, they would automatically be sent to one of the better comprehensive schools. One important advantage of this was that the parents were very supportive and interested in school activities.

One of the first things I did in the spring term was to set up in my classroom a large three-frame observation hive, given to me by the local museum.

'It belonged to Bernhard Mobus,' the curator said, 'He left it here when he went up to Scotland.'

That name again. I wanted to know more about this man!

Rival queens and the Apidictor

I brought some frames of bees from home and installed them in the glass-covered hive. Before long they were flying in and out of the hive by means of a tube which had been inserted beneath a window. Some children looked at the bees, then one took another look and exclaimed:

'Them's not bees. Them's jaspers!'

I assured them that they were indeed honeybees and not wasps, but I could understand their confusion. Even today I see articles on honeybees, written by supposed experts, in the environmental pages of broadsheets, illustrated with pictures of bumblebees where honeybees should have been.

The observation hive created a lot of interest, because the pupils could see for themselves, in safety, many aspects of colony life. Of particular interest was the issue of a swarm which was preceded by the frenetic running activity of the bees on the surface of the comb. Whilst children knew that bees buzzed, they had no idea that the queens could quack like ducks – for a few days after the swarm had left, they were able to hear the newly-reared queens which were soon to emerge from their cells making their strange piping. The 'quaaark, quaaark, quaaark' sound they emitted would help the first queen to exit her cell to find and dispose of any rivals before they emerged. If the queens emerged within a short time of each other they would fight until just one queen was left to be the new mother of the colony. Sometimes, if the colony is very strong, the worker bees prevent this from happening and hold the queens in their cells giving the first one to emerge the chance to leave the hive with a large number of bees as a small 'after swarm' or 'cast'. Often when I have been looking through colonies which have been prevented from swarming because of bad weather, I have noticed several queens emerging at once from their cells, the worker bees undoubtedly having prevented their escape.

Whenever I had a half an hour or so spare in my lunch break, I went to see old Mr Cranidge who lived not far from the school. He had been retired for a long time from his own business as a newsagent – work which meant that he had to be up early every day to receive newspapers and get them ready for the paper boys' rounds. He did well out of his business and spent all the winter months in Benidorm, returning home in late April. He was well-read and had an interesting library of books, some of which he loaned me, many written in the first few years of the 19th century. Surprisingly, as regards beekeeping practice, not much seemed to have changed since that time.

One day he promised me 'something to play with during the summer holidays'. I gave up trying to guess what he meant but then, on the last day of term, he presented me with an odd bit of electrical apparatus in a box. I asked him what it was.

'Don't you know?' he replied. 'Does the name Eddie Woods mean anything to you?'

I had to admit my ignorance.

'Eddie Woods was a sound broadcasting engineer. He worked for the BBC and was responsible for the broadcasting of the King's Christmas speech. But for beekeepers he is important for the Apidictor – that's what you have there.'

He then proceeded to tell me about Eddie's hobby of beekeeping and how Eddie had applied all he had learned from recording and broadcasting to help beekeepers predict when swarming was likely to happen in a hive. The Apidictor, he explained, was tuned into the particular frequencies of sound produced by bees.

By drilling a hole in the side of a hive and putting a microphone into it, the Apidictor with its amplifier enabled the beekeeper to hear what was going on. Eddie believed that when the queen began to lay fewer eggs prior to swarming, when the nurse bees were full of brood food for the grubs which didn't materialise, they began to produce a warbling sound with their wings, a sign of stress.

He further noticed that when the hive was tapped with the flat of the hand, the bees would give a momentary 'hiss' – but when the bees were due to swarm, the bees full of food and thus ready to leave the hive, there would be a longer but less dramatic response. By experimentation with thousands of hives over fifteen years Eddie also came to the conclusion that the piping noise made by queens both in and out of their cells was made by air passing through the bees' spiracles (breathing tubes) and not, as thought previously, by wing vibrations.

The Catenary Hive

Mr Cranidge (it was always Mr Cranidge and Mr Phipps – formal, yet friendly) let me keep the Apidictor and whilst it was too late to predict swarms we had great fun with it the following year when we connected it to the classroom observation hive. I never used it as a swarm predictor. I used the time-honoured way of simply tapping the side of the hive and listening for the volume and duration of the hiss emitted by the bees.

I received another interesting present from Mr Cranidge. It was an original Catenary Hive. The County Bee Instructor for Yorkshire, Bill Bielby, had developed this hive as a more natural home for bees. He said, quite rightly, that when bees build nests in the wild, the combs take on a catenary shape; that is the shape you get when you hold a long piece of string loosely between outstretched hands.

He made the hive by bending a very thin piece of marine ply to the required shape and fastening it to the sides of vertical pieces of exterior ply. Instead of using standard frames, the bees were just given top bars at the normal spacing to which had been added strips of wax foundation. The bees built enormous combs in this hive which needed careful handling. The boxes for honey were placed as normal on top of the catenary-shaped brood box, but again, just starter strips of bees wax were put in the top bars.

Catenary hive, designed and used by Bill Bileby, drawn by the late David Cushman

Bill developed this system for people who wished to keep bees but didn't want the expense of conventional beekeeping. When it came to extracting honey he showed that by cutting out the combs and hanging them up in a bag of muslin they could be compressed and strained without any additional equipment. Undoubtedly, Bill Bielby was the first beekeeping advisor who was concerned that the craft could be carried out in the simplest way possible and with the least expense. He was the fore-runner of those who today promote sustainable beekeeping.

I had empathy with Bielby's ideas and made another hive like the one Mr Cranidge gave me. The hives were simple enough and cheap to make, but the main drawback seemed to be the excessive amount of debris and moisture which collected in the base of the hive as the entrance was high up on one of the sides.

I continued to visit Mr Cranidge when he eventually went to live in a hospice, and up until the end of his life we had interesting conversations. His wife gave me his library of books and for several years I supplied her with honey from my own bees.

Wasps or bees?

To leave no doubt in the pupils' minds regarding the difference between honeybees and wasps, I managed to find an embryo wasp nest, with just the queen, a few workers and the small, umbrella-shaped paper comb. I fixed it inside an old chemical balance case and, like the bees, a tube allowed the wasps to fly in and out of their new home. Several of the pupils found the wasp nest more interesting and they eagerly awaited the return of the worker wasps with the mangled bodies of flies in their legs. They could also see the lines of the different coloured processed paper with which the wasps made an envelope to cover the nest and, with careful searching around the school grounds they could watch the wasps at work, scraping away at fence posts, gates, and wooden sheds with their tough mandibles.

As it was known that I was a beekeeper, I would often be called out to deal with swarms. Normally, I was pleased to do this as a free service just to help householders, as most were very anxious about the safety of their children, pets and themselves. I would put all my kit together and drive often several miles to the swarm. Usually the people were very grateful and from a distance watched with interest to see the capturing of the swarm. Occasionally, once the bees were tied up in my skep, the person I had helped would say:

'Those bees will be worth quite a lot, won't they,' in a tone which meant that payment was expected for them.

'Yes,' I agreed, 'They probably will be. Once I have fed them, that is, and provided them with a new home. On the other hand they might carry disease which could be transmitted to my bees, so I will have to find another site to keep them on. Why don't you have them yourself? I can tell you where to buy a hive . . . . '

At this point the conversation would usually come to an end. If the householder was not going to give up in his quest for money, I would continue with my well-rehearsed fall-back:

'I can't let you have the box that the bees are in, but I can shake them out again. The council will send someone round tomorrow to deal with the bees, if you phone them. If you want to get rid of them immediately, you could try Rentokil on their emergency line, but they will probably charge you a lot of money.'

I have been asked to remove bees from under the tiles of a roof or from beneath the lead in the apse end of churches, too. This work I have found to be best left for experts. Perched at the top of a ladder with bees flying round me and my clothes becoming sticky with honey as I cut huge heavy honeycombs from the nests, attempting to save the bees, is a gruelling task. Even when I manage to get the combs in pieces into a hive, there is always a residue of wax and honey left between the rafters, which will attract swarms in future years – unless a builder has made the roof good again and sealed up any cracks to prevent bees from re-occupying the space.

Sometimes there isn't a swarm at all when I have responded to someone's call – especially in areas where the houses are built of limestone. The hundreds of bees causing much anxiety have been solitary bees; although attracted to the same place for nest building, each bee has made its own hole in which to deposit its egg and to leave food for the young bee to complete its development after being sealed up in its cavity with mud. My role on such occasions is advisory – I give a brief synopsis of the bees' life cycle, assure the owners of the house that the bees will not harm them and say how useful the bees are for pollinating their flowers.

I give the same advice when I find that the 'swarm' is a bumblebees' nest, and will only move one if it is likely to trouble very young children in the garden or if the nest itself is at risk from a mower, for example. I was pleased to collect one, though, that first spring in my new school, for I installed it alongside the other nests in my classroom so that the pupils could see the wax pots, clumps of brood and bees of different sizes amongst the moss and fine grass, the bumblebee queen most likely having taken over an old mouse nest.

Over the years I think I disposed of more wasp nests than I ever collected good swarms. The problem with dealing with wasps was that I would have to make a second visit at dusk so that I could kill the nest once the wasps had stopped flying for the day. If I was able to carry away the dead nest, it provided extra instruction for the children – they could see the linear way in which the envelope surrounding the combs was made by *Dolichovespula* species (often

Wasp nest in a deserted bee hive

found in the apex of a roof, a tree, or even in a bird's nesting box) and the beautifully scalloped and more colourful envelope made by the common wasp *Vespula vulgaris*. I certainly believe that wasps are attracted to the vicinity of apiaries to nest and dozens of times I have removed embryo nests from empty hives, or even found complete nests in a discarded box of honeycombs. In my acre paddock I used to destroy at least five or six nests each year.

One very waspy year, by which time we had moved again, this time to Pilham, both Val and I were fascinated to see wasps still flying in late November, despite heavy frosts having occurred, alerted initially by a loud scraping noise in the still, freezing air.

My bees were in the orchard opposite the church and during the very cold weather when the bees were clustered together, the wasps would enter the unprotected entrances of the hives to plunder the honey stores and were also scraping at the wood of the external hive walls. This was most unusual and I decided to find out where the nest was. Using plain flour (not self-raising!), I coated the wasps as they left the hive, to slow them down a little, and eventually, by following their line of flight, I found the nest in an 18 inch bank under the railings on the north side of the churchyard.

This carried on throughout December so every day we made a tally of the wasps entering their nest, Val doing the recording at 1pm each day for a ten minute period as I was at school. Conditions were very cold, with freezing fog. When the temperature was at its highest, 6°C, 47 wasps entered the nest. At -1°C, 22 wasps were still returning, increasing to a record 61 on 7 January when the temperature was only 2°C.

Most wasp nests decline with the first frosts. The new queens will have already left the nest and found an hibernarium somewhere – usually on the north side of a building or bank where the sun's rays will not waken them too early in spring. However, the close proximity of my hive allowed the wasp nest to continue to thrive owing to the honey they robbed and the carcases of dead bees that they carried back to the nest for feeding their grubs, and Val was able to count returning wasps for a short period at the same time each day to ascertain the strength of the nest.

I sought advice from Dr Michael Archer of York University, an expert on wasps and hornets and author of *Social Wasps – Their biology and control* (Rentokil Library) who said that it  was most odd that a wasp nest should function for so long. He asked me to dig it up for him to examine. Although German wasps, for this is what they were, sometimes had colonies lasting for two years in New Zealand, it was never known to occur in England. We took the nest along to Michael's house in York for him to dissect. The results were interesting. As well as continuing to expand, and surviving and foraging under very cold conditions, it had reared a second brood of queens, of which 200 were hibernating in the nest. He said, though, that since the worker force had been considerably reduced, it was doubtful that the nest would have survived for more than a few weeks.

The face of a German wasp

Snelgrove system

My classes in this urban school took readily to anything to do with the countryside. We made many visits to farms, rambled through forests and spent three days at a time at Gibraltar Point nature reserve, just north of the Wash. On one occasion we were lucky to be there and experience the true atmosphere of a salt marsh, for the moon was full and a high tide flooded the causeway to the seashore. In the early morning mist we could hear the jingling of the halyards of the small boats in the creek, and the calls of birds which we would later see when the sun broke through – gulls, redshank, curlew, mallards, coot, moorhens and grebe.

Later, when a cold wind blew from the sea and we walked along the marram-grassed dunes, the buckthorn was alive with fieldfares and redwings which had just made landfall and were feeding busily on the berries. Beyond the shore, on sandbanks, grey seals dozed, but too far away for us to approach them. For a bit of fun, I let the children play for a while on an old fishing boat with many holes in its hull, which was stuck fast in the sand.

One of the girls called me to look inside the dilapidated wheelhouse. 'Look!' she exclaimed, pointing. The words 'port' and 'starboard' had been crudely painted in large letters on the appropriate side walls. The subtlety of this had not escaped her; no wonder that the boat had run aground!

During this time I increased my colonies of bees and harvested the honey, trying different methods of swarm control, none of them consistently successful. I finally settled on the Snelgrove system which allowed swarm control and queen rearing to be carried out in the same hive simultaneously and without the colony losing its full complement of foragers, so vital for honey production.

Too much was happening at home for much more to be done with bees just then. We now had two young children, a garden to tame, paths to be laid and sheds and a greenhouse to be erected. I did, however, enrol for the Intermediate Course of the British Beekeepers Association, which involved much night-time reading and essay writing. I had a delightful tutor, the well-respected and learned Miss Mildred Bindley who lived in Crewkerne, Somerset, who gave me very useful advice after having read my scripts.

After nearly six years of teaching in Scunthorpe, my life changed dramatically. Pupil numbers were falling everywhere and teachers were asked if they would be willing to move to schools which had vacancies. Several of my colleagues who were the same age as me had one ambition – to become headteachers – and if they hadn't become deputies by the time they were thirty, they thought they had failed in the profession. Whilst my mother and uncles were headteachers, I had no desire to follow in their footsteps; I enjoyed classroom teaching too much, and didn't want to be involved in administrative work, endless meetings and dealing with ancillary staff problems. I had other interesting things to do.

Out of the blue, the advisor for environmental education came to see me, and made me an interesting offer I could accept, decline, or even try out for two terms. The best part of this offer was that if it proved unsatisfactory I could return to my present post.

The offer was to join the staff of a nearby comprehensive school to take responsibility for a prestigious rural studies department, as its long-serving teacher was retiring. Apparently, no one had been found who was suitable for this specialist subject. My immediate reaction was to decline the offer. I had no experience of secondary school teaching and, to be honest, the prospect of working in a school of about a thousand pupils was a daunting prospect. On the other hand, I was beginning to feel a little frustrated in my present post and a new challenge would be invigorating. I decided not to make a snap decision, even though it would not be immutable.

First I met the young headteacher of the school and got the impression that he thought highly of the rural studies department; it was an asset to the country school and he would support any plans I might have for its further development. The retiring teacher showed me the laboratory, the greenhouses and the enormous well-maintained ornamental garden, describing the latter as a showpiece for the school. He was ex-Wisley and Kew, and the skills he passed on to his few favoured pupils stemmed from the time of his training.

This small group, an exam group, were his *raison d'etre*. If he managed to get just one of the pupils into a career in horticulture each year, then his mission was accomplished. I was taken to the tool store and shown the neat rows of hoes, rakes and spades, all the metal parts shining brightly, not a speck of soil anywhere. There was also a huge potting shed with bays filled with different composts and fertilizers and a soil steriliser. In its entirety the department was a horticulturist's dream. When he told me about the various teaching groups I realised that no girls were allowed to take the subject, which seemed rather strange in a comprehensive school where pupils were supposed to have equal opportunities.

Looking back, I think that the main reason I accepted the post, albeit temporarily to begin with, was that there were many opportunities for widening the scope of the subject, to make it more representative of rural studies, rather than being confined only to horticulture.

I soon found out, though, that as far as the pupils were concerned, even with all the gardening equipment in the store, their practical experience was limited. The four senior classes, less than twelve in each group, my predecessor having insisted that a dozen was the maximum, were allowed to do a bit of hoeing, clipping the edges of the lawns, with some trenching and raking in autumn. Most of the other lessons were demonstrations, with the school gardener completing the work. The younger pupils had done a lot of tool cleaning and stone picking. I had wondered why there were twenty buckets in the store room. The examination pupils, on a fortnightly rota, would be excused from their registration class and assembly time at the beginning of the school day, so that they could have practice in greenhouse management, their practical expertise being assessed at the end of the course by an external examiner.

At the end of my trial period I was happy to remain in the school. Girls would be allowed to take up the subject and start exam courses too; the old gardener had retired and a new groundsman had been appointed with a lot of his time to be allocated to my department and, extremely important for any school which keeps livestock, he would be paid overtime for weekend and holiday care. Furthermore, I had drawn up plans for the building of an animal unit, which had been passed by the county council architects; and I would have half an hour each morning to supervise greenhouse work and animal duties. I designed the animal housing so that all the units adjoined each other, along the front of which was a verandah and concrete floor, so that lessons and duties could be carried out in all weathers.

Even though I knew that accepting the post would mean a slight drop in salary I was keen to stay on but, surprisingly, I received a visit from the council's Director of Education, who was pleased with my decision, and said that under the circumstances my previous grade and rate of pay would be permanently protected.

I remained in the school for seventeen years – the rest of my teaching career. Once our animal buildings were built by the groundsman with the occasional help of pupils, as well as the construction of fences, drystone walls and walkways, we started to keep livestock. Most of the time we had pigs, rabbits, poultry, sheep, goats, a couple of calves, and a few hives of bees. The curriculum I devised was based on practical work which attracted pupils to take it up as one of their examination options. The one drawback to begin with was that the course only gave the examinees a Certificate in Secondary Education which tended to put off the more academic pupils seeking awards. I initially got round this by enrolling some of those who took up the course to do a GCE in agriculture as an extra which I taught at lunch times, a couple of times a week. When the examination system changed in England there was no problem, for the new GSCEs catered for all levels of ability and offered a wide range of modules in both Agriculture and Horticulture.

One thing I emphasised throughout the years was that we had a school farm and not a pets corner. This didn't mean that the animals we kept weren't to be given love and attention. Far from it! In fact the animals were to have the best of care, and low grades in practical assessments especially regarding the handling, feeding, and cleaning the housing of livestock would not be tolerated. As proof of our excellent standard of husbandry, our pure Welsh pigs over the years obtained first or second prizes in the bacon classes not only at the Louth and Brigg Christmas fatstock markets, but also at the Lincolnshire and Nottinghamshire County Shows, despite stiff competition from farmers who had hundreds of pigs to choose from. It gave me great pride to see pupils in their smart white stockmens' coats, who were no great achievers in other areas of their school work, gently, but authoritatively guiding the well-scrubbed pigs round the stock ring.

The same high standards were also expected of pupils in the ornamental gardens and on their own vegetable plots. Whilst usually their achievements in other lessons were closed up in their exercise books, in

my department their performance was exposed to the scrutiny of everyone. The pupils also had to show that they could behave responsibly and safely in areas around the school without constant supervision and without disturbing other classes. Trust was important. The head teacher was often showing parents of prospective pupils around the school.

He never knew what to expect when he brought them to my department. Sometimes the pupils would be spinning wool with home-made spindles and once they had a good piece of yarn on the go, instead of stopping to wind it round the base, they would climb on a chair, or even a table, unless I stopped them, so that they could spin an extra long length.

Pupil Jason Parker became a proficient beekeeper and helped to look after the school and my own bees. He had his own hives for a while but had to give them up when he became allergic to bee stings

At other times litters of baby rabbits would be on the tables, each of the bunnies being weighed or sketched by the children. And, for at least a week at Christmas time, the classroom would be littered with barley straw, baler twine and an assortment of evergreens when the pupils were making wreaths, usually to the sound of the Christmas pop music blaring from the radio.

At the end of the day the cleaner would look into the laboratory wondering where to start.

'Forget it,' I told her, 'It's going to be like this for a few days'.

It was a hard fact, nevertheless, for many pupils to come to terms with the end of a project which resulted in the slaughter of the pigs or eighteen-month-old cattle. The carcases were always returned to school and on such days, as well as learning about the various joints, the meat was weighed, priced and sold to staff and parents. In fact, even some of the pupils who had worn 'Save the Pigs' badges and one who had written to the head saying 'Mr Phipps is a murderer', volunteered for a spell in our laboratory butcher's shop when they learned that they could be excused from other lessons for the day. Most of them forgot their aprons, so I sent them off to the caretaker who provided them with large plastic sacks into which they then cut holes for their heads and arms.

Bee make-up

The bees were a valuable asset to my department and I devised a half term's course for the younger pupils. There was a full module on beekeeping in the GCSE syllabus for those who wished to take their studies further. I had a couple of hives outside my laboratory, which could be seen from the windows, as well as the observation hive where the bees' activities could be studied more closely.

Honey was extracted and sold on the school's annual open evening, as well as beeswax polish and candles which the pupils had made. I attempted to make some cosmetics with a class of girls on one occasion, having asked the deputy headmistress if they could at least wear the finished products for a while, normal cosmetics being strictly banned.

'That will be all right,' she said, somewhat amused, then more anxiously as an after-thought struck her, 'That is, if they scrub it all away at the end of the lunch break.'

Since the session was the first of the day, it would give the girls a bit of leeway, so we set to work. There were no problems with oatmeal and honey face packs, nor hand creams and lip balm. Even the black mascara was ok. But it was the eye shadow that let us down. The only colouring agent I had was gentian violet, so this was used, albeit in minuscule amounts. For days some girls were seen round the school with deep purple eyelids, the pigment was so difficult to remove. Whilst some of their classmates were envious, the deputy head was quite cool with me.

A time came when all responsibilities for the safety and well-being of pupils were passed down to individual teachers. For instance, any electrical apparatus within a classroom had to be checked weekly by pulling the cable at the plug to ensure that it wasn't loose, and light fittings, switches and sockets looked over. A record had to be kept to show that these inspections had been made. As a department head, I wasn't able to buy and use any new item from a garden centre or agricultural supplier without first submitting a risk assessment.

I was chased for a long time by a newly-appointed deputy head who demanded that I produce a risk assessment form for the three hives of bees. I never managed to complete it because we couldn't agree on some of the basic points. The bees were in an enclosed area in front of my laboratory surrounded by an eight foot high beech hedge which was impenetrable by bees for all seasons of the year. There was a four foot wide opening which led into this small area and the deputy head wanted a lockable gate fitted to prevent pupils having unauthorised access.

Beyond the hedge was the school playing field and from time to time a football might be kicked over. If a gate was there, a pupil would have no scruples about climbing over the gate to retrieve the ball – should bees have been upset in any way, any retreat would have been prolonged because of the gate, making him more vulnerable to stings.

Despite being next to the sports field, I can only remember two or three pupils being stung, usually on their feet, by old bees which had been trodden on when they were crawling home, their wings too worn out for them to fly. As for the observation hive in the laboratory, this held no real risk as pupils were only allowed inside the classroom when under supervision.

Looking back now, I suppose my entire department was a potential danger zone. Pupils were always working in the gardens with a range of implements, or doing livestock duties. I would walk around to see how well they were working and how responsibly, always returning to them by a different route. It was easy to catch those who were behaving in a dangerous way – and they were immediately sent back to the classroom.

Occasionally, there was a bit of mischief – for instance a couple of lads working near the car park couldn't help putting a big fat, slimy worm on the leather seat of the German teacher's BMW. It was a prank, which shouldn't have happened, but having to face a lambasting by her was enough of a punishment. As regards health and safety, my job was to teach the pupils how to work in the correct way and to be sure that in the interests of hygiene they washed thoroughly at the end of each lesson. It was difficult sometimes, though, to stop a farm boy chasing after a rat if he saw one, trying to catch it in his hands. It seemed like second nature to him.

Every year school leavers have to decide whether to continue their education, and if so in what way; or to seek employment immediately. Several of my pupils, especially the least academic ones, decided to find work and easily found placements in garden centres or in agriculture, working with pigs, sheep or cattle, and even as stable lads at a local racehorse stud.

Most of these school leavers already had holiday jobs with their employers, and knew what was expected of them. From an early age they had often worked alongside their fathers, and those who went to work in the stud were used to sleeping in the stables watching over pregnant mares. Each year a few of my pupils went on to take vocational courses at agricultural colleges in different parts of the UK, the girls usually choosing Harper Adams College in Shropshire, and boys Sparsholt in Hampshire where they could do gamekeeping. Several went on from the colleges to full-time degree courses at universities, and benefitted enormously from the practical experience they had gained.

As a rural studies teacher, my department became the venue for a beekeeping evening class which I taught over the course of a school year. Several members of staff became interested in beekeeping and I set them up with colonies of bees. One, a chemistry teacher, sadly became allergic to bees quite quickly and had to give up. Another, a maths teacher, never managed to prevent swarming, mainly because he could never find the queen. Indeed, in three years he never saw a queen and even now believes her to be a mythical creature. He should, of course, have joined my evening class. The 'typing' teacher was the only staff member who achieved some degree of success, but she lacked confidence and constantly needed help and reassurance. Whenever I taught adults, I misguidedly believed that they would always grasp the subject more easily than school children. This is far from true and I have accordingly reminded myself of this whenever I give presentations, demonstrations or write articles.

CHAPTER THREE

Oil Seed Rape

THE longer we stayed in our village, the more suburban in character it became. I had increased my number of hives and needed more room for them, so we looked for somewhere really rural to live where the bees were not surrounded by houses, and where the sight of beehives wouldn't cause country people any anxiety. There was another reason, too. Our young son, Jim, was allergic to cow's milk, so we wanted to find a place with a paddock and outbuildings, which would enable us to keep some goats. After months of searching we found a suitable place in a very small hamlet, with outbuildings, an acre and a quarter paddock, surrounded by a thick hawthorn hedge, and well set back from the road.

The house needed extensive restoration, which we knew would take up a lot of our money and time for years to come. We were lucky to be able to sell our house on the very same day that we confirmed we would buy the new one. The people who lived across the road from us liked the way we had transformed the house from its state of dilapidation to a magnificent Georgian dwelling, where even the sash windows had been replaced with hand-made ones, true to the original design, by a master carpenter.

I moved my dozen hives from various sites to my new orchard opposite the church, which was surrounded by horse chestnut trees and sycamores. I brought an unexpected extra colony with me, for a swarm took up residence in one of the empty hives which were stacked under the car port ready to be put in the removal van. I hoped that this was a good omen.

Beyond the church, a lane with an avenue of horse chestnuts and lime trees (still in flower) wound its way through the hamlet to a few houses and farmsteads, though the trees petered out after about five hundred yards. From then on there were just very low hedges with the very occasional ash or oak tree rising above them. There were a few acres of permanent pasture which still showed the old pattern of ridge and furrow, and a huge Victorian hall, with parkland, which belonged to the Marshall family who were famous for the steam traction engines and tractors which they had built at the enormous Britannia Works in nearby Gainsborough. Grazing in the parkland was a small suckler herd of Limousin and Charolais. In the fields, oil seed rape had already been swathed, the beans were black and desiccated on their stems and a huge crop of maize for silage had been planted for a two hundred-cow Friesian/ Holstein dairy herd which was presently pastured on a grass field, already mowed once that year, a couple of miles away.

Significantly there were one or two crops of red clover, but normally the nectar from the flowers would not be available to my bees as their tongues are too short. Once cut, and if allowed to flower a second time, the smaller blossoms would allow the bees to gain access to a late foraging source. During a quiet time before harvesting, what remained of the hedges had been cut back savagely, removing all the bramble flowers and developing rosehips, thus depriving bees and, later on, birds of essential food stores. Not only that, but trash from the flail littered the roads causing me to spend much time in the ensuing years mending the punctures on our childrens' bicycles, because of the thorns which pierced the tyres.

Although friendly, the farmers kept very much to themselves; apart from hiring extra workers for the dairy herd all the remaining work was covered by members of the family. It took a long time to be accepted in the village – even though I placed bees on farmers' crops. Indeed, when we were moving abroad after twenty-three years' residence, one farmer said to us, 'It's a shame you are leaving us; we are only just getting to know you.'

The farmers were totally wrapped up in their own world. I remember seeing a hot air balloon hovering low over our house and we chose to follow it. It moved over the hall and across the parkland, spooking the cows and calves. The farmers were out looking in bewilderment at the descending balloon, fearful that it might land in their barley field, fully ripe and ready for harvest. The farmer took off his hat, wiped his brow and, looking up at the balloon said 'Some folk have no consideration. Wouldn't you think that they would have something better to do on a beautiful evening like this?' However, when the balloon moved on and descended in another farmer's clover field, the crisis over, they lost interest in the unique event.

We were certainly not living in the back of beyond, but nevertheless there were some inhabitants of the village who hardly travelled further than the local town or nearest stock market. One nonagenarian farmer, despite his wealth, lived a very frugal existence. He was still accumulating land at his age, kept turkeys in what should have been his bedroom, slept on an old sofa in the big kitchen and throughout winter never had more than one bar alight on his electric fire. When the lock on his back door needed replacing, he just moved the sofa nearer the door at night to prevent anyone from gaining access. Each day he would walk through the village dressed, winter and summer alike, in his heavy tweed jacket, overcoat and flat cap, bent double, with either a bale of hay or barley straw on his back to feed his bullocks. We could always tell when he had passed by as he left a trail of Nuttalls mint papers along his route. He would stop and talk to us whenever possible. If it was me, he would ask where my other wife was – the one that did the kitchen work; if it was Val, after a while he would tell her to go home, otherwise I would be wondering what she was up to with him.

His day always started by opening the back door of his house, clearing the green slime from the top of a stone water trough, slapping water over his face and then, taking an enamel mug which hung from a nail on the wall, he would fill it from the trough and have his first drink of the day. In the days when he had a corn rick to be threshed, he would treat his helpers with cups of tea; after a while the drinks were declined, for they soon learned that the unwashed mugs in which the tea had been served were used for collecting the dead mice and rats which had been killed when fleeing from the stack.

Soon after moving into the house, I modified one of the outbuildings to make two stalls for the goats and a place for a milking stand and once everything was finished we bought two in-milk nannies: a Saanan (Pat) and a horned British Saanan (Gretchen). From that time onwards I milked the goats every morning and night, and each year we had two or three kids; the billys we kept for meat, the young female kids we sold on. The goats' milk had the desired effect on our son, and what we didn't drink, Val used for making curd and cheese.

As time went by we added geese, calves and pigs to our smallholding and, of course, we continued keeping chickens, thus utilising all the buildings and land available. The occasional cade (motherless) lamb came our way too, usually spending its first few days in a cardboard box next to the open lower oven of our Rayburn. As with the goat kids, our children enjoyed the bottle feeding, always surprised at how powerfully the young animals could pull at the teat. There are very few things more enjoyable when keeping livestock than the late night check to see that they were all well: the calves on fresh barley straw, their sweet cowy breath filling the air; the goats in their stalls contentedly ruminating, their jaws working from side to side; and the black and pink Berkshire pigs, lying next to each other half hidden in their bedding, snuffling away happily, tired after their day-long game of football.

The other main outbuilding which led to a big loft over the goat house (in which our cat had her kittens each year) was made into a workshop and had plenty of room for storing all my beekeeping equipment. Over the winter I spent many hours making up hive parts, especially roofs and floorboards, as I wanted to end the next season with about twenty hives. Most of the wood I obtained free of charge – a trailer full of exterior ply offcuts each time – from a small factory by the forest where I had previously bought fencing and sheds. With a simple table saw and a few hand tools it was possible to construct most of the items I needed for very little money, an important factor.

It had always been our intention to bring up Catherine and Jim in the countryside and to be able to produce as much of our food as we could. As well as having livestock we grew our own fruit and vegetables – both in the open and in a large greenhouse, with the children often helping with the tasks. The soil in our garden was a very heavy clay which made it impossible to work in early spring and then the ground became very hard as it dried out. Initially we used the pigs to clear a piece of the land before planting – they made a good job of removing the twitch and dock – and left the soil in a friable condition ideal for planting. Eventually though, I sectioned off part of the garden and made metre wide deep beds, using scaffolding planks to contain the soil and with forest bark for the pathways.

Crop-spraying and bees

The following spring, not long after the break of dawn, whilst I was in that dreamy state of not being fully awake, I heard the low distant droning of an aeroplane. Hearing planes at any time of the day or night was something I was accustomed to, for there was a small flying club nearby and novice pilots would do circuits of the airstrip, ascending and descending to practise their take-off and landing procedures.

We were also near an RAF base, and jet Provost trainers were frequently flying around us – and if we were very lucky the occasional delta-winged Avro Vulcan might pass over. However, this was a sound I was unaccustomed to. An aircraft passing by it wasn't, nor was it a trainer from the flying club. The plane seemed to be fixed in one area and the

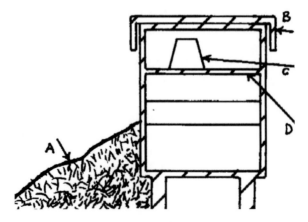

*Hive prepared to prevent bees flying during crop spraying (**see page 59**).*
A. Straw is piled loosely in front of the hive and covered with black
polythene to darken the entrance.
B. Roof.
C. Feeder filled with water.
D. Inner cover with opening which gives the bees access to water. Extra
ventilation can be given by placing a matchstick across each of the corners
just beneath the inner cover

pitch of its engine changed its tune in short, repetitive bursts. Even before
I was dressed and on my bicycle, I had realised that crop spraying was in
progress. What I needed to know was whose field was being sprayed and
whether my bees were at risk. My colonies were in units of four or five, on
the edges of fields, where the crops which were just beginning to blossom
might give me a good honey harvest. Equally, it seemed possible that if
my bees worked the fields now being sprayed, I would have a disaster on
my hands.

Oil Seed Rape

The large fields on which I had placed my hives had oil seed rape growing
in them. This was the time when a significant transition had taken
place in agriculture, a change that turned fields from being hitherto
predominantly green in spring to a very bright yellow, which contrasted
blindingly with the blue sky. Cultivation of oil seed rape was taking place
in all arable areas and on a massive scale. Like many developments in
farming, the appearance of oil seed rape in the landscape was driven by
political and economic necessity.

The EEC, wishing to be self-sufficient in many commodities, including oilseeds, gave farmers attractive subsidies to grow the crop, and the seed it produced sold at a good price. Oil seed rape was also a useful break crop in an arable farmer's rotation, as long as it wasn't grown immediately before or after sugar beet, as they shared the same eelworm problems.

For beekeepers, oil seed rape was an unexpected bonanza, for apart from beans (several acres of which were always grown near my village) the extensive fields of wheat, barley, sugar beet and potatoes were of no use for honeybees. Significant amounts of forage maize were also cultivated, though, which occasionally provided bees with pollen when there was very little to be found elsewhere in August.

The enormous increase in the cultivation of oil seed rape brought about fundamental changes to beekeeping in the UK. Like many beekeepers, I moved my hives directly onto rape fields knowing that heavy honey harvests were possible. The farmers welcomed the hives, for whilst rape flowers were not fully dependent on insect pollination, the presence of many bees speeded up pollination, resulting in more even setting and ultimately less loss of seed during swathing and harvesting. For beans, 2.5 hives are recommended per hectare and for oil seed rape, 3-4 hives give the best result.

To begin with, rape seed was produced for making a fine lubricating oil for engineering. It was neither good for crushing and making cattle cake, nor for kitchen use, as the oil contained harmful glucosinolates and erucic acid.

Eventually, scientists working in Canada produced a double zero acid variety of oil seed rape, hence the name CAN O LA, which meant the oil could be used for human consumption and animal feed. Significant advances were also made in making the oil an important alternative to diesel – and some of Lincoln's bus fleets were run on this new, 'green' biofuel (the exhaust fumes emitting a fatty smell much like the inside of a fish and chip shop), despite the fact that there are people who oppose prime food-growing land being used as an energy source, when so much of the world's population are starving.

Local farmers were particularly keen to have colonies of bees on their two main crops, beans and rape, as pollination occurred more quickly and could give a 30% increase in seed production

Whatever variety of rape, or for whatever purpose it was grown, its cultivation continued to expand with both autumn and spring sowings, so the crops could be in flower from April until July, giving bees access to a very attractive source of forage from which they could obtain high yields of nectar and pollen, over a very long period of time.

It didn't take me long to find the crop-spraying plane. I was guided by the whine of its engine as it climbed back into the sky after completing a level run of the length of a field about a mile away. The plane, in sight, by now banked, turned and swooped downwards, leaving a white trail of spray over the yellowing flowers. At one end of the field there was a man dressed in a fluorescent jacket and carrying a tall pole, who was obviously guiding the pilot towards the next swathe to be sprayed. The field wasn't near to my small apiaries – and I knew that there was sufficient forage on those places I had chosen to give the bees all they needed without them seeking out more distant flowers of rape.

Besides, I knew the farmers who owned the sites would have given me notice of their intention to spray, as they had done in previous years when my hives were on field beans. These farmers always tried to carry out their tractor-drawn application of sprays when the bees weren't flying, either very early in the morning or at twilight. Since agricultural sprays are expensive, careful consideration was given to the economic benefit of crop protection. Which would ultimately have most effect on the farming

Apart from beans and oil seed rape, there was little else for bees in our arable region

accounts, the purchase and application of fungicides and insecticides, or the loss at harvest time of a fraction of the beans? It apparently was not difficult to make this assessment with the two main problems with beans – the fungus which caused Chocolate Spot, and aphids which infested the young soft shoots of the plants. The fungicide to control Chocolate Spot was supposed to be harmless to honeybees and I can't recall any problems relating to bee losses due to its use.

However, for aphid control, two types of insecticides were commonplace then: those which killed the pests on contact; and the longer-acting systemic ones, which killed anything, pest or predator, that fed on the crop. Whilst the contact pesticides might be better for bees, their use could turn out to be more expensive for the farmer as two applications of insecticide might be necessary. There was certainly a lot of publicity by ICI promoting the use of their insecticide 'Aphox'.

At beekeeping meetings, postcards were made available for beekeepers which highlighted the fact that Aphox was more friendly to beneficial insects like bees and ladybirds, compared with other conventional pesticides, particularly the organophosphate metasystox. The postcards were meant to be distributed to farmers by the beekeepers, who in some respects were therefore acting as agents for ICI, the beekeepers' rewards being that hopefully crops would be sprayed with chemicals less hazardous to their bees, and, by adding their own contact details, farmers would be able to inform them when spraying was likely to take place.

With the increased cultivation of oil seed rape (from 25,000 hectares in the 1970s to 299,000 within a decade), pollen beetle became an enormous problem with almost all fields needing protection from the pest. To begin with, most of the insecticides were applied from the air with teams from Australia and New Zealand who were pleased to find that they could extend their flying season by working in the UK. Before spraying, an aerial survey was supposed to be carried out, the pilot informing the ground-based staff of anything he saw that might be problematic, including the presence of beehives. As beekeepers generally tried to keep their hives out of view as much possible, to prevent them from being stolen or being vandalised, this wasn't an easy task for the pilot.

During the first few years that I had my bees on oil seed rape, I lost many bees due to the crop being sprayed, even though I did everything that I could to prevent their deaths. An old beekeeping friend of mine, Ivy Jacques, who lived over the border in Nottinghamshire, showed me her hives that had been poisoned. The hives, rather shabby and old fashioned WBCs ('It's the inside of the hive that matters!'), had boards stretching from beneath the hive porches to the ground and each of them was covered with piles of dead bees.

Ivy was well known throughout Yorkshire as an expert beekeeper and lecturer who had for decades helped and guided many beekeepers to

Ivy Jacques. It was so sad to see that all her colonies had lost many bees after oil seed rape had been sprayed with insecticide

master the craft. I would listen spellbound to her stories of wagons full of bees from the heather moors speeding down the hill at Sleights above Whitby and crashing, shedding their loads. She told me about her work for the Ministry of Agriculture during the Second World War and the 'Sugar Beekeepers' and the tricks they would get up to to convince her that they had such and such a number of colonies and were therefore entitled to the extra sugar ration of 15 lbs per hive per year. It is doubtful that much of the sugar got anywhere near the bees. It was sad, therefore, to see her in front of the hives from which most of the bees had perished, creatures which she herself had protected and taught others to do so for many, many years.

To begin with, I tried moving my colonies from fields that were about to be sprayed, but it not only took a long time, it was very heavy work as the supers usually had lots of honey in them. The other option was to find another suitable site quickly which didn't have fields that were also scheduled for spraying.

Eventually, I stopped moving colonies completely, for most of the farmers I knew would only spray the crop if the amount of pests warranted such action, economically. These farmers were willing to pay for the independent advice the ministry officers gave them rather than spending money on sprays on the 'free' recommendations of chemical representatives who were always pitching for a sale. Most farmers were well aware, too, of the implications of the new Food and Environmental Protection Act which came into force in October 1986, replacing the voluntary Pesticide Safety Precautions Scheme of 1958. Under this Act, controls were imposed on the use of pesticides: none were to be used unless field trials were satisfactory; both advertising and packaging wording had to include the active ingredient of the pesticide and, where necessary, a warning that the product was 'dangerous to bees'; training had to be given to all those under the age of 25 who were to become spray operators and no one would be allowed to spray crops unless they were under the supervision of an approved, ie, certificated person.

Additionally, with beekeepers in mind, 48 hours warning had to be given of aerial spraying, though the British Beekeepers Association pushed for this to be applicable also for ground spraying. Failing to 'take precautions to protect the health of human beings, creatures and plants, to safeguard the environment and avoid water pollution' would be seen as a criminal act and those proving negligent could face prosecution.

But exactly who were the crop protection operatives to inform of their intention to spray within 48 hours? This was the nub. Part of the answer was the appointment of spray liaison officers within local beekeeping associations, who would pass on information from the farmers or contractors to those beekeepers on their list when fields in their immediate locality were going to be sprayed. However, not all beekeepers are members of associations, nor do they have to register with the ministry, which would have been beneficial not only then, but subsequently, to both groups.

Most farmers I knew had their crops sprayed at the appropriate time but not always with the least dangerous chemical. Whenever I was informed that my bees were likely to be in danger I would close the colonies up the night before. This meant opening all the hives and giving the bees some water in a feeder, then placing lots of loose straw at the front of each hive (see diagram page 54) and covering that with an old plastic fertiliser bag or black polythene. The loose straw allowed air to reach the bees, but deterred them from flying, whilst the plastic darkened the area in front of the hive and was another foil to keep the bees inside.

This system undoubtedly prevented the deaths of many bees, but it also had its drawbacks. I would return home from school to find that no spraying had been done for some reason, often because of a change in the weather, usually the wind strength, so the bees would have to be confined for yet another day. More bee deaths occurred when the rape fields were sprayed after blossom fall – when the crop was considered to be green; you don't need to walk far into a rape field to find smaller plants still in flower, stunted in the tramlines and being worked avidly by bees, all of which were at risk.

Oilseed rape honey

The cultivation of oil seed rape changed beekeeping enormously. Whereas in the past I could leave all my honey on the hive until the end of summer, this was no longer possible for the honey rapidly granulated in the comb making it almost impossible to extract in the conventional way. This meant that as soon as combs were filled they had to be extracted at once. Additionally, there was so much honey coming in from the fields that evening after evening had to be spent on this task. This pleased Jim, as he used the turning handle of the extractor as an excuse for staying up later than usual.

Extraction had to be carried out in a warm room but straining the honey through fine sieves was a very long job with constant stirring needed. One beekeeping firm produced a useful device which we trialled in school. It was called 'Strainaway' and was made up of two plastic buckets, one on top of the other, securely fastened together with a fine metal mesh separating them from each other. The honey was placed in the top bucket and once the lid was securely fitted, a simple pump very much like one used for bicycles was operated vigorously, creating a vacuum which pulled the honey through the strainer. It was even more effective if the honey had been previously warmed. I used this piece of equipment both at home and school with good success for the honey was soon cleared of any wax and other particles.

Eventually, I used a comb cutter and sold cut comb honey which had been stored in the freezer. This simple piece of apparatus is easy to use, efficient and makes clean work of what would otherwise be a very sticky and messy task

More or less at the same time as this, another firm made a honey tray which had a double stainless steel wall, inside of which was a heating element. The temperature of the water placed in this jacket could be controlled with a thermostat. Combs of oil seed rape honey which had granulated could be cut out of the frames and placed in the tray, the surface of which sloped to a tap where the melted honey could be stored in a bucket. This again, though, was a long process, and it was very important to ensure that the water temperature was high enough only to melt the wax and not overheat the honey. Whilst again, the apparatus helped me enormously, it still meant that many evenings in early summer would be occupied doing this sticky work when I would rather have been outside doing other tasks in the apiary: honey extraction is for me the least attractive part of beekeeping.

When honeybees are on oil seed rape, it is tempting to remove all the honey as quickly as possible, for the reasons already mentioned. However, if all the honey is taken and bad weather follows, which often happens, then it is necessary to feed the bees, so I eventually chose to keep all the honey on the hives until winter. Then there was always plenty of honey for the bees, should they need it, as well as for us later on, and I would save myself a lot of work during the summer months.

Having adopted this system, I no longer put sheets of wax foundation in the honey frames for the bees to build on. When the first frosts came, I would go to the hives and remove the supers of honey which were empty of bees by then and, using the tray, process the honey. I left just under an inch of comb with honey at the top of the frames which would be good starters for the bees to build on in the following spring.

Occasionally I would take some of these combs full of fresh honey in May, before the honey had set, cut them into cigarette-packet size pieces and put them in the freezer. When a piece of comb was taken out and allowed to thaw, the honey would remain liquid for a breakfast or two. A simple device, a comb cutter, made this work easier for me and, instead of wrapping the pieces of comb in cellophane, I was able to buy plastic tubs of the same size as the comb for marketing the 'cut honey'. Not only was this *(see photos opposite)* the simplest and purest way of harvesting honey, the price, per pound was much higher than that of a jar of honey and was always in demand.

Despite the problems brought about by the introduction of huge acreages of oil seed rape into the landscape, by adopting different management techniques I had the prospect, as did other beekeepers, of obtaining enormous yields of honey virtually on our doorstep, a potential that had never before seemed possible. Even beekeepers who had no rape

Jeremy Burbidge removing supers of oil seed rape honey. Normally, when moving bee hives, as can be seen in this photo, clearing boards fitted with bee escapes are placed below the supers full of honey 24 hours before harvesting

fields near them were willing to travel many miles to put their colonies on the crop, especially if there was someone who would keep an eye on them and deal with any swarms that might emerge or close them up if spraying was to occur.

My friend Jeremy Burbidge brought many hives from West Yorkshire and placed them on the field next to my garden. When he came to collect the hives they were heavy with honey and we decided to remove the honey supers before carrying the hives to the trailers. We started this work about half an hour before it was dark. The first task was to remove the bees from the boxes. Normally, this is done with bee escapes and takes about 24-hours for the bees to leave the honeycombs. We chose a very quick method which has been used by commercial beekeepers for many years.

This involved taking the roof off the hive and putting a cloth, to which benzaldehyde had been added, over the top of the frames. The bees certainly reacted in the way that they were expected to: they fled from the honeycombs and boiled out of the front of the hive. I think we had used too much of the prussic acid-smelling substance, I think it was called Bee Go. It certainly lived up to its name. I have never used it since.

Once the honey was safely stored on the trailer, we had to get the bees back into the hives, as huge clumps of them covered the outer walls.

Using smoke it took us a very long time to get them to go home. The heavy rain which accompanied a sudden thunderstorm helped in one way, but with our clothing soaking wet, the angry bees managed to give us dozens of stings. There comes a point during this type of onslaught when you resignedly decide to just press on regardless; the job had to be completed. Not surprisingly, many of the bees travelled back to Yorkshire clinging to the outside of their hives.

I was not surprised that we received so many stings – for even though the weather conditions and use of benzaldehyde might have angered the bees, it is known generally that bees are often more aggressive when working one floral source. I have found this to be true also whilst the bees are on the heather moors when there is nothing else for them to forage on.

Other management problems also occurred when I kept bees in a predominantly oil seed rape growing area. Even if supers had been added for the enormous influx of nectar at the right time, the bees would prefer to store the incoming nectar in the part of the hive where the brood was raised – where it was warmer – leading to congestion which triggered early swarming. Often, winter rape could be followed by a spring sown variety, which extended the foraging season at the end of which the colonies looked tired and worn out. As less food was coming into the hive, the queen's egg-laying was reduced and by mid-summer the bees in my part of England had little to look forward to until the following spring. I therefore had to feed the colonies to encourage the queen to keep laying, so that there would be plentiful young bees to survive the winter. Too much rape honey in the hive wasn't the best food for bees to overwinter on, for it became hard and dry, another reason why feeding with sugar syrup was necessary.

CHAPTER FOUR

Out-Apiaries

DURING the time of the rapid expansion of oil seed rape, I decided to increase the number of my hives to forty and join the Bee Farmers Association, a body for commercial beekeepers of which there were about five hundred in the UK. I looked at the price of cedarwood Smith hives, but they were too expensive. Jeremy Burbidge helped by locating twenty second-hand British Commercial hives for me, and, as for the rest, I bought twenty National hives in pine, complete with two supers and all frames from a new firm, Budget Beekeeping, at a very attractive price. The money for these items came from honey sales – most of which was sold locally to contacts or colleagues at both my own and Val's workplace. Val also bought some of the hives with money from her first pay cheque when she returned to work.

The British Commercial hives have the same external dimensions as the National hive, though their brood boxes are much deeper but their honey supers are interchangeable. The extra room provided by the Commercial hive gave more space for colony development and perhaps delayed swarming, so swarm control could be carried out in the smaller National hives well before it would be necessary to go through the same procedures with the Commercials. Well, that was my theory, and in practice it seemed to work. The bees to fill the hives were obtained by dividing up the colonies in the Smith hives and letting them rear new queens.

Except when oil seed rape was in flower, there was nowhere in my immediate locality that could support forty hives on one site, so it was necessary to seek out apiaries which would have some forage for the bees when the rape had finished. I decided to have no more than six hives on one site and to locate them on a circular route which could easily be driven around in a couple of hours. I continued to keep a few colonies in my garden as we had planted a lot of fruit trees that needed pollination, and, by watching the activities of the bees in the home apiary I would have a rough indication of what the bees were doing elsewhere for, as the crow flies, none of the apiaries would be more than eight miles away.

My home apiary - too many bees on one site! The area was really only suitable for the year-round keeping of about six hives. The apiary consisted of several types of beehives, including WBCs, British Commercial and National hives, as well as others in the bee house. Whilst this is not an efficient way of beekeeping, it allows several interesting comparisons to be made

For some years I experimented with keeping half a dozen hives in a bee house – a system which is quite common in Germany, Switzerland, Austria and Slovakia – and with the help of Budget Beekeeping I designed the building which they then constructed for me, the cost being met by a generous friend. Once the hives were installed in the building I was able to examine the colonies no matter what the weather conditions were, which was very useful in Britain's uncertain climate. However, there were several drawbacks in managing the colonies, some of them due to the unsatisfactory design of the bee house. When the windows were opened the bees from the hive being examined would leave the shed easily enough, but the windows were too small to allow enough light for me to examine the combs thoroughly and didn't give enough ventilation for the smoke from my smoker to leave.

A concrete floor would also have been better as the wooden floor meant that any movement caused vibration which easily upset the bees. However, I would – with modifications in design – recommend the use of a bee house for surburban beekeepers who just wish to keep a few hives

My Bee House

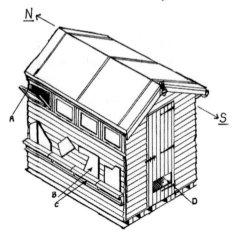

Exterior of bee house

I aligned the bee house from north to south so that the hives were facing east and west. If the weather was very warm, as well as opening all the windows, I would open the door fully.

Exterior:

A. Outward opening windows (in retrospect, these should have been much bigger).

B. Different shaped and coloured markers to help the bees to navigate back to the right hive.

C. Entrance for a bee to its hive.

D. Mesh in the lower part of the door for ventilation. Similar ventilation is provided in the apex of the north side of the bee house.

Interior:

E. Brood boxes of hives - no roofs are needed but the boxes have bee proof covers.

F. Honey supers stored beneath the stands ready for use.

G. Work top.

H. Storage space for honey extractor and straining tank.

I. Stands for the hives - raise the top of the brood box to a comfortable working height.

J. Carpeted floor to help reduce vibration.

K. An entrance tunnel fixed between the house wall and the hive entrance to prevent draughts and equalise pressure.

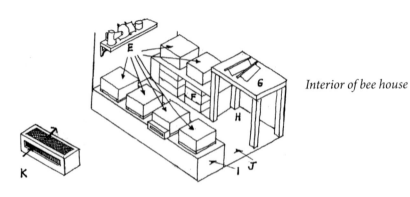

Interior of bee house

and who have only limited time to look after their bees – as they would not have to depend on the vagaries of the weather for colony examination. Also, they would have enough space in the shed to store all the equipment needed for beekeeping.

I also chose to put only half-a-dozen hives in each out-apiary because work on that number of colonies could be completed properly in a shortish time, then I would have a break whilst travelling to the next site. I am sure that when there are a large number of colonies in one place, the attention given to those at the end of the row is much less than those which are first examined. I have noticed that some beekeepers will not always add new fuel to the smoker when they are nearing the end of their work – this means that the smoke becomes very hot, which disturbs the bees – or in very bad cases small embers fly from the nozzle. The first smoker I had was the Bingham type with a small furnace and straight nozzle. The fuel I used was rolled up corrugated cardboard, the choice of many beekeepers. I had to recharge the furnace sometimes and as I pulled the nozzle away – which was tight – within a few seconds the heat would burn through my gloves. I changed to a much larger copper smoker with a bent-nosed nozzle which was hinged to the furnace so adding more fuel was easier and safer. I gave up using corrugated card when I found it was manufactured with glue and took, instead, to using old sacks which had been left to weather outside for a year or two.

I hoped this would get rid of the chemicals in the hessian as most of the sacks in our area had been used for transporting seed potatoes which had been treated – for this reason they were no longer used in schools for sack races. Since then I have used any suitable material for fuel which will burn slowly and give a cool smoke – dried grass, rotten wood, eucalyptus leaves and cow dung – and I usually add a handful of rosemary or sage to sweeten the smell.

Where to site your hives

My main considerations when choosing out-apiaries were as follows: suitable forage in spring and late summer; security; a sheltered but open position which would allow the free drainage of air so no frost pockets; and accessibility. One farmer let me have a good site which was at the end of a track a hundred yards from the main road. Behind the hives, trees gave shelter from the north and east, and the field sloped down to the west. Often beekeepers are told to have their hives facing east to catch the morning sun. I wanted my bees facing west as I was more likely to be examining the hives in the evening after work, so I needed them to be in full sunlight then.

Wet, sandy heathland

To the north-west of my village there was an extensive tract of sandy land; the sand had blown in from the coast in the 16th century. After the First World War and the setting up of the Forestry Commission, most of this poor quality and badly-drained soil was afforested with Scots and Corsican Pines, all in solid ranks five feet apart. Nothing grew between the trees except sometimes bracken, though in later years a fringe of deciduous trees was planted around the perimeter of the plantations.

The Lincolnshire Trust for Nature Conservation managed to acquire a piece of this wet sandy heathland as there were several rare species of plant and animal life which were in need of protection including orchids, sundew and a coastal species of butterfly, the grayling, as the unique grasses for their caterpillars' food was found in abundance. I tried to get a site on the nature reserve but failed, despite having helped with its management for several years. The reason was simple enough: my honeybees would compete with their wild relations and with biodiversity being the buzzword of the time, everything was being done to conserve all forms of life. Beekeepers have found that this situation still exists with conservation bodies, several of whom consider honeybees to be an alien species.

Whilst it is true that there have been many imports of different species of honeybees into the UK since the 19th century, it has been proved that honeybees were well established in the British Isles before the land bridge between us and the rest of Europe disappeared in 7,000 BC and so are native to this island. Also, bees which have been introduced and left to their own devices soon hybridise and take on the characteristics of native honeybees. I particularly wanted to place my bees on the common as there was a huge area of heathers of different species, not enough for me to get any surplus from my bees, but enough to tide them over during August and September.

Additionally, in spring there was plenty of gorse and pussy willow which would give the bees a very good start to the season. Since the outbreak of myxomatosis in 1953, the heathland was rapidly disappearing as there were few rabbits to control the pines and birches which were choking the heather. On many occasions I took work parties from school to pull up the seedling birches and in December we dug up the small pine trees to sell as Christmas Trees, our staff members preferring the pines to spruce as the needles didn't shed. Fortunately, a farmer whose son I taught helped out by letting me put bees on his land just across the way from the reserve.

Forest apiaries

I found my other sites with the help of the Forestry Commission. I already knew the chief forestry officer. There was a small rental charge for the sites, he told me: £2 per annum for five hives and 50p for each extra colony, but first he had to contact an estate that rented the forest for shooting. Most of the rides in the forest were closed off with gates to deter trespassers but there were a few public bridle paths which were well used. I don't think the gamekeepers were too keen to have me keeping bees on their rented land, but I chose sites on the edges of the forest and well away from where they released and fed their pheasants. I was provided with a key and they soon got used to my presence.

I made solid wooden stands for all the hives in the out-apiaries, with three colonies to each stand. I gauged the height of the stands so that my arms would be in a comfortable position when examining the bees, and I would not have to do much bending down.

My forest apiaries were each stocked with six colonies with three hives on each stand. The height of the stands gave easy access to the brood chambers so there was no need to stoop when examining the colonies

Despite only being a few miles apart, each group of colonies was different in several ways: the aroma coming from the hive; the range of pollens collected; the amount of stores; and the strength of the bees in each apiary. All the bees were in flying distance of oil seed rape every spring, and some of the newer varieties tended not to granulate so quickly. Some of the honey might have a trace of sycamore early in the season, or blackberry in summer and also willowherb if it was growing on the railway embankment.

On the light sandy forest soil, willowherb produced only pollen for the bees. An unkempt piece of pasture offered thistles and ragwort, too, though as noxious weeds they should have been controlled by the land owner. Some beekeepers are worried about having colonies near to ragwort, not only because the honey is said to assume a rank taste when bees have been working the flowers, but also because the alkaloids present are poisonous.

No matter where the apiaries were located, the one thing most of the colonies shared was their bad temper, with some being far worse than others. On one site I had only to park my car on the side of the road to rouse an angry response from the bees, even though they were at the end of the clearing some thirty yards away.

I have known thunderstorms make bees angry – but then most of the bees stinging are those which had been out foraging and are in a rage when they see their home being plundered so jump to the defence of their colony. Bees can be very angry, too, when working on monofloral crops like oil seed rape or heather, and also when a nectar flow suddenly ceases, but these bees were bad full-time. An explanation could have been that the hives were too near the pine trees and as the trees swayed their shallow roots would move and rock the hives, but whatever the cause, working with bees like that was not enjoyable, no matter how much honey they might provide.

The joys of checking out-apiaries

I used to drive around the out-apiaries at least every fortnight throughout the year just to check that the colonies were alright, and more frequently, of course, when there was work to be done, the route covering a distance of about twenty miles. The last hour or so before sunset or very early in the morning were the best times for me, for once I had confirmed that there was no problem with the bees, I would walk through the woods or across the common. Amongst the oaks and beeches on the fringe of the forest I would often see a pair of red squirrels, which surprisingly would not scamper off, but would circle the boles of trees and take inquisitive peeps at me. Where an apiary looked onto arable land, it was the hares that would fascinate me, the dark tips of their ears always standing proud as they chased after each other.

On a foggy winter morning I would watch the sluggish flight of lapwings as they rose from the ploughland, their ragged wings looking heavy and damp. Up they would go into the sky and, having completed just half a circle, they would descend once more to the rich earth still making their plaintive cries. From a dyke a jack snipe would rise suddenly and speed away on its diagonal path, or a woodcock hidden away would make its hollow call.

But it was the warm summer evenings on the common that were the best, for then I would be able to watch nightjars from just an arm's length away. I have seen these magnificent birds hover a few feet above the ground and pick moths out of the air, and on another occasion watched a female hover, fly around in a circle and then settle on a marker post. A male nightjar copied her performance, but whilst circling, he clapped his wings loudly together.

On frosty winter mornings I would find time to watch ferreters at work along the sandy hedgerows, netting the exits to burrows before they slipped a ferret into the only open hole. In the early autumn evenings the woodland rides would be full of pheasants waiting expectantly for the gamekeeper to turn up with their extra ration of food and along the fences I would see evidence of his work – the gruesome gibbet hanging from which were the bodies of weasels, stoats, crows and magpies.

On my site near the common was a barn in which a barn owl had set up its home. Whenever I went past I would take a look inside and collect the pellets which the owl had regurgitated. The pellets were taken to school and the bloodthirsty, budding pathologist schoolchildren enjoyed teasing the bones out from the fur or feather and, using a chart, were able to identify the small mammals that the owl had consumed, usually by their dentition. One haul included several shrews (with their red jagged teeth), wood mice and voles.

I really enjoyed the visits to my out-apiaries, they allowed me to escape from everything connected with my other life at a time when for no obvious reason I began to have long bouts of depression. There was nothing to point the finger at what was causing me the problems, my career was going well and I enjoyed being with our children, looking after them after school until Val came home from her work at the Dyslexia Institute a couple of hours later. Although at times I had to go in to school in the evening or at weekends – especially when a pig was due to give birth, it was work that I enjoyed and didn't find onerous. Driving from apiary to apiary and walking through the forests certainly seemed to help dispel my bad moods which would otherwise fester for days on end.

Disasters with the bees

Whilst keeping bees in out-apiaries was usually idyllic, there were disasters, too, that had to be contended with. On one occasion, although he had been warned by the chief forester about the presence of my bees, a contractor felling trees allowed one to fall squarely on top of two of the hives, shattering the roofs and exposing the bees to the cold winter weather. I wasn't aware of this until a couple of days after the event. The contractor failed on two points: first, to contact me before the felling, and then afterwards when my bees were in danger of perishing.

He was the kind of person you could never make headway with, so any thought of compensation was out of the question. Val and my brother, Gordon, helped me to clear the branches away so that I could get to the hives to straighten them up and put a new roof on each one. The bees were tightly clustered between the frames and luckily it hadn't rained, so hopefully they would be all right, but I wouldn't be sure until spring. I left the colonies on the site for, if that was the contractor's way of telling me he didn't want them there, I wasn't going to give him the satisfaction of moving them. His work wasn't really in that sector anyway, so I think it was a deliberate action on his part.

Worse was to come. On the night of 3 January 1976, a strong gale reached hurricane force, which at 10.45pm knocked down three pylons and plunged every house in the area into darkness. At first light I drove to the forest to see what damage there was. Everywhere pines had been

uprooted, the huge balls of soil surrounding the roots standing well above ground level. Other trees had snapped halfway up their trunks. The devastation was enormous. In all, the chief forester reckoned there were 300 acres of damage. I returned later with Val and Gordon to drag my five hives clear of the fallen branches. I was lucky. Only one was damaged but as we tried to pull it away, the bees flew

Even in sheltered locations, apiaries could be struck by severe gales

out from the broken sides and soon perished in the freezing weather. The following day I managed to return with someone who had a chainsaw, to free the hive from the branches. The bees were less agitated this time and I put the frames in a new hive and fed them with a 7lb block of candy as some of their stores had been pulverised. Surprisingly, though badly disturbed by fallen trees on two occasions, the bees survived and the queens were laying well in the spring. It is surprising how resilient honeybees are, for several times I have found that when this has happened, they have clustered together and survived despite the cold and the rain.

Woodpecker attack

A more common problem in the forests was the green woodpeckers. I knew they were about as I heard them hammering away at the trees, particularly on aged and partly hollow silver birches. I had heard their almost hysterical laugh-like calls, and seen them as they flew an undulating flight-path from tree to tree. But I didn't expect to have trouble from them so soon with my woodland apiaries. I should have checked the colonies immediately after the first hard frosts, for that is when the woodpeckers are likely to strike. They can't get at their normal food of ants when the earth is frozen solid.

A neglected apiary with hives holed by woodpeckers

Four of my colonies had been attacked by woodpeckers, each of the hives being drilled through in various places, and on the side of one hive, a piece of wood three inches by one inch had been completely chiselled away. This is one of the few drawbacks of cedar hives; they are vulnerable to this type of damage. A green woodpecker with its eight-inch tongue can soon feast on the bees once it has made a hole through the wall, but judging by the number of chilled bees outside the hives, the colony must have tried to drive away the intruder. Eventually I put wire netting around the hives as a permanent remedy, but before that I had to cover the holes made by the woodpeckers with pieces of plywood otherwise mice would have got in and completed the destruction of the colony.

With so many hives in need of immediate protection I needed a quick deterrent, so I fastened skirts made out of fertiliser bags, cut into strips for half their length, around all the hives. This cheap method seemed to work well as a temporary measure and I had no further problems with the birds. I have no enmity towards woodpeckers. They are attractive birds and were only attacking the hives out of sheer necessity. Under normal circumstances they leave them well alone.

The only other problem I had with an out-apiary, the one near the common where the bees were on the farmer's land on the banks of a drain, occurred after days of heavy rain. I checked colonies in the middle of the day and found that the water had risen over the bank and was lapping around the alighting boards of the hive. The weather was mild and the bees were flying so it wasn't possible to close the hives up. Instead, I fetched a couple of aluminium ladders from home and made a temporary stand a foot or so above the water level to prevent the bees from drowning.

Hives on the edge of the forest with protection against woodpeckers

Human predators

Other beekeepers were more unfortunate than me at that time and suffered losses of bees due to vandalism and theft. The main suppliers of bees in Lincolnshire, E.H. Thorne, lost dozens of colonies over a very short period; the world-famous bee breeder Brother Adam of Buckfast Abbey had many of his special queens removed from his mating hives in Dartmoor; and quite recently, bees being used for research in Scotland were stolen, thus ruining months of scientific work. Sadly this happens all too often, even more so when there is a shortage of bees and their price has increased. What makes it worse is that it is other beekeepers, members of the same craft, who are responsible for this criminal activity.

More recently, I have lost a few colonies in a mountain out-apiary in Greece, but this was mild compared to the problems of a Greek lady beekeeper who was having hives stolen night after night. A friend of hers noticed an unfamiliar pick-up truck at her apiary one night and telephoned her quickly. He waited for her to arrive and together they confronted the thief. He turned out to be a priest, dressed in jeans and a tee shirt, his cassock left in the back of the pickup.

'Forgive me, please,' he cried. The beekeeper wasn't having any of this and shouted:

'Yes, I'll forgive you. But only when you are hanging on that olive tree over there!'

The police took him away, but the clergy protect their own, and he got away with it, as he had for rustling cows not long before.

A beekeeping friend of mine in a neighbouring Greek village found that when he looked into his hives, instead of finding beautiful combs of honey, in their place were old, black, dirty, empty combs. It took him a long time to find out what was happening. A monk living in a cave above us would creep down, open my friend's hives and take out combs full of honey, replacing them with old empty ones. When the beekeeper became aware of what was happening, he promised not to press charges if the monk stopped this highly irregular practice.

Some attacks on beehives here in southern Greece can only be described as downright nasty. A beekeeper in one of the mountain villages started up in beekeeping and put all his hives – over a hundred of them – in his olive grove. One morning all the bees were dead, having been sprayed with insecticide. It was easy to guess which rival beekeeper was responsible, but proving it would be impossible. A more crazy occurrence took place when beekeepers throughout the Peloponnese found that many of their colonies had been killed with pesticides. Eventually, the police apprehended an Albanian man on a moped who, for no discernible reason, just went from apiary to apiary killing the bees with insecticide. As I am writing this, police are investigating the deliberate poisoning of a thousand colonies with a deadly synthetic pyrethroid in New South Wales, Australia.

Vehicles for Beekeeping

The sales manager looked just like a car dealer for farmers and countrymen should look, dressed as he was in a heavy tweed jacket, moleskin trousers, a tattershall check shirt and game conservancy tie.

'Do you pull?' he asked me.

'Um, yes. I suppose so,' I answered in a non-committal way, not understanding his question at all.

'In that case you'll need a hook fitted and wired for a trailer,' he continued. 'You already have a trailer I suppose? No? No problem; we can soon fix you up with one.'

At last I got his drift. I was buying a Daihatsu Four Track with selectable high and low four-wheel drive, a 2.8 diesel engine and was assured that it had 'plenty of pulling power' – the first vehicle I had bought specifically with my bees in mind.

Previously, I had had to rely on the Volkswagen Passat family estate car for my bees, but this didn't always fit in with our domestic life. Honey, wax and carbonised smokers don't mix very well with carrycots and clean clothes, though Val never complained about the sticky mess I sometimes forgot to clean up. Once Val was working again and we needed a second vehicle, I relied on a succession of old cheap vans to get me to school and for collecting animal food, straw and hay both for the school farm and our own smallholding, as well as taking sheep for dipping and the nanny goats to the billy.

The Daihatsu was a good powerful vehicle, but there was little room in the back so a trailer was always needed for the hives.
New varieties of clover grown for seed produce very little nectar so we never got a good crop of honey

All my vans up until now had been bought from a friendly Northumbrian who had a garage in the next village. It seems a long list looking back now – a green mini van too small for my long legs and six-foot-two inch height, a more powerful and better Ford 7cwt, a Renault 4 with everything including the gear stick and handbrake on the dashboard (and with the really useful quarter-opening door at the back of the van so that long items could be transported), and the last of my really cheap vehicles, my much-loved buff-coloured Ford Transit.

The Transit had a lot of floor space for hives and the cab was separate from the back, so apart from having to climb in the back to drag the hives inside, it was quite useful for beekeeping and carrying large loads of hay and straw. On one occasion it was used to take a dozen sixteen-year-old pupils who had purposely missed their bus from school to the technical college ten miles away for their link course. The head was well aware of the skiving which went on and wasn't going to let the pupils get away with it. Besides, if they were left in school all morning, a teacher and classroom would have to be made available for them. The head started the staff briefing that morning with, 'Whoever has that old builder's van, would they come and see me, please.' The pupils had to sit on straw bales and if there had been an accident I dreaded to think about the consequences, not just for the pupils but as regards health and safety regulations as well as my own insurance cover.

One winter some rats got into the van, attracted by that heavenly scent of the molasses in the goat's food that I was taking into school. I tried everything I could to evict them, including very thick smoke with my bee smoker going full blast. The rats had decided to set up home in the vinyl below the cab roof and, short of cutting it all away, there was nothing I could do. My daughter, Catherine, was reluctant to travel to school with me. For years she had suffered the humiliation of being chauffeured in a range of decrepit vehicles, but a Transit with rats in – that was the pits! Even Radio One, playing louder than I normally permitted, wouldn't drown out the scratches and squeaks of the rats. One afternoon our cleaning lady asked for a lift home.

'I'd like to Mrs B but there are rats in the van . . .' I told her.

'Get away wi' yer, John!' she said. 'It's just another of yer stories.'

When she was safely strapped in and we set off down the drive, I looked with horror at the scabby, scaly tail dangling from a hole above the rear-view mirror, swinging gently with the movement of the van. Mrs B. mercifully didn't see it or she would have had hysterics.

I already had been offered money for my Transit on several occasions by some local gypsies. We often stopped and talked 'Transits', and after this episode I was thankful for their offer which I readily accepted. I had told them about the rats, but they seemed unworried.

As promised by the car salesman, the Daihatsu did pull, and very well – often towing a trailer with twenty hives to local fields as well as 150 miles north to heather sites. I found that by using the regulator placed near the steering wheel, I could get the Daihatsu to move along very slowly as I lifted hives off the trailer and put them on their stands. It was much better than getting in and out of the cab all the time. There was one drawback – I couldn't open the rear door fully when the trailer was hooked up, but that may have been due to the type of bar on the trailer itself.

For general beekeeping purposes, it wasn't that useful, for there was very little room in the back for hives, so it meant that a lot of the time I had to use the trailer. The running costs of the Daihatsu were also heavy, especially when replacing tyres. Whilst I liked sitting up high in the cab and being able to see what was growing in the fields, Val hated both driving it and being a passenger, especially on long journeys. I was reluctant to sell the Daihatsu, but I knew really that a good pick-up truck would be a much better option. What happened subsequently was one of my craziest purchases.

I should have known better, of course, or at least have had a very long test drive. The pick-up I bought, although new, had its window handle fall off as I left the garage. It also had two flat spots when I tried to accelerate in first and second gear. This made turning out from a T-junction a very hazardous manoeuvre. I think I kept the vehicle for three weeks before returning it to the garage. The full name of the vehicle was Fabryka Samiochodon Osobrwych or, as you may have guessed, a FSO, the acronym for the factory in Poland where it was built. It was a modification of the Fiat 125, and certainly the worst, noticeably heaviest and noisiest vehicle I had ever driven. It was even worse if the fibreglass hood was fastened over the back of the truck. I didn't even try loading hives onto it, I just wanted to get rid of it as soon as possible.

My luck was in once again, for when I returned the Fiat to the garage, there standing on the forecourt was a beautiful red Subaru pick-up. The bodywork was good, the mileage was low, it had selectable four wheel drive with both high and low sets of gears. I liked the curve of its body from the back of the cab to its sides and immediately set off for a test drive. With no hood on the back, the Subaru flew along like a sports car with its 1.8 engine and I had no hesitation in buying it.

On a practical level I found that I could easily carry a dozen or more hives in the back despite the wheel arches taking up some of the room. The only drawback I could possibly think of was that its wheel base was low compared with other four-wheel drive vehicles, but it handled superbly on the roads and you never got that feeling, which Val had had about the Daihatsu, that you were about to roll over. It was an excellent vehicle for pulling a trailer and it served me well for several years before I left England for Greece.

Hives transported to the heather moor. The Subaru pick-up truck was undoubtedly the best vehicle I have ever possessed. I wish it was still in production. It could comfortably pull 40 hives on a trailer, with the roofs and all other equipment in the back of the truck

The benefits of expansion

The establishment of a group of apiaries made an enormous difference to the kind of honey I was able to sell. By blending pure white oil seed rape honey with other honey stored by the bees from different areas, its colour was darker and it had a more distinctive and less sweet taste. This mixture was more attractive to my customers, even more so if it was seeded with a small amount of finely granulated honey which, when stirred into the mass, gave it a creamy and easily spreadable texture.

As I now had a good vehicle and trailer I was able to move some of my hives further away from home in search of more crops on which my bees could forage. Over the River Trent in Nottinghamshire, large acreages of flax were being grown, the fields a dull, almost leaden, lavender blue in the morning when the new flowers opened each day, but by nightfall all the petals would have fallen.

The flax was being grown for its linseed oil as there was a great demand for it in the production of linoleum which was experiencing an exciting revival. I checked out what my chances of obtaining honey might be from the crop and was pleased to read that in New Zealand, where it was commonly grown, even in dry weather, nectar could literally be shaken out of the flowers. Half a dozen colonies were moved onto the crop, though the poor overcast days which followed meant that I had to feed my bees rather than return with hives full of honey.

I had the same experience with fields of white clover onto which I placed my colonies. The bees appeared to be working the flowers, but no honey was stored in the supers. Later I learned that the clover was a new Aberystwyth variety and, unlike the clovers so common in sheep pastures of ages past, nectar secretion was poor. The farmer was satisfied though with the seed set, so at least one of us was happy with my bees' performance.

One farmer and beekeeper, John Green, decided to grow phacelia on a piece of set-aside land. Phacelia is very attractive to bees and was grown principally by farmers as a green manure. It would be drilled directly onto corn stubble and usually ploughed in before flowering commenced. As the plant grew, it would take up nitrogen from the soil, thus preventing leaching, and slowly release the nutrient as it decomposed. John, of course, allowed his crop to flower and it was a joy to see his bees working in the huge mauve field beneath a light blue summer sky.

John was a frequent visitor to our house. He, too, was old-fashioned in his approach to the craft, spent no money on anything but basic equipment and cared more about the welfare of the bees than how many jars of honey he could get from them each year. As a farmer his arable land was cultivated with wheat, barley and potatoes, but a lot of the farm income was derived from the raspberries and strawberries they grew, selling them either ready-packed in punnets or as pick-your-own.

Outside the family farmhouse where he lived with his mother was a straw-filled crewyard surrounded by a range of brick out-buildings where pigs, a few cattle and poultry roamed together. Inside, in front of the fire, John's mother sat in a large leather armchair on each side of which were volumes of the farm and account books, no doubt going back for many years. John was a shy, taciturn man, but as we got to know him he would delight us with almost a smile.

We always knew when John was coming down our drive by the sound of his Land Rover Defender which would set our springer spaniel barking furiously. John always managed to arrive just as we were about to finish the first course of our evening meal and despite having already eaten, he didn't need much persuasion to share what was left with us. He was usually dressed in the best quality clothes that a country outfitter could supply and if his visit wasn't about bees, he had usually come to show me a new camera he had bought, as we shared an interest in medium format film cameras.

Hives on the moors

Just as sportsmen eagerly await the beginning of the grouse season on the glorious 12th of August, many beekeepers, too, will have their colonies of bees ready for this date for their annual trip to the moors. The journey to the heather marks the culmination of the beekeeper's season and, like my colleagues, I would have been preparing my bees for this event every year, starting in late spring, when new colonies are established, headed by the year's crop of young queens. Not only is heather honey the most sought-after hive product, thus commanding a high price, it can provide bees in many districts with the best winter stores.

Heather honey is very nutritious as it contains high levels of pollen. As such, it provides valuable amounts of protein for brood development in early spring, thus ensuring that the colonies build up quickly. Stories abound in beekeeping literature of the long trail to the moors and back, and through the course of history, wheelbarrow, bicycle, horse and cart, car and lorry have all been used for the transportation of bees.

John Green invited me to share his stance – his heather site – in Derbyshire one year, our hives securely fastened in a horsebox which he towed up to the moors above Ladybower Reservoir, beyond Sheffield. But for many years my favourite site was much further away at Grantley, just a few miles north-west of Ripon, where my hives were set down in the shelter of a dry stone wall. The sheep had usually been turned out of the field by then, though occasionally some inquisitive cows showed a brief interest in the new arrivals. The farm, Castille Farm, belonged to Mr Nicholson. Apart from a few sheep he had a small dairy herd. I would prepare my colonies the evening before my trip north by fitting each hive top with a gauze screen and blocking the entrances with foam rubber, once the bees had finished flying for the day. Over the years I tried several ways of securing the hive parts together, including lock slides which had removable wedge-shaped closures and large staples of which four had to be fitted to each part of the hive. The latter didn't stop the hives from moving apart on bad roads, but even when the bees were able to escape, they usually clung on to the hives when we were moving.

However, when it came to putting the hives on their stands at the end of the journey, the loose bees made my work far from pleasant. Best of all was a new type of hive strap which, when securely tensioned, held all parts of the hive together and I used them at once and never had the problem of bees escaping again.

I used a hive barrow to wheel the hives to my pick-up truck and trailer, and would normally be loaded up by midnight. After two or three hours sleep I would set off for the moors at about 4am, but before driving away I would spray the tops of the hives with water to keep the bees cool. At that time in the morning there was usually not much traffic on the northbound A1 and I would often reach my destination in just over two hours. As I drew into the farmyard a pair of border collies would announce my arrival, usually nipping my ankles as I made my way to the back door to let Mr Nicholson know that I had arrived.

As I unloaded the hives I could see that the heather was already turning pink, and in the sharp morning air the rich smell of its blossom was easily discernible. Many birds were flying over the moors, though it was only on rare occasions that I saw any grouse. The bees were eager to emerge from their hives after the long journey and I was excited to know that it wouldn't take them long before they found the flowers which might give me a good crop of my favourite honey. Before leaving the site I made it a rule to ensure that I had in my hands the same number of foam closures as there were hives, for once I had made the mistake of leaving a colony closed up. As it had plenty of ventilation, the colony didn't suffocate or overheat on the moors, and because it had been provided with food before the journey, nor did it starve. But I felt very bad about the colony being confined for over three weeks and was anxious never to repeat the mistake.

Mr Nicholson and his wife were very kind hospitable people and they always invited Val and me for a good breakfast in their farm kitchen. They were interesting people and told us many stories about local life in the dales and beyond. Whilst we gave them jars of our local – mainly oilseed rape – honey, it seemed poor recompense for having a secure heather site and the chance of obtaining some of Britain's finest honey.

During the time the bees were on the heather I would constantly be worrying about the weather on the

A British Commercial hive with National supers

moors and whether there would be any honey to harvest. My bees were an admixture of races and I knew that only the toughest would survive and be capable of collecting reasonable amounts of honey. If we had had a prolonged period of wet weather before the heather had flowered, followed by long, hot, summery days, my chances of a good harvest would increase. However, I would have to wait until the heather was over before I knew the outcome, for then Mr Nicholson would tell me that it was time to collect the hives.

Sometimes I would be able to synchronise the return of my hives to my apiary with a Northern Examination Board meeting in Harrogate, which always occurred in the first couple of weeks in September and during which we reviewed the recent examinations and awards in GCSE in Agriculture and Horticulture. I would drive to the meeting with a trailer attached to my Daihatsu or Subaru and, after the meeting, collect my heavy heather-scented hives with the petrol expenses paid by the examination board. It was tiring work loading the hives on my own, and as it was dark by the time I reached home I would leave the colonies on the trailer until the following morning. Sometimes my Scottish friend John Gleed would travel with me to retrieve the hives, though he would scold me when I pulled into a Little Chef on the way home for a coffee and my favourite treat – a pancake with ice cream and sour cherries. John usually loved fast food of all kinds and took advantage of what was offered on the menu, but his enjoyment of the meal was spoilt, for he thought we should be hurrying home to release the bees.

I usually returned with plenty of food for the bees for winter in the bottom box of the hive. Any surplus in the honey supers was cut out of the frames and eaten in the pure white combs, the rich reddish honey with a jelly-like consistency, smelling of the moors, making a luxurious breakfast treat.

Summing up my beekeeping progress

A quick review of my beekeeping in the early years of the 1980s would be that I had learned how to manage bees for honey production, I had been able to control swarming to some degree by using Snelgrove's methods or by making splits to increase the number of my colonies, I had standardised my hives to National and British Commercials *(see opposite)*, I had set up a chain of out-apiaries and acquired vehicles with which I could move my colonies around. Additionally, I had gained a lot of beekeeping knowledge by working through the BBKA's Intermediate Syllabus, by reading many beekeeping books and taking notice of the advice given to me by my course mentor, Mildred Bindley.

There was, however, one important aspect of beekeeping I had not touched on: the fundamental task of doing something to improve the quality of bees themselves, for they had several poor characteristics apart from their dreadful temper.

CHAPTER FIVE

The Black Native British Bee

A RATHER dashing figure, immaculately dressed in a suit complete with a silk handkerchief which overflowed from his breast pocket, took his place on the speaker's rostrum. His well-groomed luxuriant silver-grey hair, with a neat parting, was matched by a thick well-trimmed moustache. This was Cecil Tonsley, a popular lecturer both on the British and international circuits and the owner/editor of the oldest of Britain's bee magazines, *The British Bee Journal*. Long, long before the current fad of keeping bees on city roof tops, Cecil had had bees above his BBJ office in Fleet Street, and his premises had been a mecca for beekeepers travelling from abroad. During his lifetime he had achieved many prominent positions in beekeeping associations, was a respected honey judge and having a great interest in apitherapy, the use of bee products to treat medical conditions, he had written a book on the subject.

Cecil's lecture was on the importance of the Italian bee, *Apis mellifera ligustica*, in apiculture. Since its introduction into England and America in the late nineteenth century, this race of honeybee has become the mainstay of commercial beekeeping through many parts of the world including Canada, Australia and New Zealand. Waxing lyrically on the race, Cecil briefly mentioned its provenance, a valley in the Alps between Italy and Switzerland, and how beekeepers were attracted initially by the beautiful orange colour of the bees and the large easily-found queen with her burnished gold abdomen.

Whilst it was true that the colour of the Italian bees was an important selling point by some of the early suppliers, the bees had to perform at least as well as the black native bees, in order to become more than a novelty. However, he said, it soon became clear to many that they were superior in many ways and thus well worth the exorbitant price demanded by their importers. Certainly, Cecil's description of Italian bees was true of my own experience; the bees built up well in spring, were gentle to handle and, given the right weather conditions and an abundance of flowers, they produced good crops of honey. He talked about their reluctance to swarm if given plenty of room and, because they had tongues slightly longer than native bees, they could get nectar from flowers which had deeper nectaries. Whilst he acknowledged that feeding had to be carefully monitored in autumn, as the queen was encouraged by the supply of food to carry on laying eggs, he saw this as a minor problem considering the race's overall performance. He ended his talk by mentioning that although Italian queens were renowned for their longevity, beekeepers were advised to replace them after their second full year if they desired the best results from their colonies. And, of course, he concluded, good Italian stock should only be purchased from reliable breeders or their agents.

Cecil Tonsley's lecture didn't really add anything to my knowledge of this race of bee. What he said rang true, but to keep an apiary headed by 'pure' Italian queens meant buying new queens on a regular basis, which could make a tidy hole in one's profits – a queen cost the same as about ten jars of honey at that time. To me the lecture seemed more like a sales pitch for Italian queens and undoubtedly, anyone could lecture with equal conviction on Caucasian bees or Buckfast bees. Indeed, I had tried these races too. The former seemed to be much hardier and used a lot of propolis – but I liked their grey colour, the latter hardly seemed to move on the combs during examination and were very quiet and gentle.

As regards honey, I never kept individual colony records during those years, but I suspect that there wasn't a great difference between them; perhaps only that a new bought-in queen was heading the colony. Even though the temper of my colonies at that point was causing me problems, I wasn't in the market for any more queens, no matter what race they were.

The next speaker was a complete contrast to Cecil Tonsley. Though conventional enough in his clothing, it was obvious that he wasn't a snappy dresser and that he was more interested in his lecture than his appearance. He had the rather unusual name of Beowulf Cooper (I learned later that his father had been an Anglo-Saxon scholar at the British Museum). Beowulf had greyish hair, swept back, and sported a moustache which still retained some of its black colour. His subject was the native Black Bee of the British Isles, its characteristics, why it was important to conserve the race and how that could be achieved. He said that unbeknown to many beekeepers, pockets of native bees could be found throughout the British Isles and that they had neither completely died out due to the Isle of Wight Disease of the early 20th century, nor were they completely usurped by the numerous imports of bees in subsequent years. Without any reference to the previous speaker, or even a glance in his direction, Beowulf explained in a matter-of-fact, authoritative way, how the native bee was superior in almost every way to the bees brought in from abroad. For instance, their dark colour absorbed more radiant heat which enabled the bees to fly both earlier in the day and in cooler weather than lighter coloured bees.

Additionally, he explained, after examining thousands of colonies in all parts of the British Isles, he was able to see that the native bees were not homogenous, but varied according to their specific environment, brought about by natural selection. Thus, you would expect to find much hardier bees in mountain or moorland locations as they were up against shorter foraging seasons and had to work often under cool and very windy conditions. He said that only by observing one's bees closely and by honestly and objectively recording the characteristics of colonies could a beekeeper have the knowledge to decide which of his bees should be selected for breeding.

Beowulf Cooper, October 1980. This was the last time I saw him, when I accompanied him to Spurn Point, the promontory in the Humber estuary, where BIBBA planned to have a secluded mating apiary

British Isles Bee Breeders' Association

I was extremely impressed by Beowulf's lecture and took home some of the literature about his association which he had made available for the meeting. I learned that the British Isles Bee Breeders Association (BIBBA) was formed in 1964, although to begin with it had been called the Village Bee Breeders Association – so named because it wanted to express the idea that this was an association for those beekeepers who were interested in the propagation of a small-colony type of bee. The association had positive, wide-ranging and well-focused aims: 'the conservation, restoration, study, selection, and improvement of strains of honeybees of native or near-native type suitable for Britain and Ireland'.

In order to achieve these aims, beekeepers were encouraged to get to know their bees by filling in specific record cards, designed by the association, which would give information about the strength, health and food status of each colony and, from the breeding point of view, the physical and behavioural characteristics of the bees.

The items dealing with colony strength and honey stores were easy to record, as it was mainly a matter of counting the respective number of frames. Quantitative recordings (on a scale of 1-10) were also required of the characteristics of the colony which included temper – whether the bees were likely to sting, jump at you when the hive was opened, or follow you for some distance after an inspection; and how the bees behaved on the combs – particularly whether they clustered together in small groups and fell into the hive, or ran wildly over the combs.

Other things to look out for were the shape of the colony's brood nest – if it was broad or tall and whether the wax cappings on the honeycombs were proud or had an air space between the wax and honey. The bees' use of propolis also needed to be recorded and, of course, the colour of both the workers and the queen. Other boxes on the record card were to do with more complex items such as the suitability of the queen for breeding, but a lot of evaluation work over a whole season needed to be carried out first.

Hearing Beowulf's lecture and reading BIBBA material, especially on colony assessment, was for me a quantum leap in beekeeping. Whilst keeping bees and harvesting honey had its own rewards, here was something with long-term objectives which appealed to my curiosity. I must have given Beowulf my phone number after the lecture for shortly afterwards he telephoned me.

'I will be up your way to check on the eelworm situation,' he said, 'though it might not be until after 7pm. Will you be there?'

I assured him that I would be, though didn't understand what all that was about eelworms. I asked him about it when he arrived just after 10pm (he had found other people to visit on his way to me).

'Ah, that,' he said, 'I was speaking from my office and I never know who is listening.'

He explained that he worked as the regional entomologist for the Ministry of Agriculture's Agricultural Development and Advisory Service and as such travelled through most of eastern England to check on farmers' crops – as well as meeting beekeepers. 'Eelworms' was the code-word he used when talking to some beekeepers.

The point of Beowulf's first visit to our house was to ask me if I would arrange a local meeting of beekeepers who might be sympathetic to the aims of BIBBA. I said that I would probably be able to get a group of people together and, once Beowulf was satisfied with that promise, we continued to talk about other beekeeping matters until well after midnight.

'I must go,' he said looking at his watch. 'There are still a couple of people I want to call on.'

Arriving at any time of the day or night was a common feature of Beowulf's visits and invariably he came ready with his own acrylic-filled duvet and pillows if he were to spend the night. He wouldn't trust any duvet that the host might provide for him despite assurances that it was not filled with down, which would give him an asthma attack.

I managed to get a group of eight beekeepers together for a meeting one evening and Beowulf arrived early along with Adrian Waring, who later became the County Bee Instructor based at Moulton College of Agriculture. Adrian was not only an expert at handling bees, his lectures were delivered with the utmost clarity. Before the meeting, Beowulf, whilst walking around our garden with Val, asked her if I would be likely to consider editing the BIBBA newsletter. 'You can ask him,' she replied, 'but he will say he isn't capable of doing it.' 'Is he?' he asked. 'Yes, of course. He will say that he has no experience, can't write and wouldn't know where to start. But he's good at getting things out of people, can see the wider issues, and writes really well if he knows what he is talking about. Push him! Make him have a go!' So that's what he did. And thus began my editing career.

The meeting went well, for it was decided to form a local BIBBA group which undoubtedly pleased Beowulf. I tried to help Beowulf pack his slide projector and boxes of literature into his car.

'No, no, no!' he cried, 'That's no good. Leave it to me. Everything has its own place.'

A few minutes after Beowulf and Adrian had left, I noticed that Adrian had left his expensive-looking camera kit behind. I got into my car at once and sped after them. I had to drive the twelve miles from Gainsborough to Bawtry before I caught sight of Beowulf's car and I repeatedly flashed my lights to stop them. Beowulf was relieved to see that it was me; he had thought he had been followed by an unmarked police car and was about to get a speeding ticket.

Once someone showed a real interest in his work, Beowulf made frequent contact through visits, telephone calls and very long letters, his tiny writing covering every inch of space on both sides of a piece of paper. I was invited to the next BIBBA meeting at his home where I met the committee and was co-opted as the association's News editor. Other items on the agenda included preparations for a BIBBA Conference, and the mating-hive kits which the association was producing for sale.

I met a delightful couple, a retired engineer and his botanist wife, John and Gwen Rotter, who were responsible for the growing, harvesting and selling seeds of garden plants suitable for bees. Val and I once visited their beautiful, huge garden where most of the seeds were harvested. Often my family would join me on the trips to Beowulf's place and explored the local parks and countryside whilst I was in the meeting. I am sure that during this time both of our children mostly benefitted from their acquaintance with such a diverse group of people, yet brought together with one aim.

Our small local North Lincolnshire breeding group met each month and tried to tackle the rather detailed colony record cards. In order for the results to show minimum bias, we decided that when we visited each other's colonies the owner of the apiary would carry out the colony inspections though everyone would give their own thoughts on what should be recorded. Usually we had a consensus of opinion. We were an odd group of people; a power station worker, a primary school head teacher, a steel worker, a retired teacher, a business man, a part time bees' disease officer and a comprehensive school teacher.

Month by month we travelled from one site to another to evaluate colonies and fill in the cards. When we thought that we had what looked like some promising near-native colonies, we set up a small apiary in Elsham Hall Country Park, near Brigg, to the delight of the owner, Captain Elwes. This apiary was used for a BIBBA field meeting on colony assessment and BIBBA members came from some considerable distance, including Beowulf and several of the committee members.

Benefits of keeping native strains

I believe that at one time beekeepers joined BIBBA hoping that they would be able to buy native Black British queen bees. However, they were to be disappointed, for this wasn't one of the association's objectives. The message was simple: there are native strains in your own or your neighbour's apiaries as well as those living in the wild. Identify them, learn about their characteristics, and select those with recognisably suitable traits for breeding. The creation of breeding groups would increase the chance of finding suitable genetic material and cut down the amount of work for each beekeeper.

However, one interesting project which could help those who had no discernible native bees amongst their stocks was brought about apparently by a chance observation. A member had cut some comb from a hive and left it on his windowsill. A few days later he happened to notice that there were eggs in the cells, so he returned the comb to the hive. Later, when examining his bees, he found that the eggs had hatched and the cells contained healthy larvae. Today we know that the development of the bee castes – workers, drones and queens – is not fixed by a precise number of days and hours, but that some variability exists.

This is of particular significance when swarm inspections are made for queen cells at strict intervals of nine days, for a few hours can make all the difference to a beekeeper losing a swarm. The same is true of queens completing their development; an 'early' emerging queen could kill off all her rivals in minutes, a disaster if the other queens, still within their cells, hadn't been protected in some way. With worker bees there is no particular danger, but bees from eggs laid on the cooler periphery of the brood nest may take longer to complete their development.

The knowledge that bee eggs could be taken from the hive then replaced after a few days led to the new practice of sending eggs through the post. Pieces of comb just containing eggs were cut out from frames and put in the plastic boxes in which 'cut comb' honey is sold. A wad of damp tissue paper was wrapped around the comb which once carefully packed was dispatched to a beekeeper through the post. I believe the experiment had limited success, but with more trials, greater progress might have been made. I think the storing of eggs in a refrigerator was also carried out but, as often happened at that time, we had people who tried things out but didn't always write up their results.

This was extremely frustrating to me as an editor as I was always begging for copy. Members expected their issues of BIBBA News on a regular basis and lack of material made this task difficult to fulfil. I would sometimes find that Beowulf had written something in another beekeeping magazine, an article which would have nicely filled a few of our pages. When I discussed this with him he said:

'Don't worry about our members, they are on our side. We have to reach out to other beekeepers. The readers of this journal need to see that there are alternatives to buying foreign queens'.

Foreign queens were a controversial issue, for while they compromised the integrity of the native bee-sock, they certainly provided revenue for the importers. This reminded me of a comment made by Brother Adam, the famous breeder of Buckfast bees, who said he was disappointed that when travelling abroad in recent years he had noticed more mongrelisation amongst bees that were previously almost pure racial types. I thought that this was rather a disingenuous statement as for years he had been shipping his bees around the globe, the progeny of which must have been responsible, in many cases, for having an effect on the local bees.

When I look now at those early copies of BIBBA News, whilst the contents are mainly good, the production is amateur. But those were the days before computers, and for text to appear sharp after the off-set litho printing, each issue had to be typed up with a new carbon ribbon fitted in the typewriter. All headings had to be done with Letraset, a task I found very difficult, and images cut neatly to their correct size.

Once our children had gone to bed, I would take over the dining table and paste up every page on A4 pieces of card which had then to be arranged in sets of four in the appropriate order for the sheets to be folded over by the printer. Cow glue I found was invaluable for pasting as the various pieces could be lifted up again and replaced without any tearing.

Colony evaluation

Group beekeeping activities during the summer months concentrated on colony evaluation and after a whole season we had made good progress with this aspect of BIBBA's work. I had my own research planned for the winter months; I was going to find the discoidal and cubital indices of my bees – a scientific method of determining the provenance of bees.

In a nutshell, this meant that I would collect 30 bees from my colonies and, once they were dead, detach the upper right wing of each bee. The wings would be mounted in a slide mount with glass sides and projected onto a flat wall. Then from various points on the second from the top distal cell of the wing, I would take certain measurements and plot them on a scatter graph or bar graph. If the dots on the scatter graph were close together, then the bees were homogenous, if scattered widely, then there was a lot of mongrelisation *(see diagram p.89)*. Although fiddly and time-consuming, this was interesting work and gave relatively accurate information about the make-up of the colony, bearing in mind the constituents of the sample and one's measuring skills. Whilst some of my colonies verged towards the native, most of the bees I checked were decidedly mongrels. I still use this interesting method to get an idea of how homogenous a colony is, even when the similarity of the colour of the bees would give the idea that the bees were all of the same strain.

One of the last BIBBA projects I was personally involved in was the setting up of a queen mating station on Spurn Point, a secluded spot in which to breed. In preparation for this, various types of mininucs, very small mating hives, were given trials – particularly BIBBA's own model. It had perspex sides which meant that it wouldn't need to be opened to check if the queen had been successfully mated, a detachable food box and a mini cosy to keep the small colony warm. It was hoped that by taking colonies with plenty of native drones to Spurn Point, the queens from the small hives would mate within the isolated area.

Beowulf was greatly influenced by the highly-developed German system of queen breeding and rearing and he made trips across to the Beekeeping Institute at Celle in northern Germany to see their methods. So impressed was he that a BIBBA conference was held there so that members of the association could familiarise themselves with the well-tested techniques that the Germans had adopted. Sadly I was unable to attend the event, but Beowulf sent me several postcards saying how it would be good to make a series of booklets on the methods used by the German bee breeders.

Like some of the other BIBBA members, I began to use the German Jenter System of queen rearing. This entailed trapping the queen in a large plastic cage which had been cut into the comb. On the side in which the queen was enclosed were cells for the queen to lay her eggs but the base of the cells were the distal ends of plastic plugs which had been fitted into the back section of the cage. The system allowed the beekeeper to remove the plugs when the eggs hatched and fit them in rows onto bars in a normal frame and introduce them into a well-populated queenless colony of young bees, which would begin the process of rearing new queens.

I reared queens by this method with success – the main alternative of removing the larvae from normal brood combs with a grafting tool

Karl Jenter (above), designer of the Jenter frame, and (right) the Jenter system which made queen rearing more efficient and simple, by allowing the queen to lay in specially formed cells, the bases of which can be removed once the larvae have hatched, thus making redundant the more difficult task of grafting larvae for queen rearing

I found too tricky. I met the German developer of the kit, Karl Jenter, in Ireland. I bought him a pint of Guinness, a small reward, I admit, in appreciation for his providing bee breeders with such a useful piece of kit.

One October evening, Beowulf telephoned me to ask if I could attend a meeting at Spurn Point. It was a drizzly cold, overcast day when Beowulf and two members of the Yorkshire beekeepers association met up with me at a hotel just off the motorway to Hull. It was a long tortuous drive after Hull, the latter part of the journey along a single track through the dunes, a road which was kept open despite the shifting sands as it led to the lifeboat station. On such a bleak day it was difficult to visualise our drone stocks and mating hives nestling amongst the marram grass and gorse. We explored the spit of land for a while and after a few words with some of the personnel we retreated to shelter in the car, Beowulf ahead of us in his long coat which wasn't quite a Gannex, and a hat which wasn't quite a deerstalker.

And that is how I shall always remember him, for he died the following February of a heart attack. I had received a postcard a few days before he died, saying that he was working on cutting back the overgrown hedge that he now had time to attend to, work which unfortunately led to his death. There was a sense of disbelief at his funeral. It was a cold day but everywhere, both at the crematorium and in Beowulf's garden, snowdrops were in flower. And there in the most sheltered spots the odd hardy, black bee was at work collecting the precious pollen that would kick start the colony into life. Over the years when Beowulf split up his groups of snowdrops he would distribute them amongst beekeepers and my garden was full of many a patch from this source. Additionally I had good specimens of *Salix aegyptiaca*, a very early flowering willow, grown from cuttings he had given to me. Should I have told the bees about Beowulf's death? Or had Griselda, his wife, already passed on the news? I didn't ask her.

Beowulf's colony management tips

Apart from learning many aspects of bee breeding, I picked up many practical points on colony management from Beowulf, things he had himself discovered when working with native bees. A very simple but useful tip was that after smoking a colony when it was time to open the hive, the inner lid should be raised by just a tiny fraction. If it is whipped off, like I often used to do, the chimney effect of cool air entering the hive entrance would create a strong draught with the warm air being quickly expelled from the top of the hive which would disturb the bees. Just waiting a short while with the lid only slightly lifted away would allow the pressure to disperse gradually, which was then unlikely to aggravate the bees. He also contradicted what Mr Whitfield had advised me to do in my first year of beekeeping regarding the alignment of frames in the hive. Beowulf recommended that the frames should be parallel to the hive entrance, ie, 'the warm way', at least as far as native bees were concerned in a temperate climate.

His reasoning was that the bees would store most of the food towards the back of the hive and during winter would move gradually away from the entrance and thus always be in contact with their food supply. If the frames are aligned at right angles to the entrance, then often the winter cluster starts in the middle of the hive and moves gradually to one side and then to the other. If a long cold spell persists, the bees could then be cut off from their stores and starve to death. He also said that the less populous native bees could better protect their hive from robbing as the 'warm way' provided the bees with a smaller entrance area to guard. From the beekeeper's point of a view this frame arrangement is more practical as colonies are usually examined from the back of the hive. With the frames aligned parallel to the entrance it is far easier to remove them than when they are sideways on to you which entails twisting your body around.

I expected a hiatus in the activities of the association following Beowulf's death. This was not to be the case, for within a few weeks the committee arranged a meeting at the home of BIBBA's president, Professor Kenneth Mellanby, the well-known environmentalist.

Plans were made for a commemorative issue of BIBBA News, it was decided to go ahead with the setting up of the mating station on Spurn Point, and Durham Agricultural College was booked as the venue for the next conference. Not long after this, the association acquired a new secretary, Albert Knight, an ex coal mine manager who added zest to BIBBA's activities. For many years he has been the driving force, and without him the association would never have made the progress it has achieved today.

Beowulf was an inspiration. He changed my outlook on beekeeping more than any one else in my forty years in the craft. Eccentric? Undoubtedly. Unique? Equally so. As a young man he produced the definitive 'Hymenopterist's Handbook' for the Royal Entomologist Society. His work in taxonomy not only helped with his interest in bee breeding, but overflowed into his other hobbies too. He liked to collect data and discern patterns, whether it was solving the phosphor dot codes on envelopes used for mechanical sorting by the post office, or by observation carry in his head the starting points or destinations of airplanes according to their time and direction. Whilst he was able to think laterally and see connections between incidents, he couldn't understand why his employers weren't equally able to do so.

As an instance of this he told me that he was asked to go to a Royal Air Force base which was having a great deal of trouble with its jet engines. When the fighter planes came in to land the draught caused by the rotating fins picked up the snails on the runways and caused severe damage. Beowulf took a quick look at the grass on each side of the runway and saw that it was very, very long. He told them he wasn't surprised there were snails as no birds would feed on them with grass that high; birds need to be able to look around when they are feeding.

The officer in charge protested, explaining that not long ago they had someone from the Ministry, a bird specialist, who had told them not to cut the grass as this would keep birds away and thus prevent the possibility of air strikes. I don't know what Beowulf's final advice was but I am sure that it was well considered.

There is a moral here even for beekeepers. Every task that we carry out with our bees will evoke a certain reaction from them. A good beekeeper should be aware of those consequences for they can have a positive or negative effect on the colony.

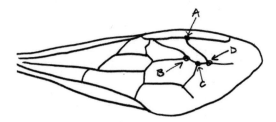

The measuring of sections of the venation of a honeybee's wing helps to determine the provenance of the bee. A large sample allows the beekeeper to determine how pure or mongrelised his colonies are and their usefulness for breeding purposes (see pages 84-85).

From: *The Honeybees of the British Isles*, Beowulf A Cooper, Edited by Philip Denwood, BIBBA, 1986

CHAPTER SIX

Going Global

WHILST I am grateful to Beowulf Cooper for giving me the opportunity of first editing a beekeeping magazine, I was able to pursue this fascinating activity thanks to Jeremy and Ruth Burbidge of Northern Bee Books, West Yorkshire. I became aware of their business when I was looking for secondhand and out-of-print books which I needed for the Intermediate Beekeeping Course. Through them I was able to obtain classic works on beekeeping by Dade on anatomy; Ribbands and Lindauer, both authorities on the social life of honeybees; and Dorothy Hodges who had produced an exquisite account of pollen collection, self-illustrated, complete with hand-painted patches which gave an accurate representation of the colour of the bees' pollen loads. I had not been able to find these, or several other important books, despite searching the antiquarian bookshops of Charing Cross Road.

As I was soon to be attending Lincoln Beekeepers' Association's annual beekeeping conference at Riseholme College of Agriculture, I asked the organisers if Jeremy could bring his books along for the event. I can't remember how successful his sales were, but I believe those attending the conference were astounded to see such a large range of books, and the ones he brought with him only represented a fraction of his titles!

Jeremy was aware of the magazine work that I was doing for BIBBA, and somehow we got round to discussing the possibility of our working together on something on beekeeping which would be published at regular intervals. I had in my possession some of Herbert Mace's 'Beekeeping Annuals', small, softback volumes, which along with most of his writings were self-published from his Beekeeping Annual Office in Harlow, Essex, between 1927 and 1949. They each contained a miscellany of articles which were no doubt of considerable interest to beekeepers during those two decades. There was information on the important beekeeping associations and a space provided for the beekeeper's hive records for the year.

My favourite section of each Annual was towards the back, for there was a list of the most prominent beekeepers, most of them clergymen, retired high-ranking servicemen, or others with long double-barrelled surnames. Each entry included a brief description of the person's beekeeping 'status' and occupation, the latter often being 'explorer'. What if we were to revive a publication something along these lines? The more we talked about it, the more enthusiastic we became and eventually a format was worked out. The new periodical would be called The Beekeepers Annual; it would be published around the time of the National Honey Show in late autumn. It would consist of three main sections: a calendar and desk diary with charts for beekeeping records, an extensive directory which gave details of beekeeping associations and organisations, and the remaining part containing a variety of articles related to beekeeping. We would also include almanac information, the dates of main beekeeping events and notes on weather lore.

In order for the Annual to be successful, we would need the full co-operation of the many beekeeping organisations in the UK, and obtaining the required data was going to be time-consuming as in 1982 everything had to be done through the post. To gauge the reaction of an association, we approached the British Beekeepers' Association who said we could discuss it with them at their convention in spring. When we met the select panel of officials, they sat behind a long table and looked at us rather suspiciously; it was a very formal interview. After Jeremy had made his excellent pitch, the panel looked at each other, and eventually the chairman said he didn't see why we shouldn't be provided with the material 'as long as it is made clear that the BBKA is the premier beekeeping association in the UK'. I remembered at this point that Herbert Mace, whose Beekeeping Annual had partly led to our proposed publication, had been kicked out of the BBKA. How had he upset them, I wondered?

We set to work. There was a lot to do but the first Annual for 1983 was ready that autumn. As editor, I gave no association pride of place; all the directory information was given in alphabetical order. Everyone I approached was more than pleased to provide me with copy, though getting the balance right was not always easy. I was trying to produce the type of book I myself would have liked to have been able to buy each year. For over thirty years the Annual has been published in the same format as we originally planned and it is undoubtedly the only publication in the world that provides a regularly updated resource in so much detail for its country's beekeepers.

Not long after the first Annual was published, inevitably some new appointments occurred within beekeeping organisations. I decided that we needed to publish something to inform purchasers of the Annual of these changes during the intervening months. I sat down one weekend and folded two pieces of A3 paper together. As well as listing new entries for The Annual's directory, I started putting some articles and pictures together, ending up with something that looked like an eight page A4 newsletter. Eventually, we published two of these with *The Supplement* as their title. Carried away by this development, we believed that we could launch our own journal, on a subscription-only basis and unlike other UK beekeeping magazines we would, because of its A4 size, have plenty of space for long articles and large photographs. Although I couldn't wait to get the *BBJ* each month, I was always disappointed as it only gave me an hour's reading at the most. I wanted to create a more substantial journal. Colour would have been nice at this point, but it just wasn't affordable. We had to wait many years for the first full-colour cover, and even longer for a full colour issue. As the number of subscriptions increased, money was ploughed back into the magazine to improve quality and increase its number of pages.

The Beekeepers' Quarterly

From the very beginning it was emphasised that *The Beekeepers' Quarterly* was a totally independent journal. I was allowed full editorial control, commissioned articles and shaped it to my own formula without reference to the publisher except when I wanted guidance, and I had no intention of being influenced by the policies of beekeeping associations and government organisations.

Starting a new magazine was exciting and challenging though it also gave me a lot of anxiety in the early years. If I had taken over the editorship of a long-standing publication, there may well have been files of copy to fall back on as well as a group of writers who sent in their reports on a regular basis. On the other hand, I might have had to work under the direction of a committee, which could have been a problem. Beowulf had entrusted me with his magazines and Jeremy was now giving me the same opportunity. As publisher, Jeremy was responsible for advertising, promotion, printing and distribution; he left editorial matters almost entirely with me. I was very fortunate.

People have often asked me what the general policy of the *BKQ* is and what its aims are. I have never formally written them down; I had had enough of producing 'mission statements' whilst working in school. But I have always had the aims in mind: to be independent and free of bias; to accept material from any beekeeper with something of interest to report; and to create a global community of beekeepers whose joy it is to share their experiences with one another. There is one thing that I have always hated in UK beekeeping; that nationalistic slogan 'British Honey is the Best'. No doubt this occurs in other countries too. To accept it as a truth is to denigrate the honey of our colleagues abroad. There is good and bad honey everywhere. The full range exists in every country, poor standards usually the fault of particular beekeepers rather than nations.

In my travels I have met many beekeepers who work with integrity doing their best without the most modern equipment but who still produce honey of excellent quality. Apart from a very occasional foreign article in the *BBJ*, the two main British beekeeping magazines were very parochial in their outlook and the only way to know something about what was happening in the beekeeping world was to obtain the expensive membership of the Bee Research Association whose journals, although of great interest, were mainly of an academic nature.

Long before computers were available I tried to contact beekeepers abroad, but my success was very limited. In my wildest dreams I thought that I might be able to become a Radio Ham and contact people all round the planet, including the southern hemisphere, if I managed to become proficient at using 'packet' radio. I was dreaming in vain, for there was no way that I could even master morse code, proficiency in that being essential to get a licence. I was an avid listener, though, of short wave radio and had a handbook which gave me the times and wavelengths of English language programmes in different countries. To improve reception, which was always tricky depending on the weather and sunspots, I constructed cobweb and long-line aerials across the garden. There was a system whereby I could sent a postcard to a particular radio station giving them information about signal strength, to which they were obliged to respond, and I always asked the recipient if they knew of any English-speaking beekeepers.

Sometimes my messages were read out on the next programme, but I never found a beekeeper in this way, though for a long time the station in Havana sent me reports of the studio cat.

The formula I adopted for the magazine hasn't changed much over the years. My editorial, in which I usually comment on points arising from the contents, is followed by letters and news, and then there are reports from correspondents around the world, and sections which cover environmental issues, beekeeping research and science, history, travel, practical beekeeping techniques, items to make in the workshop, education, bee breeding and book reviews. The turnover of writers is very low; sadly it is usually the death of very experienced beekeepers which has caused new writers to emerge. I think that I will never see their likes again, but then another beekeeper comes along with different skills, ideas and experience, who no doubt in time will be as much revered as my departed friends.

To begin with I called upon beekeepers I had known from BIBBA or through the Beekeepers Annual for articles for the first few issues. After that, people began to send in unsolicited contributions for my perusal. I would also write to beekeepers who were known to hold particular views on a subject or who had interesting colony management systems, as well as speakers at conferences I had attended. As I lived near E H Thorne's, the largest beekeeping appliance firm in the UK (they had taken over Taylor's, where I first learned about bees, and Steele and Brodie, from where I used to buy my Smith hives), whenever Jeremy Burbidge had visitors from abroad, he would bring them to meet me on his way home from visits to Thorne's factory.

International bee experts

On one occasion he turned up with Norman Rice from Australia, one of the world's most famous queen breeders, who not surprisingly called his book on the subject 'Queensland'. For his work in beekeeping he was awarded an MBE, and since that first meeting he has supplied us with articles on the practical aspects of queen rearing for over twenty years.

Another visitor was Rita Campanelli, from Italy, a graduate in agriculture who specialised in beekeeping at the National Institute of Apiculture in Bologna. She worked for the Regional Agricultural Assistance scheme, training both beginners and commercial beekeepers, as well as doing freelance work helping to establish private and co-operative apiaries. Her face expressed perceptible signs of joy and contentment as women often do during the first days of pregnancy, though it was a very wet cold June day and she must have been very cold in her lightweight Italian mac. We were invited to visit her near Rome, where on the breakfast table along with cakes, Rita had provided us with some of her very light, delicately flavoured acacia honey.

In her garden apiary amongst the olive trees, not far from the lake, I was able to inspect some of her twenty colonies, all of which were kept in the large Dadant hives with the huge porches over the entrances, much favoured by Italian beekeepers. It was good to be able to see Italian bees at work in their homeland, the prominent three bands of orange on their abdomens very much like those in my first colony. The bees were foraging on wild broom with its bright yellow flowers, many acres of it covering the hilltops above the town. I noticed that Rita was fully dressed in protective clothing, including gloves, despite the heat, though the bees were only a bit on the edgy side, probably because swarming preparations were underway. After closing up the hives, we saw a huge swarm hanging from an olive branch, which Rita collected into a box, to be hived later.

I also went with her to remove a swarm which had set up home between the shutters and windows of a holiday home, a cool dark space I learned that was often chosen as a suitable nest site by bees. Rita was working part-time so we accompanied her to the villages where she was teaching. The lessons normally started around 6pm and took place in a schoolroom or village hall. One session we watched was quite educational, not in the beekeeping sense, as our knowledge of Italian was almost zero, but in the way the group behaved. There were over twenty people, all adults of varying ages, predominantly male, who constantly interrupted Rita, volubly challenging her on particular points which would lead to heated discussions until a conclusion had been reached. Only then could Rita carry on with her planned lesson but knowing for sure that she

Rita Campanelli, a beekeeping instructor, kept her bees in Dadant hives in her olive grove apiaries, in Trevignano, north of Rome

would soon say something which would cause another disruption. I was quite shocked by the tone of the class, but now, having lived in Greece for thirteen years, I realise that what seems to an outsider to be an aggressive way of communication is, in fact, normal Mediterranean behaviour, with no malice intended.

We chose not to sit in on the following day's lesson. We were in the small hilltop village of Barbarano Romano which was enclosed by a high wall. As we walked through the tunnel-like gate-way, the heat of the day dissipated, to be replaced by cool damp air carrying the scent of musty stone. The village was a maze of narrow cobbled alleyways, with tall buildings on each side and stone steps leading up to the doorways. As work for most people was over for the day, they had collected together in small groups around their steps or were chattering from their high-up open windows, almost within touching distance. A low shaft of warm evening sunlight picked out the beautiful deep blue of an old lady's dress, and I knew I would have to photograph her. Val asked if she would pose for me. Surprised as she was, she happily consented, and stood bathed in nature's own floodlight as I clicked the shutter. The old lady turned away having indicated that we should stay where we were, walked down the steep alley and disappeared through a gate in the wall. A few minutes later she returned and carefully put into Val's hand a small warm egg, the first egg her new batch of chickens had laid.

Stanislav Muhtarov went to an enormous amount of trouble to get to our house. A Russian, living in Tashkent, Uzbekhistan, he earned more money from beekeeping than the job he was qualified for – teaching the piano. His wife Nellie was also a music teacher – she taught the violin, and their son Ildar liked mathematics and chess. Stanislav's life as a beekeeper was not an easy one.

During the summer months he lived on his hook (trailer) which he moved from one huge cotton field to another, in the flat featureless landscape, the cotton crop drawing water from the rapidly emptying Aral Sea. On the trailer was a shed where he extracted his honey which at the end of the season he sold in the bazaar in Tashkent amongst Uzbek traders. He always wrote me long interesting letters on thin paper. I knew at a glance they were from him because of the large number of low denomination stamps which crowded the envelope. If I didn't hear from him for some time, I knew the reason – his local shop was out of envelopes, writing paper or stamps. After the disintegration of the Soviet Union, Russian traders were not welcome in the bazaar.

Stanislav Muhtarov – a music teacher who turned to beekeeping

The ethnic citizens had had enough of Russians as their city had become an enormous transit camp for soldiers on the way to or returning from the Afghan war. Often the returnees had travel passes only as far as Tashkent; after that they were expected to find their own way home, but without money they couldn't move on. Stanislav went to Moscow to get a visa for his family to visit England. But then he had to change roubles into dollars; he queued for nearly three days to get 100 dollars. He rejoined the queue for another long wait and returned to Tashkent with 200 dollars – the amount of money he hoped would be enough for his stay in England. His family had already been promised accommodation by a beekeeper in Kent and with us in Lincolnshire, but 200 dollars wouldn't last very long.

Val and I met Stanislav and Ildar at Retford station. Stanislav apologised for not bringing Nellie; she was heavily pregnant and was feeling tired after their long journey. We were surprised that they had even let her fly. However, they seemed to have a good grasp of English and settled easily into our home. A lot of our conversation centred around his beekeeping work, the problems in the bazaar, and the general situation in his country – and I played chess with Ildar who easily beat me. Before retiring for the night we made plans to visit my apiaries the following morning, but sadly this wasn't to be.

Early the next day we received a telephone call asking for Stanislav. Nellie, he told us later, was not well and in a very disturbed state, so we immediately returned to the station and put Stanislav and Ildar on the train. It was a sad end to the visit for both of us. I would have liked to have seen how Stanislav handled my bees and heard his comments on how his bees differed from mine. There is often something that can be learned from discussions at the hive. I heard from him when the family returned safely home that Nellie had given birth to a baby girl, named Veronica, and both were doing well. Not long after that I understand that they all emigrated to Chicago, after which, sadly, I lost touch with them.

For a long time I was mistaken about the gender of our Yugoslavian correspondent, Snezana Popovic. My knowledge of Greek and Russian name-endings should have told me but I assumed I had been communicating with a man until I received the photo of an attractive, young, strawberry blonde woman. Snezana worked as a pomologist in the spa town of Arandjelovac, a spa town near Belgrade. An agronomy graduate with a lot of experience in fruit culture as well as in keeping bees for honey and pollination, she used hive products for making cosmetics and lotions and health creams.

Snezana Popovic, whose name, she told me, translates as Snow White

The majority of her honey was from acacia forests. Snezana found teaching disappointing as very few of her students were interested in a career in agriculture, farming being a hard and lonely occupation. They would rather sell guns or seek employment in the highly charged atmosphere of street cafes and bars. We planned to meet her at the biennial international Apimondia Congress which was to take place in Split, but this was not to be for the event was cancelled due to the outbreak of the Balkan War.

Although I still received reports from Snezana, because of sanctions imposed on her country I was unable to send her copies of the magazine. Snezana married Vellbor (Big Pine), eventually gave birth to a son, but suffered from post-natal health problems. She was unable to get the appropriate treatment as the medication she desperately needed was unavailable because of the sanctions. The imposing of sanctions on what is considered to be a rogue regime unfortunately causes a lot of hardship to a country's population who often do not support the policies of their leaders. This is brought sharply into focus when one hears specifics about it on a personal level.

Bait hives

Job Pichon is not our correspondent from France; he made this plain when he first started writing for us over twenty years ago. His reports are mainly confined to Brittany, and as a Breton he is very proud of his heritage and its Celtic connections to the British Isles. The black bees that he keeps share many of the characteristics of their counterparts in Great Britain and he dislikes the fashion amongst his colleagues, particularly commercial beekeepers, to supplant local strains of bees with Buckfast, Italian or other races. Val and I stayed with Job and his family after a long day's drive from Toulouse to his home in Brest. It was the summer holiday, and like us, both Job and his wife Annee were teachers, Job's subject being physics.

There were several hives in his town garden, large Dadants but without the fancy porches that were common in Italy, and high hedges and trees which made the bees' flight path above head-height. More hives were kept in the woods near his home village; the traditional family house there was still retained through many generations. The weather was excellent for opening hives and I noticed that the dark native bees which showed no sign of mongrelisation were very good comb builders and gentle.

Unlike British hives, the frames in the top box were not covered with a quilt or crownboard with a bee-way beneath, so large amounts of wild comb filled the space between the frame tops and roof. The wax cappings on the filled honey combs were white and convex which meant that it would be easy to uncap the combs at harvesting time, as the knife would slide through the tiny air space allowing the wax to be lifted away easily. The bees were busy working bramble flowers which were plentiful in the district, whilst other hives were on heather sites. Job pointed out several unoccupied bait hives which he had set up near each apiary to attract swarms from his own or other beekeepers' colonies.

If the bees were of a foreign race, he would kill the queen and supply the swarm with a queen he had raised that year. Job put the bait beehives over three metres up in the fork of a tree, a height which he had found by trial and error the bees seemed to prefer. Many experiments conducted since then have come to the same conclusion.

It's my theory that this is a genetic trait in bees, for in their original forest homes, bears, their natural predator, couldn't climb beyond this height. The bortniks, the forest beekeepers of Russia, made hollows in the trees for colonies to nest above three meters, no doubt having studied both the habits of bees and bears. Job also covered the hives with black plastic, as the scout bees looking for a suitable nest preferred a dark place, and the addition of old frames with black comb, which had been used for the rearing of dozens of generations of bees, added to the attractiveness

Job Pichon, our Breton correspondent, whose colonies in Dadant hives provide him with honey from alder, bramble and heather

of the site. Each year, since visiting Job, I have made use of his method of collecting swarms from bait hives with varying degrees of success.

Fresh langoustine collected straight off the fishing boat from one of Brittany's many little harbours ensured that we had a delicious traditional supper, and the following morning's breakfast continued on this theme with Breton buckwheat pancakes made by Annee, smothered in a choice of alder or blackberry honey.

I was very touched by Job's farewell comment to me, 'We have empathy with each other,' he said. I couldn't have expressed our relationship any more clearly.

'Why didn't you just say he was as tall as a lamp post?' demanded John Atkinson, after he had collected Vita from the bus at Aberystwyth, 'No other description would have been necessary!' Having left our home after a few days stay, Vita had travelled west to meet John, who was the former chief beekeeping advisor for MAFF in Wales. I had told him that Dr Vita Vydra was a beekeeper from Prague, about thirty years old, that he had worked in cryogenics and was currently working in Prague University lecturing on nuclear containment materials. I even told John what clothes he was wearing, but failed to mention his most prominent feature, his height. After 1989, it was becoming much easier for people from former Soviet countries to travel abroad, and Vita soon took advantage of the opportunity.

He wasn't all that impressed with my bees; he was expecting the colonies to be much stronger, nor do I believe he liked the rather bland oil seed rape honey which we provided for breakfast. We didn't have much time together as Val and I had already booked a holiday in Cornwall, but we allowed him to stay in our house whilst we were away, for our children Catherine and Jim were still at home. Although Catherine needed her bicycle to travel to the ice cream parlour in the next village where she had a holiday job, she said he could use it between times. This presented a problem on one occasion, as Vita had raised the saddle height so high that when Catherine tried to ride to work her feet could hardly reach the pedals. She persevered for a while, until finally, unable to lower the saddle, she pushed the bicycle to work where someone was able to adjust the seat so that she could cycle home in comfort.

Vita volunteered to help with the cooking and he proudly made for us potato soup, potato pancakes and even potato dumplings, though

Vita Vydra was our first visitor from eastern Europe. His prize hive was the huge one he made from an abandoned freezer

fortunately not all of these for the same meal. When we stayed with him in his village house a few kilometres from Prague, we were delighted that the dumplings had a plum filling.

Vita's hives were like large boxes with hinged lids, and the frames of bees were big and heavy. But his star attraction was his 'long hive' which he had written about for our magazine. In his article he had described how on the bus on the way to work he noticed that someone had dumped an old freezer by the side of the road, a practice he despised as it spoilt the beauty of the countryside. However, having changed from the bus to the city metro, the thought came into his head that the size of the freezer, together with its insulating properties, would make it an excellent home for bees.

All day the thought wouldn't leave him, but as the afternoon progressed he became anxious that someone else might have decided on a different use for a dumped freezer and that on his return journey it might have gone. To Vita's delight the freezer was still lying there so he cycled back to claim the prospective hive. With some ingenuity, or because of his knowledge of mechanics, Vita managed to secure this large, cumbersome freezer to his bicycle and somehow got it safely to his house. In practice, the chest freezer with an entrance hole for the bees and a modified roof, was proving to be a good home, for the colony looked prosperous with plenty of brood and honey in the large combs. I had never seen a recycled freezer being used in this way before, but was aware that these redundant kitchen appliances are commonly found in beekeepers' honey houses where, fitted with a light bulb, they are used to gently warm honey before bottling.

Whilst Val and Vita shared the same views on most of the topical ecological issues of the last couple of decades, Vita couldn't understand our aversion to genetically modified crops. This gave rise to many long discussions when we were together, and later via the post. Undoubtedly, Vita based his arguments on scientific and objective reasoning whilst our concerns, he thought, were formulated from an irrational fear of the new technology and an unreasoned distrust of the scientific reports.

Vita liked to have long discussions on philosophical and scientific matters, so he set off to see John Atkinson, whose erudite articles he had read in the *Quarterly* for many years. Now he would have the chance to meet the great man himself: John was undoubtedly the most intellectual beekeeper of his time which, when matched with his practical skills, earned him the respect of all beekeepers who came into contact with him, heard him lecture or read his articles, and latterly his book on bee breeding.

But long before this, John was a bee farmer, a county beekeeping instructor and the beekeeping advisor for MAFF for the whole of Wales, working mainly on the brood diseases of honeybees. John had a unique writing style; he wrote as if he was giving a lecture to well-educated students, sometimes questioning what he had just said, at other times repeating his ideas in a slightly different way. Precision and clarity were his watchwords, but he managed to slip into his text a touch of mischievous humour. Our proofreading had to be spot-on for John; every word he wrote, every punctuation mark he made, had been carefully considered, and woe betide us should we fail him.

John Atkinson's erudite articles attracted a select following of readers

John came to stay with us on two occasions. He would turn up at our house, as he did at beekeeping events around the country, dressed in his usual outfit of black leather trousers, a red shirt, and a black leather jacket. He would bring things for me to photograph, usually pieces of equipment which he had designed and skilfully made in his workshop, all of which, like his micronucs for instance, fitted perfectly into their carrying case.

After supper, we would talk for hours, the evening usually ending with a string of Welsh jokes he loved to tell, which had him doubled up with laughter. When John was away from home, he told us, his cat wouldn't eat until he had returned safely home, so he could only be away for two days. John and his wife Evelyn moved from their smallholding in Wales to Norfolk to be near their children and grandchildren. A few days before his death, I received his final article. Although very ill, he worked until the very end on an interest that had thoroughly absorbed him throughout his life.

I was pleased that I had been able to meet him a few weeks earlier when we had lunch together in Norwich. Then we went to a camera shop together as we both wanted to buy accessories for our Hasselblad cameras. John left behind a devoted group of beekeepers who were inspired by and appreciative of his great contributions to the craft. As editor of the *Quarterly*, I was privileged to know John and very proud that he had used our journal as a means of educating and communicating with other people.

He told me once 'Beekeepers must have curiosity. They have to ask *why? why? why?* when a problem occurs. Without curiosity, progress cannot be made!'

Writers from around the world

It is well over 25 years since the *Quarterly* was first published, during which time we have attracted some of the best writers on beekeeping from all corners of the world, many of whom I have been able to meet at events in the UK and Ireland. These include, from England: Clive de Bruyn and Adrian Waring, former county beekeeping instructors, who have given the best possible advice on practical beekeeping techniques; Karl Shower, who spent his career at East Malling Research Institute, and is an authority on beekeeping history; Peter Tomkins, the beekeeper at Rothamsted who was party to all the important research carried out there; Nicola Bradbear, well known for setting up the organisation *Bees for Development* and her involvement in many overseas projects; Robert Pickard whose interest in bees led to fascinating work on the human brain;

Francis Ratnieks, the only Professor of Beekeeping in the UK who in his articles compared human activities with those of honeybee behaviour; David Aston, the current chairman of the BBKA; Norman Carreck, who works alongside Francis Ratnieks and is editor of the International Bee Research Association's prestigious Journal of Apicultural Research; and Ron Brown, the most innovative of practical beekeepers who wrote several classic books on the craft.

The USA

The States provided me with several excellent authors. I met them either in London or at a conference in Dublin, and of these, four made significant contributions.

Steve Taber, sadly no longer with us, was a larger-than-life, gruff-looking beekeeper. He was an expert on queen rearing and wrote a

book on the subject. Like Atkinson, he was always asking questions about bees and would probe his hives to find the answers. For most of his life he was carrying out experiments, using the results of his work to refine his beekeeping. He was forthright with his opinions, but he could afford to be, for if Steve said something was so, you could bet your bottom dollar that he was right.

At an international beekeeping event in Dublin, I was pleased to be able to meet some of my writers. One was Ron Miksha who, as soon as he could drive, hauled trailers carrying hundreds of hives for thousands of miles across Canada and the US, for pollination and honey, each year.

Steve Taber, a tough, opinionated beekeeper, who was seldom ever wrong, much to the chagrin of some of his associates

A quiet, well-educated man, Ron now runs his own business as a geophysicist and, despite having motor neuron disease, with the help of his family he produces a huge amount of comb honey of the finest quality.

His book, *Bad Beekeeping* – as in his articles – describes how difficult commercial beekeeping is in America yet emphasises the rewards gained by being independent and having a life in the open air. Geoff Manning, from Australia, has the rugged appearance of a backwoodsman and he and his wife run a commercial honey business. This is not easy in a country with extremes of climate, floods and wild fires (Geoff is a voluntary fireman) – and the main honey crop there depends on the fickleness and unpredictability of the eucalypts. Philip McCabe, from Ireland, has held important positions in beekeeping associations and is currently the Vice President of Apimondia, the world beekeeping organisation. His tales of beekeeping in the past always add a rustic element to our pages.

Kim Flottum has the ability to write on any subject. As editor of one of America's most important bee journals, *Gleanings in Bee Culture* he is savvy to all that is going on in the States and will not dodge a controversial issue, speaking out plainly when he needs to. I see this as a very important quality in an editor as there are so many problems which crop up in beekeeping which need to be faced head-on and debated in an open forum.

Ann Harman is another of our American writers who, like Kim, can write with authority on any subject to do with beekeeping. Her curriculum vitae, which lists many years of service throughout the US as well as her work independently or with development agencies throughout the world, would fill many of the pages of this book. It is Ann who reminds me each quarter that a deadline for the next issue of the magazine is approaching and that I still haven't told her what I would like her to write about.

The Russian perspective

There is one particular person whom I must mention and that is the late Dorothy Galton. Val and I visited her in her house on the north coast of Norfolk. Dorothy was a Russophile. Despite dropping out of Bedford School and educating herself, she became a leading academic, writing several books including a *Survey of a Thousand Years of Beekeeping in Russia* which definitely awoke an interest in me of Russian and Soviet affairs and literature. In fact, most of my journeys have been to former Eastern Bloc countries.

Dorothy was an ardent supporter of communism – her father was secretary of the Fabian Society – and she became secretary to the School of Slavonic and East European Studies at the University of London. One of her friends was Prince D S Mirsky who taught at the university and who was acknowledged as being the leading emigre literary critic and historian of Russian literature. He was a supporter of Boris Pasternak. He became a communist, but not long after he returned to Moscow he was imprisoned and died in a gulag. A bigraphy of the prince includes extracts of many of the letters exchanged between him and Dorothy. When Dorothy retired, at her leaving presentation a large object was wheeled into the room – the gift was a honey extractor, an item none of the Slavs there had seen before.

Dorothy wrote articles for us on Russian beekeeping and was able to put matters right on the price of sugar. Beekeepers were complaining that whilst the price of sugar in the EEC was very high, Russians were able to buy it at a fraction of the price. To feed our colonies we were having to pay the full protected price of £480 a tonne while EEC sugar from the stockpile of 1.7 million tonnes was being sold at £85 a tonne to Russians, Israelis and Libyans. Dorothy replied that most professional beekeepers on the co-operative farms in those countries left honey on the hives for winter food, implying perhaps that British beekeepers should do the same or pay for the sugar at the required price.

However, this didn't satisfy British beekeepers who were having a bad year because of the weather, for there might not be any honey on the hives for bees and feeding was essential if the colonies were to survive. For MAFF Miss Berthoud commented 'the administrative cost of providing cheap sugar to some 40,000 beekeepers would be disproportionate to the benefit to them' considering that sugar for feeding each stock cost the beekeeper only £12. Beekeepers, like everyone who works in the agricultural sector, have to take the bad years along with the good.

Dorothy Galton, a committed communist, was suspected of being a Russian spy

Having chosen to keep colonies, their first responsibility is to ensure the bees' welfare and if that entails having to feed them, or not harvesting much honey in a particular year, so be it.

Dorothy died when she was ninety having just completed her third book on beekeeping *Honey and Beeswax in Early Historical Times*. So far, I have been unable to find any trace of the book so it is possible that this important manuscript lies in an archive somewhere and remains unpublished. Her obituary in *The Times* in October 1992 took up many column inches. It stated that as a communist, Dorothy disliked possessions and was always giving things away – her ultimate gift was that of her body for medical research. It also mentions that 'Dorothy gave a spirited interview to the BBC' in the year of her death and that it would be broadcast in the following year.

Whist searching for details of the programme I was surprised to find that Dorothy's name cropped up in files which had been locked away and released for public viewing in 2009. I downloaded the files (more than 250 of them) from the the National Archives in Kew to discover that Dorothy had been suspected of being a Russian agent since 1936 and that for many years, not only had her letters and phone calls been intercepted, but her employers and colleagues were warned that she was not to be trusted with any information. The agencies of counter-espionage were very concerned also that Dorothy would 'groom' impressionable students – especially those studying Russian –as she had a particular fondness for them. For a while Dorothy ceased working at the school to engage in 'secret work in the local communist party'.

Despite the mass of information collected, and the fact that she went on several trips to Russia, no evidence was found that ultimately linked her to any spying activities.

CHAPTER SEVEN

Back to Basics

'**O**CH, are you sure that everyone will be wanting to be reading this stuff?' asked John Gleed. He was sitting in our dining room looking through the latest issue of the Quarterly.

'What do you mean?' I inquired, for I was sure that he was baiting me; he could be quite mischievous at times.

'All this stuff on measuring bees' wings, or what's happening in other countries. Look at this,' he went on pointing to an article by Atkinson, 'Columns and columns about whether bees are domesticated animals. Will all this help me to get more honey?'

I replied that all knowledge was useful, that what happens in other countries could have great significance here, and that science was a tool to help improve beekeeping, but he cut me off.

'That might all be true,' he conceded. 'But not everyone is interested in it. You need to bring it down to the level of the ordinary beekeeper who just needs to know what to do with the bees to get some honey; the *hoi poloi* amongst us'.

John had already written several articles as Scottish correspondent, telling us about what went on north of the border. Would he like another column, I asked him, to address the points that he had made? Once I managed to get him to promise to give it a go, he said it would be good to write for the riff raff like himself, from which Val and I derived the pen name of R Raff for his new *persona*. And, bearing in mind the contents of his promised articles, we decided on 'Back to Basics' as the title of his column.

From this rather chance conversation one of the most popular parts of the magazine was born, within which R Raff railed against almost anything which didn't have as its prime objective the welfare of the bees and the quest for honey, or if he thought someone was being too pompous and clever-clever. Although he was a very intelligent man and understood fully what was written in the Quarterly, with the exception maybe of parts of Atkinson's scholarly essays, he had kept his bees successfully in the same manner for almost sixty years. John had nothing but the most basic items of equipment – his hives, a honey extractor and strainer, an old well-used but serviceable smoker, a hive tool, and a goose feather for gently moving bees off the surface of the comb. His veil was a simple affair and I never saw him wear gloves when examining his colonies. The one extra piece of equipment he allowed himself was a wooden wedge which he inserted between the boxes when lifting or lowering them, to prevent bees from getting squashed.

All the readers wanted to know the identity of this man, for they knew the writer was assuming a pseudonym, as the name was not known to beekeepers. They would never have guessed that his doppelganger was the Scottish correspondent writing in the same issues. To keep up the disguise he would sometimes refer to R Raff's articles, for instance, 'I have a fellow feeling for our contributor R Raff who finds metric measurements a trial. I imagine I am probably of a similar age and generation. Working from a diagram where all measurements are metric, I do not feel at home.

When I lived north of the Moray coast my main source of domestic fuel was peat and when it was cut and spread out to dry, in a solid carpet with not a vestige of grass or heather showing, the area covered was measured in perches. I needed twenty perches (605 square yards/515 square metres) for a year's burning. I find it sad to think that all these old familiar terms and measurements will soon be only a memory, but change I suppose is inevitable'. John once showed me his peat bank. What surprised me was how deep he had to cut into it with his long peat knife. Hefting the wet peat must have been very heavy work and then, after drying, the peats had to be transported home. The fuel gave out a wonderful heat and pleasant sweet smell and when fully burnt left very white ashes.

John Gleed beside his peat bank which provided most of his domestic heating

Beekeeping in the Highlands

John had tentatively knocked on our door for the very first time when he was staying with family in the next village to us. He had subscribed to the magazine from the very beginning and he was very interested in learning about skep making – the reason for his visit. Straw skeps housed bees for centuries, but their use is frowned upon today as the combs cannot be removed from them to check for diseases of the brood – a statutory requirement. However, several beekeepers keep an odd colony in a skep just out of interest, to preserve this traditional way of beekeeping, and to keep the skilled craft of skep-making alive. John's visit was the start of a lifelong friendship during which we all as a family shared many adventures together.

John's almost singular aim as a beekeeper was getting honey and his hobby was born out of necessity. Honey in those days when he started beekeeping occupied an important place in the domestic economy and he would even move his hives on a bicycle or in a wheelbarrow to sources of nectar.

John's mentor in beekeeping was Selby Robson, the famous Northumbrian beekeeper whose son Willie runs the 1,000 colony Chain Bridge Honey Farm near Berwick-upon-Tweed. They keep their colonies in Smith hives, are experts at producing heather honey and have over the years developed a visitors' centre which focuses on their Northumbrian heritage as well as beekeeping.

I can with ease recall our first visit up to see John in Tain. When we reached the Black Isle we first noticed that the smoke from the village chimneys smelt of burning peat, a smell we were familiar with, for on a couple of occasions Thorne moors not far from us had underground fires in the peat which smouldered away for many weeks. The small town of Tain has a beautiful sheltered harbour and not far from it is the distillery of Glen Morangie, one of the first places John took us to see. I made the mistake when looking into one of the vats of taking a deep breath to smell the fermentation. The full force of the carbon dioxide I inhaled sent me crashing to the floor; I felt as if I had received a powerful electric shock, so instantaneous was its effect. However, the free samples of whisky we were given offset the frightening experience.

John and his wife, Irene, were excellent hosts to all our family and during all our visits north we were looked after and taken to see interesting places. All mealtimes were started with a prayer and at least one evening a week and most of Sundays, whilst they were at their church, we were free to walk along the dunes or explore other places for ourselves. I think John has been the only person that I have met who I could really describe as being a god-fearing man. Being a staunch Protestant he was most put out when we bought some raffle tickets for him and Irene, on which we had left their name on the counterfoils in the village shop. We must have caused them an enormous amount of anxiety, for as an elder of the church, like its brethren, no involvement in gambling was allowed.

Most of John Gleed's hives were home-made including the long 'coffin hive'

Although I had initially trained as a divinity teacher but was now an acknowledged atheist, John never pushed religion down our throats, though he did say that he would pray for us. It was later that I understood that he was also a fundamentalist and believed literally in the creation story, but we never argued about such matters – we had enough to talk about concerning bees.

John's apiary was in a clearing in a wood a few miles from Tain. All the colonies but one were kept in well-maintained National hives, the British Standard hives, the other in a long hive, his 'coffin hive' with twenty frames. John had made most of his hives using his circular saw, and they were treated annually with creosote to protect the wood. Often John would apply the creosote on cold dry winter days when the bees were tightly clustered inside the hives. It was instructional to watch him at work: using the minimum of smoke at the entrance he waited a full two minutes before gently and slowly removing the roof. The frames were taken out with care with no sudden movements or jarring, the combs quickly scanned to see that all was well. The bees were completely under his control though should an errant bee sting his bare hand, he would merely flick away the embedded sting, and showing no concern would continue with his examination of the colony. With no agricultural crops of any importance to bees within range of his apiary, his honey came from wildflowers and trees, particularly sycamore, and in late summer from heather. On one walk through the countryside in very early spring he showed me huge clumps of butterbur near a stream where hundreds of bees scrambled amongst the flowers collecting the much-needed pollen for colony growth. In summer I was taken to a 'secret' place where giant hogweed grew in profusion, each of the dinner plate-sized heads covered with nectar-collecting bees. Giant hogweed is listed as a noxious plant which should be destroyed, for if the foliage is touched it can result in severe and prolonged itching. Hidden away, though, in the clearing of a large wood, I doubt if it would trouble anyone.

John was a very generous man to others, but as regards himself he was frugal. We were sitting in a cafe in Forres one morning, the sky grey, the strong wind cold, and heavy rain was lashing the windows; not unusual for an August day but hardly suitable for our planned visit to Pluscarden Abbey, a Catholic Benedictine order, to look at their bees. I was looking forward to a hot cup of tea to warm me up, but when it arrived watery grey and with globules of fat around the edges of the cup, I desisted from drinking it. John's was much the same.

'You're not drinking it?' I asked him.

'I've paid for it, so I'll drink it,' he replied. 'It's no so bad. I've had worse!'

We were expected at Pluscarden in the forenoon, John said, so off we set to find the beekeeper monk. Brother Dominic was waiting for us, dressed in a creamy white habit, complete with hood which he used to cover his head in the pouring rain. Following him, we squelched through the muddy monastery garden, where just beyond the vegetable patch was a row of hives in front of a stone wall. They seemed to be National hives and it didn't look as if there would be much honey in them as no supers had been added for its storage. The hives were in need of repair and painting, and instead of being numbered they each bore on their front

Part of the old apiary at Pluscarden before it was modernised by the local beekeeping association. The monk's hives were named after Catholic monasteries: in this case, Pittenweem and Applecross

wall above the entrance the name of a Catholic monastery. One or two dark bees made short flights but soon returned to the hives. Obviously we weren't going to be able to open the hives, and being aware that Brother Dominic was getting soaked, his sandaled feet were already caked in mud, we began to depart.

'You have been invited to stay for lunch,' he said directing us towards the refectory. 'Just join the queue of monks.' The refectory was large and light with rows of long tables. We waited for the monks to take their customary places (if indeed this is what they did) and found two empty places for ourselves. After the chanting of the pre-meal prayer we sat down and turned towards a raised lectern behind which a monk was standing. His chosen book for the edification of his audience was General Sir Peter de la Billière's *Storm Command, A Personal Account of the Gulf War* which was probably being serialised for each meal. Although there was a rule of silence in the refectory, the monks expressed their reaction to the text with a chuckle, a laugh or anything else as long as it wasn't a recognisable word. The meal was vegetarian, starting with a thick soup followed by pasta and finished with a milk pudding. Towards the end of the meal, the monks took a chunk of bread from the basket on the table and began to wipe it round their used plates, dishes and cutlery. Once their 'washing up' was completed they each wrapped the items in a large white napkin and stored them in a drawer below the table.

John and I looked at each other and raised our eyebrows – for we weren't permitted to speak. But driving back to his house later we wondered who might previously have been sitting in our places in the refectory and how many tongues had licked the plates – and what nasty germs they might have been carrying. Since our visit to Pluscarden many years ago, the local beekeeping association has renovated the monastery apiary and made pathways through to the stands which are now occupied by new modern hives.

German beekeeping

Ever since I first read Bernhard Mobus' newsletter it had been my intention to visit him at his work place – the North of Scotland College of Agriculture, near Aberdeen. Bernhard had been a German prisoner-of-war and like many of his compatriots he chose not to go back to a homeland occupied by Soviet troops. He found work on a farm in a small village near Scunthorpe and looked after a pedigree herd of Jersey cows which produced some of the best quality milk in the area. Whilst he was a herdsman he had colonies of bees, studied for the highest qualification in apiculture and was awarded the National Diploma in Beekeeping. When I began the *Quarterly*, Bernhard was one of the first beekeepers I approached for copy and he always presented me with long detailed articles on the practical and scientific sides of the craft. Bernhard had the advantage of having access to German magazines and brought to readers' attention new discoveries and ideas which were not commonly known or practised in the British Isles.

John Gleed knew Bernhard very well, for Bernhard would visit local beekeeping associations to give instruction and demonstrations, and often ended up at John's home for refreshment. Bernhard had been

a member of BIBBA since its formation and one of the things he was doing at work was selecting and breeding a line of native bees and distributing the 'Maud' queens, or ripe queen cells, in his district.

Bernhard was everything that I expected him to be both in appearance, with his shock of white hair; and in his temperament – excitable, enthusiastic and with a questioning smile. He certainly was eccentric and posed for photographs with his head almost buried in skeps of live bees until he was sure that I had the picture I wanted. Part of the apiary contained many small German styrofoam hives in which were

Bernhard Mobus, one of the most well-informed beekeepers of his time, though many people were unable to appreciate his odd sense of humour

newly-mated queens. Without smoke he gently took off the lids so we could see the beginnings of each queen's developing brood nest. This is always a sight to look forward to, for after weeks of careful planning and husbandry of breeding colonies, poor weather could spoil everything. Even when the queen has safely emerged from her cell and been placed in her mating hive, there is the worry that she might not return from her nuptial flights, as many birds are always trawling the skies for insect prey. To see the new queen standing proud of the combs on her slightly longer legs, her abdomen swollen with developing eggs of which she can lay two thousand a day, one experiences a real sense of fulfilment. A young queen in pristine condition is truly a sight to behold.

In one part of the apiary was a sheltered outdoor feeder into which pollen trapped from beehives, or a pollen substitute, was placed in early spring so the bees would not have to fly far on cold days for the essential protein food to nourish the brood.

Beekeepers seemed either to like Bernhard or dislike him intensely.

I liked Bernhard. Many of my beekeeping friends are eccentric to some degree, and so as far as I was concerned he was just another individual who had his own way of doing things and expressing himself. If there were failings on his part I could see beyond them and appreciated the wealth of experience and knowledge that he brought to our journal.

Catherine, our daughter, played the oboe in the county youth orchestra and since Scunthorpe is twinned with Luneburg in Northern Germany, the orchestra was invited to play at the town's bierfest in August. I had

seen postcards of the heather moors there – the Luneburg Heide – which Beowulf had sent me, and pictures of nearby Celle, where he had spent time at the Beekeeping Institute gathering information on bee breeding techniques. John Gleed, his wife Irene, Val, myself and Jim, decided to go on a beekeeping trip to Germany, while Catherine travelled by bus with the orchestra and stayed at the youth hostel.

Harold, my English contact there, introduced our party to several beekeepers and between them, they transported us from one immaculate and well-organised apiary to another. The Carniolan bees, favoured by German beekeepers, were gentle, we could open the hives without using veils and the only smoke given to the bees was from a commercial beekeeper's cigarette. The Germans, I was led to understand, had adopted the Carniolan race as their national bee and were thus able to preserve its good characteristics, including gentleness, as foreign imports

Catherine, at an earlier age. Whilst she liked dressing up, bees were of little interest to her

were discouraged to prevent mongrelisation which would have negative consequences on what they saw as a national asset.

Bee alcohol!

At every apiary we had a picnic in preparation for which car boots were filled with food and crates of Pilsner and cans of Fanta. We ate well, for piles of sausage and pork dripping sandwiches had been made for us. Since Val didn't drink beer they brought her some home made Barenfangs

Bee shelters on the Heide – the heather moors near Luneburg, north Germany

The hives were opened from the back and as there was little room for adding extra supers, combs were removed as soon as they were full of honey

(Bear's Teeth) and, as the name suggests it has a real bite to it. She really liked it! Knowing this, they presented her with a bottle to take home. It is worth knowing the recipe because it makes a lovely warming winter drink. Firstly, one brood comb full of pollen should be minced up and put in a demi-john. Next, add one pound of warm, preferably dark honey (try different types, especially heather) to a litre bottle of Korn (schnapps), mix in about two teaspoons of ground propolis and put the mixture in the demi-john. Finally fit a fermentation lock and leave for two months, but swirl the demi-john around each day.

From the apiaries in the woods we moved to the Luneburg Heide. The heath is very different to the moorlands of Britain. It is very flat and low lying with scattered conifer trees. The Heide is criss-crossed with paths for hikers, cyclists and horse riders and for those feeling less energetic, expensive carriage rides are available. Not many beekeepers have licenses to keep bees on the heath, probably because it has thousands of tourists, but those who are licensed, keep their colonies in bee shelters. Inside, the hives are arranged in tiers, their entrances facing outwards, the beekeepers working them from behind, inside the beehouse.

Each hive had only two chambers, one for the brood and one for the honey, separated by a queen excluder. The frames were placed at right angles to the entrance and were removed from the hive for examination by sliding them towards the beekeeper. As no extra storage was available, combs of honey were removed as soon as they were filled, and replaced with empty combs. Between the door of each hive and at right angles to the brood and honey combs was a 'building frame'. From this frame the beekeeper was able to read the condition of the hive without disturbing the bees. It acted as an overflow for the hive and when drone comb was being built, it signified that swarming time was not far off. An attempt was made by a manufacturer to sell this type of hive in the UK some years ago. It was given the name The European Hive, but it was heavy and expensive and never caught on.

Not far from the bee houses was a traditional heather apiary, with hundreds of hives, most of them straw skeps or basket hives. The huge shelter in which they were housed was made of timber and roofed with thatch and made up three sides of a courtyard. In front of the shelter was a clearing for twenty yards and then a narrow strip of woodland. In order to look at the bees we would have to approach the hives from their front, which is never a good idea, for being in the bees' flight path stinging is bound to occur. John, myself and one of the German beekeepers took a risk and began to close in on the hives, only to be driven back by an onslaught of stings which had us running for the shelter of the trees where fortunately the bees gave up their attack. It is known that the aggressiveness of bees manifests itself more noticeably when they are working one floral source, and is often remarked upon by beekeepers when their colonies are wholly feeding from oil seed rape or heather.

At the beekeeping institute near Celle, the director took us on a tour of the laboratories, apiaries and museum. Everything was in impeccable order. Between the buildings, vast beds with many varieties of heather in shades of pink, white and purple not only added beauty to the grounds, but also provided the bees with a source of food.

The apiaries were in well-maintained walled gardens with brick archways leading from one section to another. Several of the hives were made out of high density styrofoam and painted in bright attractive colours and no matter where we walked, the bees made no attempt to

Traditional skep beekeeping on the Heide

sting us. The museum was mainly devoted to skep beekeeping and the straw hives covered with cow dung were of all sizes and shapes, many of them depicting a human face, with the entrance to the hive at the mouth. Tongs, knives and wooden presses for harvesting the heather crop were displayed with information about the artefacts in English and German. As I was walking around the exhibitions, I was pleased that traditional skep beekeeping was not a craft confined to history but still existed prominently on the Heide. When Beowulf was in Germany he met a beekeeper who had 2,000 straw skeps which he moved to the orchards for pollination in spring, then on to the colza (rape) and finally to the heathland.

My son Jim accompanied us on many beekeeping trips. He liked playing with the smoker and helping to extract honey, but preferred to keep away from the bees

We took a bus ride up into the Hartz Mountains where John spent some time gazing to the east. In the far distance the Iron Curtain divided Germany, and trapped beyond the barrier was Wolf, a wartime friend of John's. They had kept corresponding with each other by mail for more than forty years and John found it very tantalising to be so near to the border but unable to visit his friend. Happily, they had only just over a year to wait, for in 1989 when the Berlin Wall came down, they visited each other's homelands.

Skep-making

When John came down to Lincolnshire he would bring his skep-making tools – an old sack needle and a slice of the middle part of a cow's horn. A farmer I knew let him have armfuls of long rye for the skep, as the stalks of other cereals were too short. When he was unable to get rye, his skeps were made out of very fine reeds which made much tighter coils. Traditionally, for stitching the coils together, bramble stems would be used, but it was a tedious and often painful procedure to remove the barbs and split the stems so, like many skep makers, he made use of that great agricultural waste product, baler twine. Unlike my attempts, John's skeps were beautifully proportioned, perfectly symmetrical and passed the ultimate test – setting the skep on the ground and jumping on top of it without it losing shape. My coils were never tight enough and when tested, the skeps would collapse. I lent John a huge bell jar from my laboratory which he placed on a skep that was well stocked with bees. The bell jar was used as a super for honey storage and the bees filled it

My home made cottage hives made from recycled bedroom doors. Fortunately, the boards from the door were very wide

with beautiful white-capped honeycombs. To protect the skep from bad weather he covered it with a wooden barrel, the cork having been removed to provide an entrance hole. When I made some cottage hives out of the old bedroom doors that we replaced, John worked alongside me and made all the wooden supers.

John tried to coincide his holidays in Lincolnshire with the BBKA Convention at Stoneleigh in Spring, or the National Honey Show in London during the autumn so that we could travel together. Despite his aversion to buying any equipment that he could make himself, he finally succumbed to buying ten pre-shaped pieces of metal with which to replace the old felt on his hive roofs. He was so pleased with his purchase that he hardly noticed their weight when we wandered around London after the show. If he happened to be around when the Lincolnshire or Nottingham BKA auctions were taking place, then we would have to go, for a beekeeping sale for both of us was entertaining and educational.

Beekeeping auctions

In order to be successful and run smoothly when hundreds of lots are up for auction, the organisation has to be spot on and both the associations referred to became accomplished professionals in this aspect of the craft. The sales are held on their county agricultural showgrounds at the beginning of the beekeeping seasons and a foul brood officer, employed by MAFF would have inspected live bees beforehand so that the colonies were cleared as being free of the two most infectious diseases of honeybee brood. It was always surprising to see what was brought along to the auction, in fact anything that might be useful to beekeepers for the apiary, garden or workshop, or a collector of 'museum' pieces might find an item of remarkable interest. The hives and general beekeeping equipment

Beekeeping auctions held by Lincolnshire and Nottinghamshire beekeeping associations were well-organised and attracted people from all parts of the UK – for bargains as well as unusual beekeeping items

are usually to be found in three categories: things which someone was clearing out and generally not in a very good state; oldish items which had been given a lot of attention and might also have been given a fresh coat of paint in order to attract high bids; and newish equipment in very good condition.

In the first few auctions we visited, beekeepers were getting rid of the old cumbersome double-walled hives and using the money they raised to buy modern beehives so the WBC's and their like were not so numerous in later years. Electrical equipment including honey extractors and circular saws are inspected by an electrician beforehand and any faults are clearly marked on a sticker. The items could still be sold, but the buyer would be made aware of any problems to do with safety. Beekeepers mostly end up with good bargains, but some get frightfully carried away when the bidding is brisk, and they end up paying well over the odds for items. I was delighted to see at one auction exact copies of the cottage hive that I had designed and reproduced plans for in the Quarterly, even more pleased when I saw that they fetched a good price.

The bees are usually sold towards the end of the auction and this is when prices go well over the top, especially when there is a shortage of colonies. We witnessed six combs of bees going under the hammer for £130, which although on a par with nuclei today, I am talking about twenty years ago! Hundreds of beekeepers and their families travel great distances to these events; they are fun occasions, especially if the auctioneers like the ones I know have a good sense of humour. Along with refreshments, cake and plant stalls, not forgetting the commission on articles sold, the auctions really help swell association funds. There must have been a collective sigh of relief at the end of the long day when the organisers and their helpers viewed an empty, swept clean warehouse.

It was at one of these events that, as John put it, my beekeeping empire came to its end. He helped me pack everything I hadn't already given away into my Subaru and trailer for the two journeys to the Lincolnshire Showground. It was a sad turning point in his life, he told me, for in a few months I would be leaving England to live in Greece. John continued to write for me both as the Scottish correspondent and as R. Raff, though eventually he said it was time for a younger hand to take over the Scottish writing. R. Raff was resurrected for the 100th edition of the BKQ, of which John saw a copy in the last few days before he died.

He wrote: *'Like Bobby Ewing in Dallas, I have returned from the dead, but have no fear, there will be no rocking of the boat [as he was wont to do – Ed]. Our editor was kind enough to invite me to pen a few lines for this memorable edition and once that is done I shall sink again into oblivion'*. He went on to relate his involvement with the Quarterly, the time we spent together and how he had mastered firstly an Amstrad word processor and then a proper computer so that he could send copy to me via the internet. He wrote that even after our departure to Greece he continued to visit our acre field where we used to work together with the bees until at last that, too, was sold. So, *'that was it. The last chapter was closed and my close connection with the birthplace of the Quarterly was severed. Very sad.'*

We saw John two or three times during our visits back to England. He was well into his eighties by then, though with a daily dose of glucosamate for his arthritis he still managed to cycle some miles to his apiary. Eventually I received an email that his empire had also come to an end; for the first time in sixty years he was without bees. The last time we saw him was in Lincolnshire at my sister's house. He was taking a great interest in her electric bicycle and he readily accepted the chance of a ride. Off he went, his back straight and with a happy grin on his face as he raced up and down the village street, and that is how I last remember him.

CHAPTER EIGHT

Honey as a Business

THE huge yellow fields of oil seed rape which continued to increase in number every year almost guaranteed a good harvest of honey every season and, apart from one or two exceptions due to poor spring weather, I normally had plenty of honey to sell. My workplace provided an important outlet, sales from my gate were usually good, and one or two local shops and a garden centre would each take a couple of dozen jars at a time. Selling wholesale to shops nearby was not easy though, as many of them had procured their honey from the same beekeeper for many years, so it was really a case of waiting for dead men's shoes, if I was to be their main supplier.

In the few places that I managed to sell my honey I often wondered what service I got for the 30% profit the shop owner received. There was no real attempt to promote my honey and it was sad to see the jar lids gathering dust in a corner of a gloomy shop. I often mentioned making some sort of display, but no interest was shown; after all, my honey was just another of the hundreds of commodities that the shop had for sale.

I was really envious of Jeff Rounce in Norfolk, a retired teacher, who had plenty of time to devote to his bees. His apiaries were the most organised I have seen anywhere, with all the hives on stands in woodland clearings and preserved with fresh creosote. He was equally meticulous with his management and it was obvious that his bees were given the best possible care. Jeff's wife was the village postmistress and undoubtedly some honey was sold from her Walsingham post office, but Jeff's major outlet was the Shrine Shop of Our Lady of Walsingham, the Shrine itself attracting over 10,000 visitors a year. Not surprisingly, Jeff depicted the Shrine's Anglican church on his honey labels, to good effect.

I could easily have sold honey in bulk to a small honey co-operative, but the price was very low. Tesco's was another possibility, for they were trying to promote local produce. They would pick up the honey from certain locations, take it to a central processing plant and then deliver it back to its supermarkets in the original area with the local county label pasted on the jars. Neither of these options were to my liking for I wanted complete control of the marketing of my honey. My aim – a very

Jeff Rounce's Walsingham honey

ambitious one – was to sell the honey to one of the top stores in London and throughout the whole of the UK, but how was this to be achieved? Val and I discussed this for many weeks and together we decided that we would set up our own honey business.

Way back in the 1950s Manley, one of Britain's finest beekeepers who had apiaries in the Chilterns, stated that in order for a beekeeper to be able to make a successful beekeeping business, three factors were of great importance: having the right amount of experience; having the capital needed; and having a good market for the hive produce. Essentially all three of these are needed concurrently. There was another factor to be considered by us, too; where we would find the time, for we both had responsible full-time jobs. Another factor, but of not such great importance just then was that my health problems as regards depression were not improving – but my mood was generally lifted when I had something new or exciting to think about.

The only 'assets' that I could put into the honey business were my experience of keeping bees and selling honey on a small scale for about twenty years and what I thought to be some very good ideas. My plan was firstly to cut my colonies down to just fifty hives to give me more spare time and, secondly, to buy small amounts of many different types of honey, monofloral if possible, from elsewhere. I had already stayed with beekeepers in several different parts of Europe by then and very much liked the honeys which they produced.

I would then 'downpack' the imported honey – as well as my own – mainly into miniature 28g pots for which I would design my own packaging. The packages would then be sold either in 'up-market' food stores or by mail order as the latter, even before internet sales, was becoming increasingly popular for anniversaries and celebrations. By downpacking honey, although there would be more work, the honey would sell for a very high price and manageable amounts could be bought in as required. Hopefully, customers who tried our range of honeys would then want to buy full size jars of the honey varieties that they particularly liked.

Val had already decided on a business name, 'Honey Hunters', the very ambitious idea behind it being that eventually we would try and locate the source of any honey that was requested. We had an idea for the logo too: it would be based on a carved wooden bear we picked up in an antique shop in Goslar, Germany. As the bulk of the honey would be put into plastic 28g pots I decided to develop two types of packaging; one would hold twelve pots, the other thirty pots (a month's supply of honey for breakfast or tea time).

The smaller box was very simple. It would be rectangular with space for three rows of four pots; it would have a strong lid which could be removed and slipped under the box bottom so that the contents could be displayed; and there would be an inner, clear, perspex cover which would protect the pots.

The second type of packaging was much more complicated. I wanted it to be in the form of a dispenser which could be hung on the kitchen wall. It was to look attractive and resemble the pine tree from which the forest beekeepers cut out their combs from wild bees' nests. Each morning or afternoon, the recipient of the gift would be able to open the door in the tree hive and take out a pot of honey. As there were to be 30 types of honey in the dispenser, each day's honey would be of a different type and a surprise for the consumer – who would soon realise just how diverse honeys were in taste, aroma, colour and texture.

Once my ideas were on paper, complete with the appropriate measurements, I contacted several box manufacturers before choosing one particular firm in Bradford for the work. They were extremely helpful throughout, except for one almost disastrous flaw at the end of the project. All the artwork – the logo design, the box decoration and tree motifs, as well as labels for the mini pots was done by a local bank manager's wife who was starting out in that line of business. We had already set up a list of honey types which we knew were available and provided the artist with a supply of pictures to help her with the work.

Honey Hunters packaging

I needed cash for the project – about £10,000. I needed to go to the bank (Manley would no doubt have shuddered at this point). However, I had security, plenty of it: a secure job and a good property. And £10,000 didn't seem that much anyway; it was only the cost of a new car. One week after driving a new car you have lost a lot of money but I knew that my business plan looked good and I would make a healthy profit.

Different packaging options for the honey jars

The bank manager thought so too, even though he knew nothing at all about honey. He was either captivated by my enthusiasm or knew that the bank's money was going to be safe enough, given some security. The money would cover all the packaging and labels, the first batch of honey, the setting up of a honey house and equipping it, and a bulk supply of pots and jars in different sizes. It would also pay for the launch of the enterprise.

Before spending any money at all, I carefully weighed up the advantages/disadvantages of being VAT registered. There was no doubt in my mind that although it would perhaps take years before I reached the threshold when I would be compelled to register, doing so straight away would be to my advantage. Not only would I receive the VAT back on all my purchases, this would extend to (though proportionally) my telephone bills, running my pick-up truck, etc, yet I would not have to charge and eventually repay VAT on my products as they were classed as food. One disadvantage, of course, was that there would be more paperwork and that returns would have to be made each quarter. However, I thought that doing the paperwork regularly would be a good discipline to keep on top of the business. I also employed an accountant who showed me how to keep my books, checked my VAT return and completed my annual tax return.

Just before I started on the design stage of the project, I had contacted several beekeepers who advertised in the magazine *Abeilles de France* and asked them to send me samples of their honey. The greatest and most interesting range of honeys came from Joel Schiro, a beekeeper in the Pyrenees, near Lourdes. As we had friends in Toulouse, we booked flights for a short holiday in the region and allowed ourselves three days with the beekeeper, who was just a couple of hours away by train. In that short time we learned a lot about French beekeeping, travelling from one large apiary to another, and spending time in the huge honey house, sampling even more varieties of honey.

We put together a first order – just 15 x 35kg tubs and settled all the paperwork there and then. Each pail of honey contained clean, well-filtered honey just ready for bottling and some of the types we chose were honey from rhododendron (not the poisonous variety!), fir trees, bell heather (moorland), ling, sea holly, lime tree, sunflower, lavender, cherry, and spring mountain flowers. We also arranged transportation. A haulage firm across the road from us in our village made the trip down to Spain once every fortnight and would collect the two pallet loads on the way back – only adding an hour or so of driving for the slight diversion.

On our return to the UK we also ordered honey from British packers thus adding to our list of honeys: Mexican, Orange Blossom, Caribbean, New Zealand Clover, Tasmanian Leatherwood, Guatemalan, Chinese, Australian Bluebell and Canadian – all of which were available in 25kg tubs.

Within a short time we added many French 'herb' honeys to our list and manuka, from New Zealand, which was in great demand after Peter Nolan's work on this honey and its curative effect on stomach ulcers.

My own 'honey house'

A purpose-built honey house was needed, but time and money were at a premium. Fortunately, I already had a concrete pad next to our house which would make a good base. It had formerly served as a base for a greenhouse made by the previous owner (I pulled it down as it was hideous – it was made of panels of perspex of different thicknesses and shapes gleaned from an old Lancaster aeroplane factory). I chose the easiest and cheapest solution, a pre-cast concrete garage 5m x 3m, but with a standard door fitted to the front instead of a full-width one for a car. I painted the inside walls and the floor, as the surfaces were very powdery, and made a false bee-proof roof. Both water and electricity were nearby so fitting these was not a problem.

Three banks of power points were fitted and all lights were shielded with plastic shades. I had a large galvanised sink, big enough for washing 35kg containers, made to my own design at a local metalworker's yard. One side of the honey house was for storage of large honey pails, an extractor and steel shelves for finished products, whilst opposite this was a bench for uncapping combs or bottling honey. Under the bench I had a row of honey warming boxes, bought from Thorne's, but extended

Oil seed rape honey was plentiful and didn't always attract a good price. 'Creaming' the honey so that it had a soft creamy consistency, and using attractive packaging improved both prices and sales

in height with 'lifts' so that they would accommodate the larger tubs. I bought two pieces of equipment for the honey house: an electric zapper to kill flying insects and a Danish bottling machine which could be calibrated to fill even the very small 28g pots.

Before I used the honey house I asked the local environmental health officer to come and inspect the building. Legislation for honey processing rooms and their inspection was quite new at the time of the officer's visit. He knew nothing about honey except that it was in the 'low risk' category of foods. I soon realised that anyone fearing an inspection has no need to worry – as long as their honey-handling premises are clean and tidy.

The important things were all in order; washing facilities were good (both hot and cold water), worktops, walls, ceilings and floors were all easy to clean, light bulbs were shielded, there was adequate light and ventilation (but who opens the honey house window during extracting?), electric points were safe and earthed, and the inspector liked the zapper and first aid kit which, apparently, weren't essential.

I was given a score of 100%. I asked him how low the mark needed to be for an inspection to fail. He said if I had scored 60% he would have had to put me on his list for a visit in a year's time. Even hotels and restaurants in that category are given a chance to improve, but in a shorter space of time. Even then, though, the inspectors must make an appointment, they cannot make spot checks, so I was left thinking how limited the inspections were. I was amazed; this was the first time I had achieved a perfect score in anything!

Launching the business

One of the difficulties of introducing a new range of products onto the market is that you cannot hawk them around to shops until you finally have the finished products in your hands. It's no good going to retailers and saying 'I'm thinking of expanding my range of products. I'm going to put them in packs like this ... are you interested?' Nine times out of ten you will be told to come back later. I knew that there would be some time between having my products to show potential customers and sending them to food magazines and Sunday supplements before I would get any return on my investment.

However, I had, I believed, one golden opportunity for launching the business – the Lincoln Christmas Market. Thousands of people from many parts of the UK, and abroad, are attracted to this annual event. From the picturesque castle and cathedral area and all down Steep Hill crowds throng amongst the craft and food stalls. Food, beer and gifts from Germany, hot potatoes and chestnuts, French crepes, roast boar, speciality foods, Christmas Carols, Morris Men – the range of products and entertainment is enormous. What an opportunity! I paid my £200 rent space and constructed a market stall out of iron and plastic at the front of which would be an enormous trestle table that I would borrow from my school potting shed.

Ten days before the market I began to panic. The boxes I had ordered still hadn't been delivered. All the honey was waiting on shelves – hundreds of pots of 30 varieties of honey, all labelled and ready for packing. The filling of the small pots had taken a very long time for the Svienty machine either delivered plus or minus two or three grams each time; in order to work properly it needed a constant stream of honey at the same pressure.

I had to resort to using a hand dispenser on a 28lb honey tin, which was a monotonous and painful job. After a series of phone calls I was told that the boxes would be brought the following evening. That was OK, I thought, as I still had one weekend before the market. The packaging looked superb when at last it arrived. When filled with a dozen varieties the rectangular presentation boxes looked really attractive. I then began to fill the 'Christmas Tree' dispenser – and realised very quickly that something was wrong – this box would only hold 28 instead of the labelled '30 varieties'.

I had a problem – or the company had. To this day, I believe they made the wrong measurements as they had the empty pots to take back to their design room. I suppose I could have, then and there, said – 'Take them back, they are not what I ordered'. But I had all the honey on the shelves and the prospect of a good market just a few days away. The director (he'd overseen the whole project from start to finish and had delivered the packages himself) absolved himself of any responsibility and said that he would have a new label produced for the following day and sent over by courier – and that this could be placed over the incorrect printing. I wasn't happy – I had planned for a 30-day supply of honey – and based my costings on 30 pots, but I was in a very difficult situation. I opted for the new label and I'm sure the director sighed with relief. A teaching colleague, who had himself been in business, knowing that I was under pressure, came one evening with his wife and helped us to fill the boxes ready for the market.

The Lincoln Christmas Market was a spectacular failure. I was unfortunate enough, like twenty other stall-holders, to have a very bad position in a small car park at the side of the castle. It was at this point that many people disembarked from their coaches and used the park as a thoroughfare. Many people stopped briefly for a cursory look and said that they would return later. Some commented on how pretty our products were and some said what a pity I wasn't selling jam! We stood and stamped our feet in the cold thick fog for one evening and two whole days hardly selling a thing.

On the second day, the seller of baked potatoes sold all his potatoes to a man who had a better location in Castle Square; the latter had already sold what he thought would be enough potatoes for the three days. Both my wife and I joined the Breton pancake-maker from time to time, exchanging products instead of cash, strangely comforted by our joint disappointment in lack of trade.

And what had people bought chiefly at the Christmas market? The top seller was a Christmas hat carrying the title of a song, by Right Said Fred, which was then top of the pop charts, 'I'm too sexy for my hat'. Enough said!

Needless to say, we were totally numbed by our lack of success at what should have been an extremely lucrative market. If you can't sell gifts like the ones we had designed at Christmas time then the future of the whole business looked pretty bleak. In an attempt to get some cash back I managed to sell some boxes to some garden centres and up-market delicatessens, but local sales were very limited. I had already sent out gift packs for review in magazines and newspapers, yet I knew I couldn't afford to sit around and wait for the outcome; something more positive needed to be done and that quickly, for the hefty bank loan needed to be paid each month.

For the short term, we placed some adverts in the Sunday newspapers saying that we would send our gift boxes directly by post to the intended recipients. The cost of each box, including package and postage was just £7.75 – cheaper by far than chocolates, flowers, or Stilton cheese! We had a good number of responses which was encouraging. However, we soon realised that this method of sale was only good if we persisted with our advertising – but the rates were really too expensive.

Our next line of attack was one that we had intended to do all along but had no time to do before Christmas, trying to get our gift boxes into one of the top London stores. We tried three. All of the buyers were impressed with our range and packaging – but in each case the answer was the same: 'We will get in touch with you'. Feeling flat, but not totally disappointed, we got on with more bottling and packing and I had time to produce a brochure which attempted to give interesting descriptions of each of the honeys we sold. The information included the geographic area the honey came from, their nectar sources, descriptions of the taste, colour, aroma and texture, and also some ideas how the various honeys could be used.

Within two or three months, several top food writers wrote favourable descriptions of our products and the market picked up a bit. Buying over the telephone was a problem for many customers as we were unable to accept credit card payment. In the case of emergency we sent out the product before a cheque arrived – and only once did we not receive payment.

One afternoon, unexpectedly and much to our delight, we received a telephone call from one of the prestigious London stores. They wanted to see us as they wished to order some of our products. Sadly, although they liked the gift boxes, they had something else in mind. They were building a new top-floor 'grocery' shop to compete with another famous nearby store. They wanted to stock all our range – but in one pound jars. Their requirements were specific as regards both the jars and labels. The jars had to be glass and square and the labels both plain and simple. The initial order was to be large and after that they expected to buy about 1,000 jars from us each month.

We went home with a lot to think about. It was good to receive such an order, but it meant changing the way our business was intended to go. By down-packing honey into 28g pots I was getting a very good return on the 336g in each gift pack – some 150-200%. The problem was though,

I wasn't selling enough of them. On the other hand, I would have the opportunity of selling my own two lines of honey in a top-notch store at twice the price that I could get locally. I thought, too, that it must be important to have a flexible approach to business; surely, being adaptable and taking opportunities when they crop up is a key to success?

We decided to go ahead with the store's requirements, except we had to compromise on the pots – we used square polycarbonate ones which were obtainable locally. Val was asked to go to London to train the staff on how to sell the honey and how to answer questions customers were most likely to ask such as 'Why does honey go solid?' and 'How long does honey keep for?' Also, not long after the new food department opened, we went to London again, this time to set up a honey-tasting stall in the shop.

Fixing labels on square polycarbonate jars in our honey house

It was wonderful to see row after row of our square jars of honey with their distinctive yellow labels on the shelves of the grocery department, occupying a large and prominent position. We found, though, that our experience with customers confirmed our belief that the gift packs would sell. Whilst we found that the shoppers tasted some of the honeys and then went and bought a jar or two of the one pound sizes, most of them wanted to buy the gift packs which were not for sale. Many of the people who came to our stall were not the Saturday grocery shopping crowd, but tourists or business people looking for a gift to take home and our boxes were far more interesting and would travel better in suitcase than a jar of honey. We could not convince the floor manager at the end of the day – but at least we had managed to hand out some of our brochures which might attract some attention.

On one of the tasting sessions, a gentleman with his whole family sampled honey after honey, eventually settling for one they all really liked. We pointed them in the direction of the shelves and they came back a few minutes later enthusiastically waving several pound jars. 'Oh, dear!' I said. 'You've picked up the wrong variety.'

'Yes! But these are the most expensive,' came the reply as they went off happily.

Television coverage

Eventually, the media really tuned in to our small business. Radio 4 wanted a sample box for their food programme and Carlton TV wanted to make a film about our honey. The BBC telephoned me just as I came in from work. They wanted the box the next day to be opened live on Derek Cooper's *The Food Programme*. I took a package straight away to the local village post office so that I could arrange for next day delivery. It was impossible. I was advised to go to the main post office in Gainsborough. I made it by 4.45pm. There was a long queue and out of the five positions behind the counter only two were manned. I don't know how I kept my patience – I knew that for guaranteed next day delivery the package had to be at the counter by 5pm.

My turn came seven minutes after that – 'You're too late,' the woman said, 'It cannot go by Express post – you will just have to risk it getting there by First Class Post.' It was immutable. I was speechless! And cross, having waited for more than twenty minutes only to be disappointed. Fortunately, however, the honey arrived in time for Derek Cooper's programme, and received a favourable review, following which we had a fair number of enquiries from many parts of the UK.

The television programme was a success too. We had a very pleasant day with Tony Francis, who directed and produced *Heart of the Country* for Carlton TV, and his team. They came to our home in Lincolnshire and we looked into beehives together, when unfortunately the novice reporter received a couple of stings despite excellent weather and a good nectar flow. Despite the pain, being a true professional, she continued with her commentary as soon as the stings had been removed.

The team sampled the types of honey, on camera, as well as items of food and drink prepared by Val using monofloral types of honey. Interestingly, after the film was aired, we received requests for full-size jars of honey relating to the recipes Val used for the televised food – lavender honey for ice cream, dark fir tree honey for the fresh pineapple and yoghurt, lime tree honey for the honey lemonade, mild rhododendron honey for tea, and Caribbean honey for the rich, spicy walnut and honey cake. If people catch on to a recipe they will demand the right type of honey and in this way a market can be created.

The uniqueness of our honey business caught the attention of the staff of *Farmers Weekly*, and Ann Rogers who wrote the farm life column came up to interview us together with a photographer. Subsequently, an article covering two full pages appeared in the weekly magazine, which not only covered our honey and beekeeping activities, but also my work locally as a rural science teacher. She also noted my criticism of MAFF policy which at the time restricted the movement of bees to control the spread of an invasive exotic pest.

As the pest spread further from its original point of infestation in Devon, the Ministry gradually demarcated areas from which bees couldn't be moved. Since the mite, varroa, was going to spread eventually throughout the UK, as it had in almost every other country – and rapidly – despite restrictions on colony movements, the policy seemed senseless in a small country like Britain and meanwhile was going to make it very difficult for commercial bee farmers who needed to move bees for pollination contracts, or like myself and hundreds of other beekeepers, to take their bees to the heather moors. Ann also gave some of Val's hints for using honey in cookery, together with some of her recipes.

We had started our business at a very difficult time – in the middle of one of the worst recessions. However, with orders coming in from London and with slow but steady sales of gift boxes, we were quite hopeful about the future. We asked the London store how things were going – and they were pleased to say that we could confidently order more honey so that there would be no lack of continuity in supply. This was extremely important. Some of the honeys we procured from the Pyrenees and Provence could not be relied on every season and one of our main suppliers was going to cut down on some of the specialist monofloral honeys as he had trouble selling them in France. He saw his future in putting most of his 3,000 hives of bees onto sunflowers and going for bulk sales. I had to buy more honey very quickly to keep in store – and in so doing, made my biggest, but unavoidable, mistake. I went back to the bank.

The bank saw no problem in supplying me with more cash to meet the honey bill. The manager had been a couple of times to our house, had seen what we were doing and was pleasantly surprised that we had one of England's most prestigious stores as a customer. I placed a large order with my French supplier. When I went to arrange collection with my haulage friend whose business was just across the road from me, I had a shock. Their lorries were no longer going to the southern border of France and Spain. As a result of minimum wage agreements, the catalogue supply company was no longer buying clothes and leather goods from Spain and Portugal as the labour costs were too high – they were now sourcing their goods in Asia.

However, I was given a couple of contacts of hauliers that operated in that area and managed to get the honey, but at double the transportation cost. I continued to supply London with the honey but two months later they did not re-order – ever! We found out, although they did not tell us, that they were now procuring the honey themselves from the Pyrenees, bottling it in the cellar beneath the store, or one of their warehouses and selling it under their own label. Of course, we had no written contract with the company, for that is not their policy, despite the fact that, fool that I was, I had allowed them the distinction of being sole suppliers of our range in London. I learned that in the same week, a new floor manager had decided to have a change and got rid of a whole collection of bone china that someone had produced specifically for the shop, so I was not the only disappointed supplier.

Admittedly, one of my biggest mistakes had been to put most of my stock into one store. I should have heeded the advice of Val's uncle, a businessman, whose mantra was never to put more than 20-30% of your stock in one outlet. However, we were in a depression and times were hard and it had been too easy for me to swallow the bait. I knew of commercial beekeepers who were almost doubling their mileage each year in seeking out and supplying retail outlets as the local demand for their produce had diminished.

Out of the blue came one glimmer of hope. I received a fax from Malta for 1,000 jars of honey – and if they liked it they would order more. I had not contemplated exporting before and had a lot of paperwork to sort out before the deal could be completed.

All was ready when I received another fax – apparently from the one of the food ministers in Malta – which requested a health certificate stating that the whole consignment of honey 'must not have come from any colonies which had had any disease or pest of any type for the three years prior to harvesting'. This included the very contagious diseases of honeybee brood, which I could understand – plus diseases of adult bees which are endemic in most apiaries throughout the world, but could not be transmitted via honey. This was an impossible request as all the problems, apart perhaps from foulbrood, are endemic in most apiaries throughout the world. I faxed my supplier. He had 3,000 colonies in many apiaries from the Atlantic seaboard to the Mediterranean.

Three days later, much to my surprise I received a certificate of health from the French veterinary service endorsing the fact that all the colonies had been inspected and that they had been in excellent health over the last three years! The French authorities thought nothing of signing the certificate, no matter how dubious the declaration. My customer in Malta was pleased with the honey – and wanted more. However, unreasonable officialdom, or more likely pressure from a local honey supplier, made further exports impossible so I was still left with a huge amount of honey and no discernible market.

Eventually we decided that the only way that we could dispose of our honey was on a market stall. This was well before farmers' markets were in vogue, so we rented a space each week in the old indoor Butter Market in Newark, about 25 miles from our home. This meant we had to be preparing our items for sale on Friday evening and making an early start the next day to be at the market by 8am. For eighteen months, with Val's creative flair, we made the stall as attractive as possible and gave away free sample pots of new varieties to our regular customers and enjoyed talking to everyone who stopped by.

Val made unique candles which she had covered with dried pressed flowers and tiny leaves that were then dipped once more in wax for a protective, transparent coat, which became very popular. Also, to increase our turnover, we combed market stalls, car boot sales and even antique shops for candlesticks – and old brass ones, complete with beeswax candles, were snapped up very quickly. A good range of cosmetics made by my friend Willie Robson's Chainbridge Honey Farm were an additional attraction – the peppermint foot cream, handcreams and lip balms all selling well.

It was important, too, for us to use our time at Newark to educate people about bees. By trying our honeys, visitors to our stall soon realised that honey was not just sweet and sticky, but had a full range of tastes – fruity, spicy, and almost rank or bitter. Naturally, enquiries were made about what we added to our honey and when we answered, 'Nothing!'

*Honey Stall at
Newark Butter
Market*

and that the taste came from the flowers that the bees visited, there was incomprehension that the honey didn't taste like the fruit or flower of a plant. I took an observation hive to the stall each week so that our customers could watch the bees and learn about colony life and for many people this was the first opportunity they had of seeing bees close-up.

Whilst the days on the cold concrete market-floor were long, they seemed to pass by relatively quickly, for our regular customers always wanted to talk for a while and there were the other stall-holders with whom to chat. There, in the middle of the recession, they would work hard at selling their crafts, antiques, books and clothes though always, it seemed, the odds were against them. Each week they gave themselves a reason why they had made little money – it was the third week in the month and the people hadn't been paid yet; it was the beginning of the school term and money had to be spent on school uniform; it was summer and people were saving for their holidays: always there was an excuse.

No matter what, they kept cheerful and confident, turning up each week and ever hopeful of a better time ahead. We didn't have their tenacity and when our range of products diminished and our debt was just about paid, we left the market forever. We also had a steady income from our full-time jobs, something most stallholders lacked; it was their main income.

It is easy to look back now and analyse what went wrong. Undoubtedly, we made mistakes but we were trying just too hard when market forces were against us and eventually we had no energy or wish to continue with our honey business. If internet shopping had been available at that time, we might have emerged from the depression with good postal sales, but after spending half a weekend for eighteen months selling honey, on top of our everyday jobs, we were tired and needed a rest. I still think our ideas were sound and if taken up by beekeepers today they would make a success of such a business, especially in tourist areas. I was doubly disappointed as I thought that one day my beekeeping would enable me to have a successful business should my Rural Studies department come to an end, as the new General Certificate in Secondary Education syllabus demanded more time in the school curriculum leaving fewer slots in the timetable for pupil options.

Have we regrets? Surprisingly few. We learned many aspects of developing and running a business and came into contact with people whom we would never have met otherwise, including someone who was inspired by our efforts to take up beekeeping and has made it a very successful livelihood. We are very open-minded people but not naive; we tend to trust people until they let us down. And we prefer it that way. We were able to utilise our creative and communication skills effectively, and of great importance, we made many, many friends.

It was a short time of our lives that we look back on with nostalgia and not regret; and some of those contacts we made are still friends today. Indeed, one of the people we met was David Cramp, ex-RAF Russian linguist whose services weren't so much in demand after the end of the Cold War. The RAF certainly looks after its own and arranged for David to do a post graduate course in Apiculture as a means of rehabilitating him for civilian life. David made good use of his time there and went to Spain and kept bees for several years before moving on to a job as manager of a huge apiary in New Zealand, whose main honey crop was from the highly regarded tea tree which produces manuka honey. He has written several excellent books on the practical side of beekeeping and for years has been our correspondent, firstly from Spain and subsequently New Zealand.

CHAPTER NINE

Greece

GREECE? Whatever do you want to move there for? Our family, whilst supportive, couldn't understand why we would want to live in a 'backward' country; our friends and neighbours were surprised that we wanted to move from the village that had been our home for twenty-three years; and Jeremy, the publisher of The Beekeepers Quarterly, was definitely worried that there might be adverse repercussions for the magazine if I left the UK.

As we had both taken early retirement from our professions on health grounds, Val and I, on doctors' orders, needed new horizons and a complete change of environment. We also needed to move out of our house, which was too big and expensive to run on our very reduced income.

After increasing problems with depression I had, at last sought medical advice, and had a short stint off work. The doctor had asked me what he should put on my medical certificate – fatigue due to a viral infection? I said no, depression and stress – so that is what he wrote. On returning to school, no one talked about my illness, mental illnesses were not openly discussed, though there were occasional references to my health after particular courses or activities with the deputy head saying sarcastically 'I hope that wasn't too stressful, John'. Of course, other remarks were along the lines of 'pull yourself together' and 'don't take the job so seriously – it pays the mortgage'.

Things were getting difficult in my department as we had vandalism of some sort or another most weekends and little was done to prevent it; also plans were being made to build a sports hall where my department stood, something I knew nothing about until I saw some surveyors with measuring tapes. One day I drove to school and just couldn't turn into the gateway – and that effectively was the end of my career. My emotions were very mixed but were chiefly anger and guilt.

After various visits to a specialist, my problem was diagnosed as bi-polar disorder; I was not surprised as my father had similar symptoms and the condition is said to be familial. For over a year I tried three courses of medication, each lasting about three months, until I found one that seemed to help. The effects of these drugs in the early stages of treatment are experiences that I hope I will never have to suffer again.

Val's job was the Principal of the Dyslexia Institute in Lincoln and her area covered a large part of Lincolnshire and Humberside. She left work before me and came home much later as often, as well as teaching, personnel and office duties, she had to give many talks after her normal hours. Her health began to deteriorate, and her symptoms were forgetfulness, fatigue, stress and anxiety and she was initially treated accordingly. Things only began to change when we had been in Greece for a couple of years and a problem with her wrist led to a visit to the emergency department of our local hospital. All examinations in the casualty department are done thoroughly and as well as x-rays, many other routine tests are carried out. The blood test was revealing – it showed that she had a severe thyroid problem, an easily diagnosed condition that was treatable – and that it was this and not depression which had led to her resignation from work. Understandably, Val was furious, for she enjoyed her job enormously – and would still have been in employment had the illness been spotted in England.

Although we had given up our honey business a few years previously and I had cut down my colonies to about 20, I still enjoyed working with my bees as they gave me some physical activity and a routine which is often needed when retirement comes along. I was fortunate, too, having intellectual stimulation and contact with people through my magazine, without which my life would have been much the poorer. However, there existed – and still exist today, times when I just cannot face the work and rely on sudden spurts of energy – usually engendered by an event or a contact – to stir me into a protracted spell of action. Fortunately, Val helps enormously with some of the sub-editing and all of the proofreading, so my work is less arduous.

Finding a property

We decided that we wanted to live in a place which wasn't primarily arable, far away from fields of oil seed rape, preferably in a mountainous area with easy access to heather and not too far from the coast. My choice was Northumberland, but Val needed a warmer climate with shorter winters, less damp, and where the sky wasn't usually overcast and grey. We had been to Kefalonia several times, long before Louis de Bernières had popularised the island by writing *Captain Corelli's Mandolin*, though Greece, in general, had originally attracted us after we had both read John Fowles' *The Magus*. Kefalonia is undoubtedly a beautiful place, but for us there were two major disadvantages: it is an island, which means that at times it is cut off from the mainland due to stormy seas and turbulent winds; and many of the islanders who work in the tourist industry leave at the end of each season, usually leaving their olive groves untended, reducing the population dramatically.

An advert in one of the Sunday broadsheets, advertising an old olive mill from which the machinery had been taken away and was suitable for conversion into a dwelling, attracted Val's attention. The location was in the southern part of the Peloponnese, an hour's drive from Kalamata, near the village of Stoupa. We arranged with the property agent to view the press and booked a week's holiday there to look at it and other possible properties. Before our departure I was 90% sure I wanted to stay in the UK, whilst Val was 90% in favour of buying a house in Greece.

The agent, an English woman, kept us waiting for a couple of days before we managed to see her. She was invariably late for appointments, which annoyed me intensely and, since the olive press had already been sold ('These places are snapped up quickly' she told us), we were taken to see houses that were in various states of decay, usually way off the beaten track, and properties which were not yet on the market, though we were assured that if approached in the right way the owners would be pleased to sell. One house 'belonged' to a man who had won it in a game of cards, though it is doubtful whether without all the paperwork he would have been able to sell it legally. Sometimes a house 'for sale' after someone had passed away needed the permission of countless relatives before any transaction could be completed and, as they were quite likely to have emigrated, the process could either be very lengthy or quickly terminated by a negative answer from just one distant relative.

All the houses we looked at needed extensive renovations and although we had completed such work on both of our houses in England, we didn't wish to repeat the experience, especially in a country where we knew neither the regulations nor which tradesmen to employ. Also we needed instant internet connection, mainly because of the BKQ. Eventually we decided to buy a beautiful plot of land on a quiet lane at the back of the village of Neochori which was only 3km from the coast, about 300 meters above sea level, surrounded by olive groves and with views of the Messinian Gulf to the west and the Taygetos mountains rising to 2,408 meters to the east. We went to the village kaphenion (café) which belonged to the owner of the land and said that we would buy the plot at the price he had told the agent, albeit some time ago. However, as land prices were constantly rising in this popular part of the Mani, he had made a slight increase. The agent was furious, and despite the fact that we were happy to pay more for the plot as it was well within our budget and despite our instructions to the contrary, she said that the original price had to stand; it was a matter of principle for her. 'Don't worry,' she said, 'He'll drop his price now that he knows he has a firm offer!' To be on the safe side, we looked at a house on the edge of the village which had its outside stone walls just completed.

This plot of land sloped down towards the sea and had an excellent view of the coastal villages below, the most western finger of the Peloponnese across the gulf of Messinia, and the mountains behind. This was to have been the builder's own house, but as his wife wished to live in Stoupa he had decided to put it on the market. We looked at the plans which seemed fine to us and, having talked about how long it would take to complete the building work, we told him we would make our decision when we had returned to England. We didn't see any more of the agent that week; in her own words she had 'More bloody Brits' to meet. 'And thank you, too!' I thought.

Bee-friendly Greek flowers and herbs

By the end of the week, when we flew back to England, Val would have happily stayed in Greece there and then. My position had changed – I was now only 10% against the idea of emigrating. What had changed my mind? It wasn't just the climate and the beautiful landscape with its unique combination of coast and mountains, though for many people this might have been enough. It was the real feeling of being made welcome, a genuine and practical expression of the local Greek's *philoxenia* (our daughter was quite cynical about this, but after thirteen years we still feel the same and our closest friends are Greek). People had time for each other but nevertheless things somehow got done, for Greeks do work very hard, despite the current view of the nation.

Although we were to live in a tourist area, it was very quiet and just a couple of miles up in the mountain you would hardly meet anyone except for the shepherds with their flocks of sheep and goats, and collectively the villages themselves were an unspoilt rural paradise. Also, of course, as there was no arable farming in the region I wouldn't have to worry about agricultural sprays, for the bees I was sure to buy would be producing honey from a multitude of wild spring flowers and aromatic herbs.

Furthermore, honey in Greek supermarkets was selling for the equivalent of £11 per kilo! This was more than twice the price I was getting in the UK and with a few hives I would have enough honey for my family and friends, with a little more to sell to pay for journeys connected with beekeeping. I no longer wanted to produce honey on a large scale. I wanted time to experiment with my bees, try out new techniques and equipment – with articles for the magazine in mind – and also work with local beekeepers who would appreciate the help.

We had only been home for a few days when we received some unwelcome news from the agent. She had been wrong: the kaphenion owner would not accept the lower price for the plot, much to our dismay and even now, each time we walk past the land we regret that the agent had acted as she did and he regrets not selling it to us. But we went for the other option of the land with the plans already drawn up.

We got on very well with our builder; he spoke some English and after a while we dispensed with our agent as a go-between on building matters, although she was extremely helpful with all the official paperwork. The builder managed to get his Albanian men to work through the hot summer by paying them extra so that the house would be ready for occupation in mid-autumn, though like many of his colleagues' buildings, the house doesn't completely resemble the original plans. For instance, some builders make cellars beneath the house which can give an enormous amount of storage space but will not be declared in the overall square meterage of the property, which must be known for tax purposes. A house is signed off by an inspector from the electricity company, as house and local taxes are collected via the electricity bill, so the full electricity supply is not connected until the inspection has been satisfactorily passed. Before the inspector arrives, cellar doorways and window spaces may be filled with stone, and once he has gone the stonework can be removed and doors and windows fitted. The authorities are well aware of this scam. It is reckoned that 60% of houses in Greece fall into this category, the onus being on the owner, not the builder, to get the plans re-drawn to make them legal, which can cost upwards of €10,000.

As we had plenty of time and had already sold our property in Lincolnshire, arranging for the transport of all our effects to Greece and their temporary storage until our new house was ready went smoothly and items we wouldn't need including greenhouses, sheds and bicycles we gave away to our friends and relatives.

All my bees and beekeeping equipment not already given away I had disposed of at the Lincolnshire and Nottingham beekeeping associations' auctions in spring, a task in which my old friend John Gleed reluctantly participated. All I took with me to Greece in the way of beekeeping were my Sherriff bee veil, an old copper smoker and my books and magazines. My British hives would be no use to me in Greece as they all conform to another pattern – besides, it would be good to have a clean start.

Part of my 10% uncertainty revealed itself the day before our departure. Whilst neither Val nor I had any older relatives to care for, there was still that lingering feeling of guilt in my mind of leaving our now adult children behind. Both our daughter and son had settled jobs and were living in London. They had friends and were long used to living independent lives. We were staying in Broadstairs for a few days before starting our long journey by car from Dover when my son Jim telephoned us. Whilst he had been the one who had encouraged us to 'go for it!' and live in Greece, the reality of our leaving had just struck him and he was very upset. We had a very difficult and sad day together in London, and a long and tearful farewell, slightly lightened by our one-year-old dog, Meg, who was emigrating with us, but we did leave him much comforted with the realisation that he could still see us whenever he needed to.

We had been extremely lucky to get Meg. She is seven-eighths border collie and one eighth springer spaniel, a delightful combination.

Departure for Greece

We departed from Dover by car on a gloomy Monday morning in August. The sky was overcast and threatened rain and by the time we reached Langres, a small pretty hill town still partly enclosed by its ancient walls, near Dijon, in the late afternoon, the heavens had opened. The Hotel Europa welcomed Meg and the waitresses in their smart turquoise suits made a fuss of her. When we went down to the restaurant for a meal of duck and cranberry sauce, they were surprised that we had left Meg in our room, as other dogs were sitting by their owners' tables or even on a chair beside them. I suppose this could only happen in France! The following grey morning we set off for Italy, via Lyons, and as we exited the long alpine Fréjus tunnel we were suddenly dazzled by bright sunshine and the clear blue, cloudless sky. We stopped overnight at a small hotel in Bussoleno, just off the motorway, near Turin, where Meg was welcome 'as long as she is quiet'. The last part of our journey through Italy to Ancona was mostly on the motorways which was a bit of a nightmare. The road surface was often pitted, the camber dreadful and heavy lorries sped along taking no notice of the lane demarcations.

The three hour wait for the ferry we had in Ancona was made bearable by watching the many boats and the huge ferries in the harbour, the late warm afternoon sun bathing the church and roof tops in a rosy pink hue. To us it felt very foreign and exotic. The overnight ferry crossing to Patras in Greece gave us some rest from driving and after disembarking, the journey onwards to Kalamata on quiet country roads was very relaxing after the ordeal of Italian motorways. The final leg of the journey to Stoupa though, a distance of 40 km, was extremely hazardous. The road was narrow and poorly constructed with no discernible edges and had innumerable double bends. For most of its length, the land fell away steeply into deep gorges which had been scoured by rain and rocks for thousands of years or down to steep rocky cliffs bordering the sea. We were tired, darkness had fallen, and we sighed with relief when we reached our temporary rented accommodation after four days of travelling. Val secretly vowed that she would never make a journey on that stretch of road again, although after a few days' rest she got back in the car and made the double journey to conquer her fears.

Now we love the route, stunningly beautiful at any time of day and in most weather conditions. We had thought of selling our car, flying to Greece and buying a new one there. But we needed to feel our separation from England in terms of time and distance, which a flight wouldn't have given us. Besides, we were only offered £3,000 for our two-year-old Subaru all-wheel drive which gave us excellent service on the rough mountain roads of Greece for over ten years. Admittedly, we had to pay a tax of well over a thousand pounds to the Greek authorities to change our license plates, despite its being contrary to EU law. Apparently the exchequer gains more money by imposing the illegal tax than they have to pay in EU fines.

As soon as we had settled into our house we began work on the garden, which needed several loads of topsoil as the land was very rocky immediately below the surface. We excavated craters and planted orange, satsuma, peach, apricot, nectarine, olive and lemon trees in the garden which was bare except for two small mulberry seedlings. Part of the plot was turned into a herb garden in which we put many plants which would be of use to us and my bees when they arrived. The remainder we used as a vegetable garden. We found that after the rains of September and October, it was sowing and planting time for many vegetables, so we watched what the Greeks were doing and followed suit.

Keeping bees in Greece

My next priority was to find some bees; local bees that were suited to the area. I knew this wouldn't be difficult as most Greek families had at least one beekeeper amongst them; and this was true of the Marabeas family, one of the most prominent in the village. Whilst the majority, including the present and previous mayors of the district, kept only a few hives, one couple with three young children who lived very near to us made their living from beekeeping alone. They were very approachable people and although Vangelis spoke little English, his Greek-German wife, Irini, had a good command of the language, a bonus as although Val and I had already started to have Greek lessons, our progress was slow, and what we knew then was extremely basic. They invited me to join them when they were working whenever I wished, so I often found myself squeezed inside the front of their pickup truck, along with their two-year-old son, Dimitris, who had to be taken with them everywhere. Often we would be joined by Vangelis' father, Iannis, who had been a beekeeper as well as a builder for most of his life.

The Marabeas' apiary near the coast

At the turn of the year the Marabeas' 140 colonies of bees were taken down to the coast near the village of Trachila for the first spring flowers. Like almost all beekeepers in Greece, the Marabeas family kept their colonies in hives of the American type – Langstroths – the first and only modern hive used in Greece, the boxes for brood rearing and honey storage being of the same deep size. I first examined the bees when they were working *Oxalis pes-caprae*, Bermuda Buttercup, which grows profusely in the olive groves. On the rocky hillsides, several varieties of spurge provided plenty of forage, followed a little later by vetches, clover, mountain sage and lupins. Although our locality is primarily known for its huge plantations of olive trees, most of the groves are less than sixty years old.

Prior to this cereals, wheat, barley and oats had been grown on well-tended terraces and cattle grazed on the uncultivated rocky slopes. To provide additional food for the livestock, the cereals were undersown with forage crops, and now that both cereals and most of the cattle no longer abound, these continue to grow wild, providing bees with extremely valuable sources of nectar and pollen. The lupins were originally grown for their seed.

However, in order for them to be made edible for cattle and people the seeds were packed into hessian sacks and lowered into the sea for many days. Treated lupin seeds are still commonly sold in Greece as a snack. Recently, on the BBC's early morning farming programme, it was revealed that there was to be an expansion in the cultivation of lupins to help Britain to become more self-sufficient in protein feeds for livestock, as the cost of importing soya is too high. If this happens it will also be a fillip for UK beekeepers.

The Marabeas' bees were of the local type, Cecropian, which are dark in colour, generally good-tempered though prone to swarming if the brood area is compressed by using a queen excluder. The hives we looked in often had three boxes and it wasn't unusual to find brood in all of them which I thought would make the harvesting of honey very difficult. In fact, as soon as the flowers began to fade in Trachila and it was time to move the bees to a new location, the honey had to be removed otherwise the hives would have been too heavy to load into the pickup.

Whereas in England we put boards fitted with one-way bee escapes beneath the honey supers, waiting until the next day when all the bees have left the combs before removing them, in Greece the frames are examined one by one and the bees shaken off those which contain honey. These are put in a box ready for carting away. For me this was unsatisfactory, for it took a long time to go through each hive, the bees were badly disturbed and most of the frames were not full of sealed honey, though they were shaken first to see if any loose unripened honey fell from the combs. If this happened, the combs would be put back in the hive as unripe honey, ie one that hadn't had its water content reduced to about 18%, so it would ferment over time, would have a frothy appearance in the jar and have a yeasty, beery smell. This would make it unfit for sale except for the confectionery or bakery industries.

When the nectar flow at the coast was all but finished, the bees were moved over 3km away up into the mountains to a height of about 350 metres. The same types of plants which the bees had already worked on at sea level were now in flower and given good weather a second honey harvest was possible. One more move upwards was made later with half the colonies, the others remaining in place for the thyme which flowered in June and July. At the beginning of autumn it was possible to take the bees even higher up the mountainside, if the state of the road permitted it, for the bees to store food for winter from the heather. It was a great surprise for me to find large stretches of heather not only growing in Greece but close to my village. Honey from the heather is one of my favourites though most Greeks dislike its strong taste. Honey which isn't left on the hive for the bees is sometimes extracted by beekeepers and sold to manufacturers who add it to fondant and sell it in beekeeping shops as winter food for colonies.

Vangelis' and Irini's apiaries each contained scores of hives. Unlike England, there was plentiful flora to support the large number of colonies and, as I was used to dealing with one apiary of half a dozen hives at a

Feeding bees the Marabeas way. Syrup from a tank was hosed into 10 litre buckets which contained straw for the bees to grip onto, the buckets being placed on top of the frames and covered with a super

time, the prospect of going through sixty hives without a break in the heat of the day was a daunting prospect. Irini was a hard taskmaster. Vangelis would look at me knowing that I was tiring and say sympathetically, 'She has the German temperament, not Greek!' I liked it best when Vangelis and I were working alone; we would take our time and rest when we needed to. When we had finished Vangelis would say to me 'Have you much work to do when you get home?' 'Yes', I replied unenthusiastically. 'Let's stay here for a while then and have a longer rest'. I was happy to oblige.

Irini was expert at queen rearing and, in particular, in transferring day-old bee larvae into prepared cells, a job which needs good eyesight and very steady hands. In that first spring she gave me one of the new queens which had been installed in a six-frame nucleus of bees; my first Greek colony, which I proudly put in my garden. I knew it wouldn't give me honey that year, but at last I was keeping bees again.

Both Val and I helped their two oldest children with their English – Val teaching Maria more formally, whilst I did a series of projects with the younger Iannis. We bought chickens and rabbits after I had supervised him in making the coop and cage, and his carpentry and language skills developed simultaneously. Not long after this Vangelis and Irini quit beekeeping. For all their hard work the income they received from the honey wasn't enough to support their growing family and they turned to the building trade with the help of both of their fathers.

I bought ten of their 140 colonies and had a good crop of honey from the mountain sage and other wild flowers. I would have liked to have followed the nectar flow, for having bees in just one location would only give an average of ten kilos of honey per hive per year. I was unable to buy a pickup truck, for in order to have a commercial vehicle in Greece it is necessary, by law, to have a full-time job that demands such a means of transport. The type of business is painted on to the wing of the vehicle for it is only permitted to transport materials associated with that type of work. We were stopped by the police once for towing a small wooden fishing boat by tractor. To avoid trouble we just spoke in English. The officers looked at each other, shrugged their shoulders and went back to their car.

Historic hives

I am not a believer in fate or destiny, but unbeknown to me when we chose Neochori for our home, the village was the location of the best preserved old hives in the whole of Greece. In a ravine just below the village are three sets of stone hives built in tiers dating from the late eighteenth century. Altogether there are 257 hives down there, plus another four on the inside of the wall of the cave where the beekeeper lived. The hives are simply made with slabs of pourri, a form of limestone, soft when excavated but hardening with exposure, and marbelite, a harder transitional stone. The slabs of stone are between six and eight centimetres thick and the hives have internal dimensions of 55.5cm deep, 21.5cm wide and 28cm high. The front of each hive has a small opening at its base, the latter projecting slightly to give a landing area for the bees. Many of the hives have Christian symbols carved into the front walls and one carries the message 'Jesus Christ is winning the war against evil'.

Irini was able to give me a lot of information about the hives as they belong collectively to the Marabeas clan. She was uncertain as to what was history or what was myth but altogether it made an interesting story. Apparently, in the middle of the 18th century a member of the Marabeas family who lived in the nearby village of Nomisos walked over 60 kilometres to Kalamata to seek work. Soon after reaching his destination

One section of a wall of stone hives built towards the end of the 18th century

he was insulted by a Turk whom he promptly slaughtered. This was not a surprising act, for people who live in the Mani are renowned for their fierceness, independence and uncompromising behaviour (the war of independence against the Turks began in this region). In order to escape from the scene of his crime and avoid punishment, he followed the example of many men in a similar situation – he fled to Mount Athos and became a monk in the Russian Orthodox monastery of Agios Pendelaemonas.

Here he learned about beekeeping. Some years later he wished to return to his birthplace and with 'bees in his hat' (this can be taken literally, for the stove-pipe hats of monks and priests could easily contain a nucleus colony) he set sail for his home. It is said that occasionally bees escaped from his hat and the alarmed co-passengers would jump into the sea to be avoid being stung, remaining there until the bees were secured. No doubt everyone was relieved when he left the boat just below Neochori, made his way up the ravine and took refuge in a cave. The cave provided spacious living quarters and by filling in part of the entrance with stone, it provided good shelter from the strong winds which occur in these parts. Over the years more hives were constructed as well as a church at the top of the gorge which was consecrated to the saint whose name he had taken as a monk; Pendelaemonas.

These hives remained in use until the 1960s and from the age of fifteen Vangelis' father Iannis helped his two uncles to look after the bees. Iannis' father died during the campaign in Albania during the Second World War, like many of his compatriots from exposure due to the very bitter weather in the mountains. Iannis was expected to work with his uncles, but it wasn't an easy job, for neither of the uncles would speak to each other. Iannis had to pass on the screamed messages to each uncle in turn and people walking up to Neochori hearing the commotion below would nod to each other and say 'The Marabeas are looking at their bees again!'

I walked down to the hives with Iannis and he told me how the bees were managed. It was very simple. His job was to wait for swarms to emerge and then collect them with a stick on the end of which was an open pyramid-shaped funnel made from woven straw. The bees were carried to an empty hive from which the stone back had been removed. They were shaken in and the stone was sealed in place with cow dung. Most beekeepers know that this instant-hiving of bees isn't usually successful; it is better to catch the bees but not put them into their new home until the evening. However, this was the method that was adopted so Iannis was often catching and hiving the same swarms that had absconded from their new homes. At the end of the season some dry rotten wood or cow dung was lit and allowed to smoulder on a piece of tile. The back of each hive was opened and once smoke had been blown over them, the combs full of honey were cut out, enough being left for the colony's needs. Interestingly, all the bees built their combs at right angles to the entrance, the same way that most beekeepers in the world orient the frames in their hives today. On average about one kilo of honey was harvested from each hive and taken into the cave where the beekeeper and his family might live during the summer months. It was the men's job to squeeze the honey out of the combs into earthenware pots, the women then carrying the 25kg loads up to the top of the ravine to their homes in the village.

Two UNESCO culture officials, looking mainly at our enormous number of Byzantine churches with beautiful murals, were surprised to see such a collection of well-preserved hives showing proof of beekeeping on a commercial scale in 18th century Greece and said that everything should be done to preserve them. Now they are almost completely surrounded by newly-built houses and apartments.

Visiting Mount Athos

I was intrigued by the tale of Pendelaemonas and wondered if my local bees had the same characteristics as the bees in Mount Athos. I could easily use the morphometry methods which I learned from my time with BIBBA to check for any similarities, that is, if I could get some samples of bees from one of the twenty monasteries on Mount Athos. Visiting Agion Oros, the Holy Mountain, is not easy, for only one hundred Orthodox and ten non-Orthodox men are allowed on to the promontory each day, that is if they have already applied for a permit from the Metropolis of Thessaloniki, which can take many months to be processed, and have been given a date on which they must present themselves at the Pilgrim's Office in Ouranopolis, the port of departure.

Three other beekeepers were interested in joining me on the visit; Mike Thornley, an architect and beekeeper from Helensburgh, Scotland (who later became my Scottish Correspondent); Roger White, a bee breeder and our Cyprus correspondent; and Dimitris Vogopoulos, a honey and queen producer from Crete. Much of the work to do with organising our visit, especially for arranging a meeting with the Protaton, the elected head of all the monasteries for one year, was conducted by George Schismenos, who unfortunately was unable to join us. He died tragically, not long afterwards, in the plane which crashed into a Greek mountain, when all the crew and passengers succumbed due to cold temperatures after systems aboard the aircraft had failed.

On the day of our departure we all waited outside the Pilgrim's Office to get our 'diamoninitiron', the special passport which would allow us to gain entry to Agion Oros. Fortunately, we had arrived very early and we managed to get our permit well before the morning boat departed for the main embarkment point, the small harbour of Daphne. Many pilgrims were on board, mainly priests or monks, several of whom were selling walking sticks, or crocheting black elasticated wristbands which they would bless, thus conferring protection to those who wore them. I had been charged with the task of obtaining many of these for friends and acquaintances and ended up with an armful by the end of my visit. Other passengers were extending their hands upwards allowing the seagulls following the boat to grab pieces of bread out of their hands. Many of the young monks were from former Soviet Bloc countries, and I wondered why, at such an early age, they had chosen this way of life. Was it simply to escape the poverty and difficulties which had befallen their countries after the collapse of the Soviet Union, just as did hundreds of thousands of ex-Soviet women who sought partners of any age in the west? I would never know.

We sailed down part of the western coast of the 50 kilometre promontory, the landscape verdant and fresh with many trees, sometimes offering us a glimpse of a monastery on the shore line or in the folds of the hills. Particularly impressive was the Russian monastery of Agios Pendelaemonas, with its verdigris cupolas, which sadly wasn't on our itinerary. A bus took us up the very steep and long road to the secular village of Karyes, which had a police station, a post office, shops and accommodation for the many labourers, mostly Albanians, who were working on building projects in several of the monasteries. We soon found the headquarters of the Protaton and were immediately invited in to meet him. Fortunately he spoke English, for in his former life, he told us, he had been a Cypriot banker. In the beautifully-furnished room with rich carpets and the sun streaming in through stained-glass windows we were treated to a typical English tea whilst he answered many of our questions about life on Agion Oros. It surprised me to learn that each monastery was self-regulated and independent. Some were very rich, some were much poorer, but they rarely co-operated with each other unless a particular commodity needed to be bought or bartered for from another monastery.

Roger reminded the Protaton that we were there to look at bees. If we found suitable breeding material, maybe we could buy some queens? He was unable to answer the last part of our question, but immediately sent someone to summon two beekeepers who had hives nearby to come and meet us. They arrived, looking suspicious and not very friendly, but took us nevertheless to see their apiary which wasn't far away. This contained dozens of colonies, each with three boxes, most of which were in a long row beneath flowering sweet chestnut trees, others scattered about amongst the bracken. As we walked amongst the hives, Roger and Dimitris managed to collect about thirty stings between them, not surprising, since they bent down right in front of the hives in order to look closely at the bees at the entrance. But when the colonies were smoked and the hives opened, the bees were quiet enough so no protective clothing was needed.

The two monks, 'Brown Eyes' and 'Blue Eyes', took us to their apiary in the shelter of some flowering sweet chestnut trees

Disappointingly, despite showing many of the characteristics of *Apis mellifera macedonia*, the presence of many yellow-banded bees showed that there was a large degree of hybridisation, so queens from these stocks would not have been useful for breeding, not that the monks would have parted with any of them. Brown Eyes and Blue Eyes, the names we gave the monks, didn't live in one of the main monasteries, but a 'skiti', a simple dwelling, and they had an agent on the mainland who sold their honey for them. How much of the profits from the sales were passed on to their monastery I didn't dare ask, though they certainly looked after themselves and had a huge newish 4WD pickup truck which would be the envy of any beekeeper.

The reason why the bees had become hybridised became clear to us during the following days. Contrary to what we believed, there were several large apiaries belonging to beekeepers who had been allowed to bring their hives onto the promontory – at a cost. We met one beekeeper who had moved over a hundred hives; he had paid one thousand euros for the privilege. He was busy putting new frames into each of

The hives were opened up for us to see the bees

his colonies so that the bees could fill them with chestnut honey. Mount Athos is a beekeeper's paradise for not only does it have the early spring flowers, but lime trees, chestnuts, fir, pine and heather, so the bees could be storing honey throughout summer and autumn. It also had a useful amount of rainfall and fast flowing streams criss-crossed the peninsular, sometimes tumbling down steep cliffs in magnificent waterfalls which usually descended into huge rock pools. On one hot afternoon, Mike, unable to resist the temptation, stripped off his clothes and plunged into an icy pool feeling, he said, much refreshed afterwards. I thought he just looked slightly blue.

Agion Oros, according to the Athonite tradition, is the earthly paradise of Mary the Mother of Jesus. The story is that when travelling with Peter to Cyprus, the ship was blown off course and they landed on Athos. Astounded by its beauty, Mary prayed to her Son that she might have the place as her garden, a wish which was granted to her. This may well be the reason why no women or female mammals are allowed there, for she is still believed to visit her garden from time to time to protect the monks.

We only had a permit to stay for three days and had to move to a different monastery for each night. Whilst Roger and Dimitris continued in the search for pure Macedonica bees and wanted to travel by bus and taxi, Mike and I hiked to each of the monasteries we had been booked into. The stone donkey paths in the shade of the trees which often formed a long green tunnel gave us delightful walks, though on one occasion, when we were at sea-level Mike promised me that the ascent to the next monastery was very short and after that the route was straight and level. It turned out to be the longest, toughest, most precipitous climb of my life and, wretched in the unbearable heat, carrying a full backpack, stumbling over the rocks, I tried my hardest to keep up with Mike who was galloping along ahead of me. Before coming to Greece Mike had read and been immensely inspired by Robert Byron's *The Station*, which included vivid descriptions of his walks on Mount Athos and the architecture, subjects dear to Mike's heart.

Only later though did he tell me that the route we had taken from Agios Dyonisios to Agios Gregoriou was dismissed by Byron as being too difficult. My reading had been primarily Kazantzakis' 'Report to Greco' in which the author describes his month-long travels on Mount Athos and quotes words spoken to him by a monk at Agios Pavlos: 'We entered and looked at the cells which circled the courtyard. The monk extended his hand. 'Behold God's beehive', he said sarcastically, 'Behold the cells. Once they were inhabited by bees who made honey; now by drones, and what a sting they have... May the Lord protect you', he added and burst out laughing.'

I was quite willing to accept this statement as being part of the truth of life on the so-called Holy Mountain. Often in the newspapers I had read accounts of dodgy land deals between the government and the monasteries, as well as ugly stories of police being called to intermonastery strife with opposing monks setting fire to buildings, fighting each other with fire extinguishers and any implements which came to hand. Whilst I knew I would enjoy the visit on an aesthetic level I was rather cynical as to what the monks themselves might be like.

I needn't have worried though. At each monastery we were greeted by the guest master and offered mint tea, loukoumi (which is really Turkish Delight, but the Greeks would never use this term) and some raki, and given excellent accommodation. We were expected to go to the Katholican, the church, in the small hours of the morning for which we were woken by a monk repeatedly striking a simitron, a long piece of metal or wood. As Mike and I were not Orthodox Christians we were not allowed in the churches for the services but we were perched on a seat similar to a misericord from 4am to almost 7am from where the chanting of the monks was barely audible. When the services ended, we were invited in to see the magnificent splendour of the interior of the churches as well as the monastery's hordes of religious relics including skulls and other bones. At Agios Gregoriou, one monk took me to a shadowy corner where I could see the much-kissed icon of the Virgin Mary feeding Jesus, which clearly showed an exposed nipple: apparently one of only very few icons of this kind.

We followed the monks into the large refectories after the services and the food served depended on whether it was a fast day or not. As no goats, sheep or cows were kept, there was no milk or butter, so the brown bread was eaten dry, though feta cheese did appear on one occasion. The fruit we were given was produced at the monastery and included apricots, apples and peaches which were obviously organic as they had maggot holes, scab and were very pitted; though the cucumbers, tomatoes and olives were perfect. A cold chickpea soup we had one evening wasn't at all appetising, but we made up for this the following morning with chips, fried courgettes and sweet red wine.

As at Pluscarden Abbey, we were read to during the meals, but when this was finished and the abbot stood up to leave, we all had to follow him out and leave our unfinished food on the refectory table. I then realised why the monks gulped down their food and stashed what remained in their robes as soon as they stood up.

Agios Gregoriou, where I heard the most beautiful chanting in the monastery garden

After walking all day, it was lovely to stroll around the monastery grounds and relax. Once, at Agios Gregoriou, I came across a group of young monks practising their singing, the beautiful chanting in the monastery garden spiritually uplifting. At dusk the gates to the monastery were closed and as we had our early morning call with the simitron, we usually slept shortly afterwards.

Although the beekeeping part of our visit wasn't a success, our time on Mount Athos provided us with a rich experience. The peace and tranquillity, the outstanding natural beauty, the stunning size and grandeur of the interior and exterior of the monastery buildings, the exquisitely maintained gardens and orchards and the general helpfulness and friendliness of the monks will remain in our minds for ever.

In the monastery of Iveron which we visited, there was one book which I would have loved to have seen, one of the great treasures of their library. It is an Arabic translation of Discorides' *De Materia Medica* the original of which ran to five volumes and is considered to be the first systematic

Western herbal. Discorides was one of the greatest early physicians, a Greek, born in AD 40 in a place that is now part of Turkey. He studied medicine in Egypt before joining Nero's Roman Legion and during his numerous travels he gathered an immense amount of knowledge on plants and substances, including honey, used for medicinal purposes from a wide variety of cultures. Whilst early editions of his books were lost over time, some copies were preserved in the Muslim world and over a thousand years later his ideas were re-introduced into Europe by the Arabs. Within the book, amongst his many descriptions of the preparation, properties and testing of drugs, he writes that a pale yellow honey from Attica (near Athens) in Greece was the best, being good 'for all rotten and hollow ulcers'. Aristotle, an earlier physician (384-322 BC), also referred to pale Greek honey as being 'good as a salve for sore eyes and wounds'.

Undoubtedly, both Greeks were referring to the famous Hymettus honey which is gathered from mountain herbs, particularly thyme.

Medical research and hive products

When the first International Symposium on Apitherapy took place in Athens I was very pleased to be invited. Doctors, vets, pharmacists, scientists and beekeepers from many parts of the world attended the event, the purpose of which was to accord the treatment of health problems with hive products – honey, propolis, royal jelly and bee venom – the same standing as conventional medicine. The participants were well aware that their research had to stand the scrutiny of scientific and peer-reviewed journals, and those who presented papers were armed with a wealth of data on the work that they had carried out over the years.

Dr Bogdanov from the Swiss Bee Research Centre gave an overall appraisal of the health benefits of eating honey; Dr Nolan, from New Zealand, described the long process of formulating manuka honey dressings which would not slide off wounds; and Behnam Kaviani-Vahid, from Iran, showed that lining the mouthparts with honey prevented burning when patients were given radiation treatment above the neck. He also presented us with the case history of a man with multiple myeloma (cancer of the bone marrow) and the excellent results that had been achieved by using bee stings on acupuncture points.

Papers on patients with eye problems revealed that a simple preparation of 20% honey in water used as eye drops three times a day for those with keratopothy improved visual acuity and the status of both the conjunctivae and cornea: that a blueberry and royal jelly product 'Viziovitalis' was effective for patients with myopia and retinal degeneration; and that a combination of pollen and royal jelly was helpful in age-related macular degeneration. There were so many convincing reports on hive products to improve both human and animal health, from reputable people, it would have been churlish to dispute their claims.

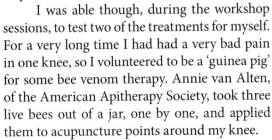

Bees stings give effective relief from chronic pain especially on acupuncture points

I was able though, during the workshop sessions, to test two of the treatments for myself. For a very long time I had had a very bad pain in one knee, so I volunteered to be a 'guinea pig' for some bee venom therapy. Annie van Alten, of the American Apitherapy Society, took three live bees out of a jar, one by one, and applied them to acupuncture points around my knee.

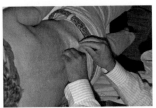

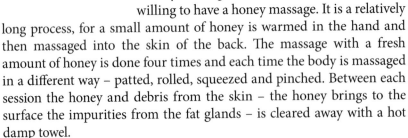

Honey is an excellent skin cleanser

The bees naturally stung me, but I was not allowed to remove the stings for about ten minutes, thus allowing all the venom to be pumped into me. There was very little swelling, my body being well used to stings, but I was pleased and surprised to find that before the end of the conference I no longer had any pain in my knee, nor has it returned. Stefan Stangaciu, from Romania, President of the German Apitherapy Society managed to find someone who was willing to have a honey massage. It is a relatively long process, for a small amount of honey is warmed in the hand and then massaged into the skin of the back. The massage with a fresh amount of honey is done four times and each time the body is massaged in a different way – patted, rolled, squeezed and pinched. Between each session the honey and debris from the skin – the honey brings to the surface the impurities from the fat glands – is cleared away with a hot damp towel.

At the end of the massage, a final cleaning takes place and the person is allowed to relax under a warm towel for twenty minutes. The amount of grime removed is considerable and if the person is a smoker or has eaten garlic mushrooms for instance, the smell is extremely unpleasant. However, the skin is clean and smooth and soft; the treatment works well.

The final demonstration was a massage with bee venom cream. A lady was already lying on the table for this when she realised that she was allergic to one of the constituents of the cream. Nobody seemed to want to take her place so rather than this part of the workshop being cancelled, I volunteered for this as well. It was just twenty minutes in duration, but as the bee venom cream was massaged into my back an enormous amount of heat was created. The bee venom not only spurs the adrenal glands into action but increases the blood flow, which can help repair diseased parts of the body. Stefan uses this type of massage for diagnostic purposes and he told me that any parts of my body which felt painful might mean that there was a problem with an organ in that region. A massage of this type is warming and relaxing, though Stefan advocated that it should only be administered a couple of times a week unless one had a painful joint when the cream could be used more often.

The conference was a huge success. As for me, not only had I learnt a lot and met and conversed with eminent people from around the world, but I had returned home with a painless knee. Apart from wax for making candles and polish, I had never made much use of other hive products such as pollen or royal jelly, but I did find that a tincture made from propolis was a useful item for cuts and other open wounds. When our spaniel had a long, open wound that wasn't responding to antibiotics, twice daily applications of propolis (which had been dissolved in alcohol) over two weeks resulted in a complete cure.

Prokopovich in Russia, Dzierdzona in Poland and Langstroth in America, are all famous 19th century beekeepers who invented moveable frame hives which allowed beekeepers to remove frames from the hive to assist colony management and to harvest honey without damaging the bees' nest. The secret was simple, as long as the moveable parts were no more or no less than the 'bee space', ie about 3/16ths of an inch, then the bees would not secure those parts to the hive walls.

Early Greek Top Bar Hive

Between the faces of the combs the bees left a double bee space, thus allowing them to work back to back. Whilst this was a major innovation, with each of the inventors being regarded as the 'Father of Beekeeping' in their respective regions, the Greeks had stumbled upon this phenomenon several centuries before.

In fact, Greek beekeepers discovered that not only if the wooden strips onto which the bees built their combs were appropriately spaced, but also if the sides of the hive sloped inwards, the combs were built without them being attached to the walls. The hives, made from reeds and daubed with cow dung, resembled waste paper baskets, the flat tops being covered with tiles and straw. Surprisingly, though, the use of these hives that were very advanced for their time and made managing bees easier, didn't spread throughout Greece. The beekeepers preferred the hives they had traditionally used for centuries in their own regions using materials available locally, ie stone, wood and clay.

Greek beekeeping today

Modern beekeeping came to Greece in 1903 with the arrival of Langstroth hives and by 1912 three thousand of these hives were in use compared with a quarter of a million traditional hives of all varieties. Both world wars had a significant effect on Greek beekeeping and by 1946 the industry had been virtually destroyed. The Greek bank and government gave beekeepers a fresh start by donating 93,500 hives, 3,000,000 frames and 3,100 honey extractors.

Almost all hives in Greece are Langstroths

Today there are nearly one and a half million beehives in Greece owned by 32,000 beekeepers, many of whom have more than a thousand colonies. Greek honey production stands at about 14,000 tons each year, making it the third largest producer after Spain and France. The European Union has given this sector of agriculture important funding over the years for beekeepers to expand their enterprises, replace lost stocks, buy vehicles and to improve honey-handling premises.

A local beekeeper who has over a thousand colonies and who supplies many shops with honey as well as selling in the market with his wife twice every week, has just installed a honey extracting plant with the best stainless steel equipment. Everything complies with HACCP standards and of the €500,000 it cost, the EU supported his venture with €135,000. In the UK, EU money is not given directly to beekeepers; they benefit from the services which FERA supply, the latter being the recipient of the funds.

An EU grant to help beekeepers to produce more honey in the forests of Greece has led to a mass migration of colonies throughout

160

many parts of the country several times a year. As soon as word gets around that there is a flow from the honeydew (source of 60% of Greek honey) in the forests of pine and fir, thousands upon thousands of hives are quickly loaded onto pickup trucks, trailers, or in several tiers on large flat bed lorries, and transported hundreds of kilometres, even by ferry if necessary, so that a suitable site is secured. Speed is of the essence, for often there is no space available for the great number of colonies, though latecomers will think nothing of setting down their hives on land on which notices are posted saying *No Bees!* More often than not, hives are placed on both sides of the roads, on the asphalt, leaving little space between for cars to drive along; and the numbers of bees make it a no go area for cyclists.

There are problems for beekeepers who practise this type of beekeeping, for hives can be stolen, subjected to infection from other colonies, bees can drift away from their home hives, they can suffer from lack of water, and there is a need to provide the colonies with plenty of frames of pollen as there is no ground flora. Sixty percent of Greek honey comes from the forest trees: 'elato', a creamy, toffee-like honey from fir trees, which if isn't harvested quickly is difficult to extract; and 'pefko' from the pine trees. The source of the honey is the sweet and sticky exudations from the sap-feeding insects, particularly the scale insect *Marchalina hellenica*. This creature has contributed so much to the Greek economy that the EU gave grants to beekeepers to help them to spread *Marchalina* to forest areas where they weren't present. The project was a great success, the *Marchalina* thrived, much to the beekeepers' delight, and honey production increased.

There is a flip side to this story, however, causing a continuing controversy between beekeepers and environmentalists. *Marchalina* is blamed for the deaths of thousands of conifers throughout Greece. The dead trees can be seen covered with the white cotton wool-like material secreted by the insects, undoubtedly showing that they were present in great profusion. At beekeeping conferences

Bees collecting honeydew secreted by Marchalina hellenica, a scale insect which sucks the sap from pine trees. In the UK honeydew sources are generally the secretions of aphides. Honeydew is transformed by bees into a dark, nutritious and health-giving honey

some scientists favour the beekeepers' opinion that *Marchalina* is not responsible for killing the trees; at the meetings of conservationists, an equal number of scientists argue that *Marchalina* is indeed the cause – aided and abetted by beekeepers!

If the conservationists are right, then this is the only example I know of beekeeping having a detrimental effect on the environment. The government has acted – chiefly favouring the conservation lobby – making it illegal to spread *Marchalina* to new areas. In towns and cities, councils are allowing affected trees to be sprayed with insecticides. In the countryside forests this is a move likely to be fought vigorously by Greek beekeepers.

Traditional methods

Although beekeeping in Greece is a very modern industry, there are a few diehards who keep their bees in koffinia, or basket hives, similar to the old British wicker hives daubed with cow dung. In one apiary near Kalamata, an old beekeeper works with his son; the father uses koffinia hives, the son Langstroth hives.

Surprisingly, this combination of beekeeping methods works well. The father spends late March and April in the apiary waiting for swarms

Some beekeepers still keep their bees in traditional wicker hives – koffinia.

A swarm is transferred to a Langstroth hive

While traditional Greek beekeepers use koffinias to produce swarms which they then house in Langstroth hives, thus increasing their number of colonies, in the UK and much of Europe, skeps (right) are used for capturing and transferring swarms to modern hives

to emerge from his hundred hives. When they do, he takes one of his son's Langstroths, already prepared with combs, and holds it beneath the swarm so that the bees at the bottom of the cluster are just in touch with the top of the frames. He invited me to watch what happened next. He began to whistle, slowly and softly, whilst holding the hive steadily, and the seemingly mesmerised bees moved down and disappeared between the frames. The swarm was taken to a long, long line of other hives, swarms he had captured on other days and which would eventually be taken to one of his son's apiaries.

Herb honey

Some of the finest honeys I can produce in my locality are sage and thyme and they are in great demand, not so much by tourists, but the Greeks themselves. Honey is used in many Greek dishes, with yoghurt, sweets and cakes which are often floating in it. Selling ten kilos at a time for €150 is not difficult. There is a ready market for good honey especially if it is known that chemicals aren't used in the hive. In the twelve years that I have been here I have noticed a steady decline in honey production locally.

One small reason is that the building boom has led to the destruction of large areas of land which were formerly covered with sage and thyme. The other, as local beekeepers as disappointed as I am keep saying, 'It's the weather. The climate has changed. We used to get a lot of honey ten years ago!' This is true. We have noticed the difference in climate during the last decade. When we first came to Greece we would normally have a cold spell around and just after Christmas and maybe another one when

Easter was early. From January the flowers would begin to cover the olive groves and mountainsides, reaching their peak at the end of March and decreasing gradually after April.

Over the last few years the bees have foraged well during January and February, then we have had prolonged cold and wet weather in mid-March until the beginning or even the end of May, so not only have the bees consumed what might have been a honey surplus, they have needed feeding as well, always hopeful that the feeding would boost the hives' populations.

Beekeeping with Socratis

I no longer keep more than a few colonies of bees, up to about a dozen normally – though this can increase in summer if some of the bait hives I put out attract swarms. If I get enough honey for my family and friends I am happy. I use my colonies to try out new equipment, new techniques and for photography; playing with them, I suppose.

I do help a couple of other beekeepers though, particularly Socratis, the husband of my Greek teacher. His apiary is in the village of Exohori, which for me is a delightful drive through the mountains, though access to the hives is difficult as he has placed them at the top of a steep slope. His mother's goats have made the path to the hives very precarious and yet Socratis manages to carry heavy hives and supers of honey up and down with no problems. He has 1,500 olive trees and is a mountaineer, even having climbed Mount Ebrus, the highest mountain in Europe with, he says, heavier backpacks than the weight of hives. It is several degrees cooler in his apiary and if there is a slightly fresh wind, the bees, the same strain as mine, are the very devil to work with. Socratis believes that a veil should only be used as a last resort, that is when he has been stung many times and can hardly see what he is doing any more. In summer, I can examine my colonies in just sandals, shorts, a T-shirt, and a very light veil. I never need to wear gloves because the behaviour of the bees doesn't warrant it. But, in Socratis' cooler apiary, I need more substantial clothing.

For all the years that I have helped Socratis, his bees have produced three times more honey than mine, although we use the same management system. Our apiaries are only 12km apart as the crow flies, and to look at, there always seems to be more abundant flora within flying range of my bees than his. Last autumn we started a small test. I bought four queens, two Buckfast and two Caucasian, from the same breeder. These were installed into small queenless colonies and fed throughout winter. In very early spring we transferred the bees into full-sized hives. Two hives, each with a different queen, were taken to his mountain apiary and the other two to mine. In mid-July, when we removed the honey, we had the same result as in previous years, so it was clear to me that my district is now a very poor one for honey production. I think that apart from the general climate change, the main problem that affects honey production for me isn't the bees, nor the flowers, but the very strong turbulent winds which curtail foraging and dry up the nectar in the flowers.

The hot weather together with the wind dries up the foliage of many of the plants by June and wild fires, occurring by accident or design, get out of control very quickly. On one occasion I was asked to go across to Areopoli ('the city of Mars' and former capital of the Mani) to report on a fire. Long before I reached the scene I could smell scorched earth and burnt wood, the creosote from the burnt telegraph posts particularly cloying.

Half way up a completely devastated mountainside I saw a forlorn beekeeper looking at what remained of his hives, in most cases just a twisted metal roof or queen excluder amongst the wood ash. A few of the hives which had not been burnt had suffered from the tremendous heat of the fire for inside there was a gooey mass of honey, wax and bees. The fire had started when many of the bees were already out foraging and having returned they flew around not knowing where to alight.

Socratis Galineas who keeps his bees in a mountain village not far from mine; we usually work together

It was a terrible sight. Even the wire fence and the metal store had been twisted out of shape, a scene more fitted to a war zone than a Greek mountainside on a sunny summer's day. 'I had ninety hives,' the beekeeper told me, 'You can see the few that are left. It happened so quickly, I didn't have time to move any of them.' I offered him my sympathy. He shrugged his shoulders and said, 'I have been a beekeeper all my life – you will have seen my stall by the side of the road. That's it. I am too old to start again.'

CHAPTER TEN

International Beekeeping

ROMANIA

It was nearly midnight on the long crowded platform of a railway station in Prague, where Val, Vita and I were waiting to board the Pannonia Express to Arad, in Romania. The train with its high carriages was already late, and when the doors eventually opened, the passengers surged in, temporarily blocking the doorways with old suitcases tied around with string, huge cardboard boxes and plastic bags full of food for the 14-hour journey. The six-berth compartments were cramped, so our luggage had to be stacked on our beds. There was little chance of sleep, for whilst the train progressed through the night at a comfortable fifty miles an hour, it would squeal to a stop at many of the stations en route. Border officials and customs officers entered our carriage before crossing into a neighbouring country, and this was repeated with a new set of officials over the border.

On each occasion tickets and passports had to be presented and our identity checked with a beam of torchlight shone on our faces. At an officer's whim, passengers were told to open their luggage for scrutiny despite the hour of night, and whilst Val and I always escaped this attention, the other occupants in the carriage, including Vita, were subjected to a full search. Although the Iron Curtain had fallen several years before, travellers were still in terror of those who wore uniforms, and were deadly silent with anxious faces until they had moved on to the next carriage.

As soon as it was light the three of us stood in the corridor to watch Slovakia and then Hungary, waking up to a cool, clear dawn. For hour after hour we traversed the flat Hungarian Plain where the earth met the sky in the far distance and where patches of corn were being harvested and collected by peasants, the cobs stacked onto racks for drying. Often the train followed the course of the Danube, leaving and meeting it again as it meandered along. As we crossed into Romania, the industrial buildings looked old and dilapidated, compared with the more modern plants in Hungary, with smoke belching uncontrollably from the chimneys.

George Tamas, a Romanian beekeeper, met us at the station and took us to his apartment in the centre of the city which he shared with his mother. George was a hobby beekeeper with just a few hives, one of which he kept on his balcony. His full-time job was in the city's main boilerhouse, which supplied heat to all the houses. Ceausescu had dictated to the boilermen to what temperature the homes could be heated each day. Often the heating was far from adequate in winter and those whose apartments were at the end of the system suffered terribly.

Our first conversations were to do with the Romanian economy, the orphanage problem and life under Ceausescu. No happy news came out of these topics though we did during our time manage to visit a German-run orphanage, which was well-funded and provided excellent living and learning conditions for the children; they even had their own gardens, orchards, poultry and pigs.

Part of the orphan problem was that Ceausescu had expected each woman to have five children, which was unaffordable. It was common for a mother to give birth to her baby in hospital and once the nurse had returned to her bed with the baby all washed and swaddled, the mother had already fled. During the summer holidays under the Soviet system all children had to go to Pioneer Camps. These facilities no longer existed but many of the orphanages still closed for the summer, so most of the young teenagers lived on the streets, some not returning to the orphanages when they re-opened.

The Romanians held Winston Churchill in high esteem, but thought very little of the Queen and Prince Philip, saying that Princess Diana, whom they revered, was treated badly by them. They couldn't understand the stiff upper lip of the establishment, though I believe that secretly they were disappointed that I was not a little aloof and formal.

The next day we were joined by Stoyan, a Bulgarian beekeeper, his wife Keta and their daughter, from Jambol. Maria worked as a translator for the few days we were in Romania. We had many discussions on beekeeping, showed each other various pieces of apparatus and medicants for treating bee diseases, some new very efficient straps for fastening hives together for transportation, and, of course, we sampled each others' honey. Stoyan had brought with him an almost pure coriander honey, for the crop was grown for its seed in his south-east region of Bulgaria.

As we were keen to see Romanian bees, we all travelled to Lipova in the hills where the vineyards begin and where a beekeeper called Constantin had a large apiary. It was a beautiful late summer's day and Constantin was already at work when we arrived. He had an open-necked shirt, no protective clothing of any kind, and was standing at an open hive, one of many in a long multi-coloured row. The hives were mainly large Dadants, but some were long old-fashioned ones, with hinged lids and integral compartments for feeding and pollen trapping. The honey from all the hives had already been harvested; acacia honey, which is water-white, mild flavoured and one of the honeys which doesn't granulate for a long time. Constantin makes his colonies as strong as possible for the flow from acacia and gambles everything on this source alone; there is a strong demand for it and the price he receives for the honey makes it worthwhile. Many of the colonies were being joined together for the winter, with sheets of newspaper between boxes so that the bees would unite peacefully. We watched Constantin examine some of the colonies. Very little smoke was used and although wasps were flying around everywhere and trying to land on the open cells of honey, the bees were very quiet and gentle. The lightish grey bees were not, as I had first thought, Carniolan, but Carpatica, and I was impressed with their behaviour.

Besides trapping pollen to feed the bees in spring to stimulate colony growth, Constantin removed combs which contained plentiful amounts of pollen and placed them directly over the cluster, giving the bees easy access to this valuable breeding food when conditions were cool. Apart from the usual pest, varroa, Constantin's only other problem was with chalkbrood, the many mummified bodies of the developing bees being found on the floor of the hives in spring. Just as in any apiary visit we could have stayed and talked for hours, but Constantin had a lot of work ahead of him that day, so after a couple of hours amongst his hives, we left him to his labours.

I had always wanted to go to Timisoara where the Romanian Revolution began and since it wasn't far from Arad we all visited for a day. I was shocked. It was not at all like I had expected it to be. I thought it would be an old, backward, out-of-the-way place with crumbling buildings and with an air of desperation about it.

I was completely wrong. Timisoara is a beautiful garden town, full of parks and boulevards, magnificent buildings including a Roman Catholic and an Orthodox Cathedral, as well as an Opera House. In the square in front of the Opera House, young people smartly dressed in jeans and miniskirts stood around talking and drinking Fanta, whilst close to them was a rink which had been set aside for a roller-skating competition, sponsored by the company whose drink they were enjoying. I wondered how many of those young people who were sitting on the steps of the Martyrs' Memorial were aware of the sacrifice that had been made to give them the freedom which they now enjoyed. Yet it was only

Constantin preparing his hives for winter. The weaker colonies were combined with the stronger ones using the newspaper method. Despite being harassed by wasps, the bees were good tempered and no veils were needed

a few years since a large number of people stood up to defend the right of the outspoken pastor, Father Laszlo Tokes, opponent of the Ceausescus, to be reinstated in his parish – only to be shot down by shells from tanks and armoured cars.

It is known that Ceausescu had exported much of the country's agricultural produce to get rid of his foreign debt, leading to many food shortages for the Romanian people. I was given a slightly different slant on this policy. The people charged with the task of projecting harvest yields, sycophants, habitually overestimated the figures so that they would be seen in a good light. When the targets weren't achieved they plundered the crops which the people had grown for their own use to make up the shortfall. I was very interested, therefore, to have an opportunity to visit the local market to see how things were now for those who grew crops and raised livestock. It was obvious that we were on the right road, for old battered cars, lorries, trucks, horses pulling carts and people carrying sacks or cardboard boxes of produce were all making their way to the edge of town where the covered stalls, tables, blankets on the ground, or the open wagons and boots of cars served as a market selling fruit, vegetables, meat, cheese, animal feed, including straw and hay, clothes, shoes, besom brooms and other household goods, and livestock; as thriving a market as any that you would find in Western Europe.

The quality of the produce was excellent and displayed in rows or pyramids to make a good show. One old lady had a table full of white cabbages, every one as large or larger than her round head. Another woman, dressed like most of the others in warm homespun clothes, a colourful pinafore and headscarf, was selling sauerkraut from a big wooden barrel, doling it out, a kilo at a time. One man who wore a traditional black hat, bowler-like but with a much higher crown, had a stall devoted to cheese; huge rounds of it from sheep, goats and cows. But it was the livestock area to which I devoted most of my time, surveying in particular piebald piglets being sold from the back of old Dacias, the purchasers carrying them home in hessian sacks. A pair of weaners were fetching hefty prices; thirty pounds a pair, about two thirds of a month's wages. Some hogs for breeding filled the whole of a wooden cart, whilst red milch cows with white faces were tied to the back. A lot of the produce had been brought in from the local villages, many of which simply consisted of a double row of identical one-storey houses with a wide mud road between them. Here all types of poultry pecked, scratched and grazed. These were the lucky ones, for most country dwellers, who had been the butt of Ceausescu's paranoia, had seen their villages bulldozed and had been moved into horrendous suburban concrete tenements, this policy of systemisation allowing them to be kept more closely under observation.

Although food was now plentiful, and life freer, there was still general mistrust of the government for remnants of Ceausescu's former administration were still in power, people who would no doubt have been put up for trial had not the president and his wife's execution been so swift. What was still lacking in Romania was the cash that so many wanted in order to have a more western life-style; the branded goods which they wished to wear to give them standing amongst their friends. Not surprisingly, the longest queue in the market was the one which led to the lottery kiosk.

We were well fed during our visit, though I doubt whether I ever want to eat such a large mamaliga (polenta covered with melted cheese) again. It covered a huge dinner plate and even with the help of plentiful red Romanian wine, it was difficult to reach the end of the meal. For those who wanted it, a bottle of Tuica, home-brewed plum brandy, was on the table from morning to night, many Romanians drinking it several times a day for medicinal reasons!

BULGARIA

Almost a year afterwards, we again flew to Prague and, having enjoyed a late night walk around the city with Vita, we all three took once more the Pannonia Express to Arad. There were some improvements to our accommodation in the carriage this time – we had a spacious three-berth compartment with washing facilities and rails on which to hang our clothes. Vita told us we would be chasing bad weather as a deep depression was moving eastwards across Europe. Sure enough, once it was light we saw that the huge Hungarian Plain looked at times as if vast lakes had been created on the flat land. We had a short break at George's house, where his mother asked us what we would like to eat before our long journey and, before I could stop him, Vita begged her to make another mamaliga. We left Arad in the early hours of the morning for Bucharest where a connecting train would take us into Bulgaria. Bucharest railway station was probably one of the most colourful in Europe, for over the concourse line after line of flags stretched from one side of the high roof to the other. In our carriage a mother with her daughter were sitting across from us, and after a while the young girl took a rabbit out of its box and let it roam over the seat and the floor for the length of the journey.

After a long wait at the border post of Giurgiu, we finally crossed into Bulgaria at Ruse, along the two and a quarter kilometre girder bridge, thirty metres above the Danube, stopping for the whole train to be sprayed with disinfectant. The bridge, built with Soviet funds, was completed in 1954 and given the name 'Friendship Bridge'. However, after the collapse of the Soviet Union it is now just known as the Danube Bridge. I had seen beautiful panoramic pictures of this bridge before leaving for Bulgaria, but on that wet day, with overcast clouds, the river was a dirty grey, the banks looked black and greasy and lined with derricks. Despite this, many fishermen were standing at the river's edge, so there must have been some life in its depths. Three hours later we reached the end of our train journey at Gorna Orjahovica, where we were met by Stoyan's cousin Pavel who drove us to Jambol, two and a half hours away. Late in the evening we reached our destination at last – the 1800km journey having lasted almost exactly 48 hours.

Our correspondent from Ukraine, Dr Alexander Komissar, had arrived before us, having travelled from Kiev, by bus, via Burgas. He too had seen the effects of the floods; in places the torrents of water had been so bad that cars had been washed off the roads. If we thought our journey had been long, it was nothing compared to Vitaliy, from Chelyabinsk in the Urals. He had been travelling by train for almost six days.

Vitaliy's father had been in the Russian army stationed in Kazakhstan at the time when atomic weapons were being tested. He and his comrades were lined up from time to time to witness the remarkable force of the distant explosions, with no extra protective clothing. When he left the army he was in a very poor physical state and could hardly walk without getting out of breath. However, he completely changed his lifestyle when he returned to the Urals. He lived in the countryside, obtained many colonies of bees, ate honey, grew his own food and exercised daily. After two years he was able to run for several kilometres through the nearby forest and, with the occasional help of his son, he increased his beekeeping operation.

It was good to meet Stoyan's family again. Maria had already stayed with us in England for nearly a month and not only had her

171

They were large single storey hives, the one of the left divided into several parts for the raising of nuclei. These hives were kept permanently in the apiary

English improved enormously, I had taught her to be proficient in word processing. The family's living accommodation was on the first floor, above their butcher's shop and the workshop in which Stoyan made his hives and any other equipment for his apiaries. Some of the large hives that were being made took Dadant frames and had a unique construction – internal walls of plywood, an inner layer of polystyrene, and an outer covering of sheet metal. To reach the steps to the apartment we had to go down a dark narrow alleyway at the end of which their fierce guard dog was chained. It was let loose in the yard during the evening, but just to make sure we weren't harmed, Vita and I, gentlemen that we were, teasingly always let Val out of the door first. If there was no barking, we knew it would be safe for us to follow.

Our first visit was to Stoyan's village apiary. The twenty large, one-storey hives were colourfully painted and well-maintained, each holding two colonies. These stocks always remained in the apiary and were chiefly used for queen rearing, or frames of bees and brood were taken from them to boost the honey-producing colonies housed in a large mobile bee house and moved from crop to crop.

The latest honey, from sunflowers, had yet to be harvested, and to stem a spate of robbing which had broken out, Stoyan set to work and fitted reduced-entrance closures to each of the hives. The 48 hives in the bee

Stoyan's huge mobile bee house could be moved between sources of nectar

house were in two tiers and lined both of the long sides of the walls, the brood boxes containing fourteen frames. There was sufficient height in the bee house for both tiers to have two honey supers per hive.

In addition to sunflowers, Stoyan expected to have honey from the spring flowers and coriander, but that year both had been disappointing. The wild flowers in spring had been plentiful enough, but the bees were repelled by the blossoms because of deposits left on them by acid rain and other pollutants believed to have been due to the NATO bombing of the nearby country of Serbia.

Like most Greeks, the Bulgarians objected strongly to NATO's strategy, even more so when bombs landed in their own territory. Coriander, which flowered later, might have given much better yields, but instead of the 4,000 hectares which were usually sown, only 700 hectares of the crop had been cultivated. Normally, Stoyan expected to harvest around four tonnes of honey each year, but this season's harvest was likely to be in the region of just one and a half tonnes. The ground floor of Stoyan's original home had been converted into a honey-extracting house and store. Whilst we were there, his brother-in-law and his wife were starting to extract the sunflower crop using an enormous radial extractor. After filtering, the honey was stored in metal tins and later run into kilo jars of which 500 were sold every month, at about one pound sterling each, to a shop in Sofia.

Stoyan's brother also kept bees. He used single-storey long hives each containing nineteen frames, and had a row of them in his parents' garden next to the orchard in which apples, pears, nectarines, peaches, almonds, walnuts, figs and vines were grown in addition to the plums which were indispensible in a Bulgarian home for making raki. The quality of the chilli and sweet peppers, aubergines and tomatoes was far better than I could manage in my greenhouse, and of course, during our stay, most of the food we ate had its origin in this garden.

Stoyan was a butcher by trade and had his own small modern village abattoir. The family reared pigs, cows and sheep – the milk being used for butter, cheese and sour milk. The slaughtered animals were for family use as well for stocking the butcher's shop they had in town. Although the Bulgarians lacked money, the village gardens provided the families with a wealth of good natural food from crops which flourished in the favourable climate.

All the bees we encountered either when we walked around the apiary or were looking inside hives, were perfectly behaved, making no attempt to sting us. Only a minimum of the sweet smelling, cool smoke was needed to drift across the tops of the frames during hive inspections to completely calm the bees. I did wonder about the source of the fuel used for the smoke and soon realised where it originated; she was stubborn, shoulder-high, likely to kick out with her back legs unexpectedly, had enormous ears, and lived in a stable at the side of the house!

After supper, and many toasts of raki, we held our evening meetings, each of the beekeepers having brought with him something to talk about. Vitaliy brought along a wonderful video of beekeeping and the countryside in his part of the Urals that he had made, with an English commentary over the background sounds of nature. This depicted most of the honey sources, including buckwheat. I love the strong taste of this honey, which I had first tried in Brittany. Whilst the Bretons use the flour from the grain to make pancakes, for Russians the whole grain is used to make a staple food – kasha – which is eaten in the morning as porridge with butter or honey, or as a substitute for potatoes with meat or fish dishes.

My contribution to the meeting was on the marketing of honey and I was able to show the various types of packaging which we had used in our own business as well as samples from UK beekeeping suppliers. Vita showed us special frames in which hexagonal combs of honey could be produced and the packaging into which these sections fitted perfectly. Alexander's contribution didn't get underway until past 11pm one evening, but he still had us interested in the slide show of his development over the years of multi-nucleus hives for queen mating. He told us that a hive with 16 compartments, with carefully shielded and different coloured entrances, would be sufficient for the needs of hobby beekeepers. For commercial beekeepers, he said, he had developed a 36-unit version, and as its description and management would need our full attention, he ordered coffee for us all and made us have a short break before he completed his presentation.

Our last day was spent on the Black Sea at Nessebar with its golden sandy beaches and deep blue sea (sadly for swimmers, full of many jellyfish). Formerly, this was the holiday place of high-ranking Soviets and favoured people in the regime, the skyscraper apartments built to accommodate them not far from the water's edge. Behind these modern atrocities was the old medieval town with its Byzantine churches and walls and the thriving market place, where 250g of honey could be bought for the equivalent of 30p, in Coca Cola bottles, and women sat by their stalls or in front of their houses making lace. As Pavel drove us back to Jambol we were treated to another repertoire of songs, started by his wife Rosa, and very soon accompanied by Vita, Vitaliy and Alexander: Val and I listened spellbound.

So far, most of what we had seen in Bulgaria was wonderful, but then something happened which made us modify our opinion of at least one aspect of the country's resources. Maria, it was believed, had a heart murmur and feeling ill one day was taken very quickly to the hospital in Jambol. When we went to visit her, many patients in their dressing gowns were wandering around the unkempt gardens of the hospital or sitting on the few available benches. The ward into which Maria had been admitted was a small room so crammed with beds we had to crawl over others in order to sit near her. This was the ward for heart patients. There was no sign of any nursing staff, nor medical apparatus and we found that there was only one electric socket in the room. Fortunately, Maria's problem was not serious but we left Bulgaria wondering what else there was to uncover below the surface of all that we had seen which had been so pleasant.

The long train journey from Bulgaria went via Budapest where we had a few hours spare before our connection to Prague. We arrived there at about five in the morning, seeing dozens of homeless people being woken up so that the station's platform could be swept. For the first time in our lives we were pleased to find a MacDonalds which was open, knowing that there would be clean toilets and that we could have a good wash. Vita was hesitant, though, as he had never on principle set foot in one of their establishments before. However, he gained something from the visit as he realised that the standard polystyrene beaker in which Val had been served her tea had just the right volume for measuring the number of bees to be put into a mating hive. After leaving MacDonalds, cleaner and refreshed, we had enough time to cross the bridge from Buda to Pest and climb the hill as the sun rose, its warm rays casting long, rosy shadows over the roof tops and tinting the surface of the Danube. Our next train was a new European one which sped on to Germany after Prague, all stainless steel and spotless, with a magnificent restaurant car. On the Bulgarian train all I had been able to buy was a Mars bar, which had melted and solidified day after day, but I had eaten it nevertheless.

UKRAINE

I had to wait nearly twelve years before I embarked on my next trip to Eastern Europe, where I wished to visit Alexander Komissar in his home city of Kyiv. He had retired as a Professor of Apiculture at the University and at last had more time to spend on the journal he edited, his bees, and inventions that he had described for us in *The Beekeepers Quarterly.* Alexander, little changed since I last saw him except in girth, was waiting for me with Masha, his daughter-in-law at Boryspil airport. She drove us along the fast newish road to the city, where in his fourth-floor apartment I met his wife Irina, his two sons and grandson.

Breeding solitary bees

In the morning Alexander opened the doors of his balconies and the noise of bees was colossal. Hundreds of bees were flying to and from the cherry trees in the street below and many flew into the rooms. But these were solitary bees (not honeybees), *Osmia rufus*, so-named because of their reddish colour. The term 'solitary' seems to be an inappropriate description to the casual observer of these insects, for they choose to make their individual nests in soft limestone walls or in sandy soil, in close proximity to each other, and are often mistaken for swarms of honeybees.

Alexander preparing reeds

Examining his reed nests for the solitary bee, Osmia rufus

This species of bees can be encouraged to nest in hollow stems of plants, so every winter Alexander cuts thousands of pieces of reed to a length of about 25 cm, one end being naturally closed by a node, the other, the entrance, cut at a sharp angle.

Handfuls of these prepared reeds are fitted into boxes or tins, on a horizontal plane, ready for the bees to nest in them. In late winter, the previous year's reed nests would be cut open, the cocoons from which the bees were due to emerge being put into cardboard trays. The cocoons have to be carefully selected though, for many can be parasitised by flies which gain entrance to the tubes and

Bees lay several eggs, provide them with pollen, then seal the tubes with mud

lay their own eggs within them. Each nest can produce several new bees, for when a bee emerges in spring and locates an unoccupied tube it will lay several eggs in each one, separating them with a wall of pollen which will serve as each larva's source of food. Once completed, the entrance is sealed up with mud.

Alexander supplies boxes of cocoons to people who want pollinators for their gardens and to commercial growers whose crops are under glass. In the latter he will also set up banks of new nesting sites for the bees to use once they emerge. Osmia bees have several qualities which make them more attractive to gardeners than honeybees for pollination; they are unlikely to sting, they forage at lower temperatures, in wet weather and in poor light (from early dawn to dusk), and if someone is willing to have the time and patience to make the nests, they can be obtained freely if the species are present in the neighbourhood. In England a few years ago, nest kits were supplied by the Oxford Bee Company to gardeners, with great success. I spent a lot of time with Alexander shaping and cutting reed tubes, taking them to sites where newly-emerged bees were flying, and standing beside tubes which were already being used, catching and squashing the parasitising flies.

Alexander had to prepare his presentation for a meeting we were to attend the following week, so Irina took time off work from her job as an entomologist at the university to take me for a long tour of the city. Kyiv is partly built on hills and bisected by the Dnieper river; its streets are lined with horse chestnut trees which were about to burst into flower, white blossomed cherry trees, lime trees, birch and plane. Much of the city could be traversed by walking through one park to another, though we spent most of our time walking around the beautiful campus of the Polytechnic and the enormous Botanic Garden where similar tree species were often grouped together in its hollows and hills.

Whilst the perimeter of the garden was devoted to natural woodland, fresh leaves unfolding in the spring sunshine and under which dandelions, violets, celandines and red nettle were already flowering, there were long vistas planted on each side with huge beds of roses or herbaceous plants. One path led to a magnificent monastery church with its golden cupolas resplendent against the clear blue sky. Exiting the botanic garden we found ourselves in another park with views over the river where a bridge over a stream had its railings entirely covered with padlocks of various shapes and sizes and ribbons of all colours, each object declaring one person's love for another. We went home via the metro which has the deepest escalators in the world. The trains arrived punctually every two minutes. I was impressed.

Trip to Chernobyl

The following day was set aside for visiting Chernobyl. Alexander was going to accompany me, although he had visited Chernobyl both before and after the disaster and even had a couple of hives there. He had been sent by his university after the meltdown of Reactor No 4, on 28 April 1986, to collect samples of the migrating ducks which stopped in this very wet and marshy area before moving on to the north. His findings were that the radiation levels in the ducks were extremely high so they were not fit for human consumption. The main problem was the difficulty in passing on this information to hunters in the countries where the ducks would eventually settle and breed. Some work was also done on the honey from the hives in Chernobyl. He told me that the honey itself was all right, but that the pollen was heavily contaminated.

A minibus picked up our small group early in the morning. Apart from Alexander and myself, there were three other British men who thought they may as well 'take in' Chernobyl. It was a long straight road that we travelled for over two and a half hours, tossed around each time the minibus hit one of the many large potholes. The land was very flat and where it wasn't marshy and covered with small lakes and reeds, villagers were planting out their rows of potatoes and other vegetables in the black soil. Frequently, we passed huge stands of trees or seemingly endless forests, slanting shafts of sunlight lighting the edges of red-barked pines and the white peeling bark of silver birches.

Thirty kilometres from Chernobyl we stopped on the border of the Exclusion Zone, where a young man in camouflage uniform joined us as our guide. He spoke perfect English and had just finished university specialising in tourism. He told us that he worked for fifteen days at a time showing people around Chernobyl but after that, like many people on the plant, he had to leave the area for two weeks.

We were given some simple instructions: Don't touch anything; keep to the roads as much as possible as they are cleaned frequently and the radiation is much less; and avoid walking on herbage, particularly moss which has the highest levels of radiation. After a while we stopped alongside the forest road where we could just make out a building amongst the trees. We took a narrow path towards what had been a kindergarden, passing a small playground with rusted swings and collapsed fence almost obscured by thick foliage. I wasn't prepared for what was inside – metal bunk beds with piles of sheets and blankets on the sunken mattresses, childrens' toys strewn abandoned on the floor, dusty school books still on their shelves and exercise books still open to show the last lesson of that fateful day. The uncurtained, dirty windows masked the full effect from the sunlight, but as we stirred the dust by our movements, millions of specks floated in its beams. It was a sad and depressing place and I was pleased to leave it.

We journeyed on, reaching the twenty kilometre exclusion zone where our papers were diligently checked and not long afterwards stopped directly outside the power station. It was impossible to believe on this fine sunny day, with a clear blue sky and trees everywhere coming into leaf, that we were at the scene of the world's greatest peacetime nuclear tragedy, for the plant, quiet and lying at peace, with just a few personnel strolling around in hard hats and overalls, belied its past destructive history. The only sign of work was the lorries which rumbled back and fore from the cement works as a new casing was being added to the old crumbling sarcophagus which entombed Reactor No 4. In line with the reactors, huge derricks still rose to the sky from the half-completed Reactor No 5, the construction of which had been suddenly terminated exactly twenty-six years and a day before.

Outside the main offices the memorial depicting the firemen who never knew what it was that they were up against was bedecked with fresh flowers from the commemoration service the previous day. A stone's throw away a copper-coloured angel of metallic rods blew its long trumpet to the sky. Beyond this a double row of posts, bearing the names of villages in the danger zone which had been bulldozed to the ground and forever covered with earth, petered out into the distance. Beneath the damaged reactor there was very little to see apart from the new casing which was designed to shield the site from further radiation for decades.

A few kilometres down the road from the plant we came to Pripyat where the workers from Chernobyl and their families had lived. These were privileged people, high earners, who were given good apartments and had everything they needed – schools, good medical facilities, shops, theatres, spacious

Reactor No.4, Chernobyl, which caused the 1986 nuclear disaster

squares, all surrounded by beautiful forests and lakes for fishing. Ready for opening that May Day was an enormous playground, with dodgem cars, slides, boat swings and a gigantic ferris wheel, never used. Nature had flaked away their paintwork, twisted the slides into grotesque shapes, stranded each of the boat swings on to one rusty chain and blown the dodgem cars on their sides into a heap. The ferris wheel alone stood tall and proud, its gondoliers so corroded they no longer rocked in the wind.

Between cracks in the pavement and on the balconies of the apartments, trees and shrubs were reclaiming the town. In one school, enormous posters and placards for the May Day parade still leaned against the walls, unfinished. In the streets and squares, signs that the people had left in a hurry; a single shoe, a doll with its limbs missing, a toy gun, odd pieces of clothing. They had had only two hours to collect essential items together, for then they had to be on board one of the 200 evacuation buses. Almost all of these people never saw their homes again. Masha's family was amongst them; her father had a good job as an engineer at the plant, and Mashuka, just two months old, joined them on the bus to a new life and temporary home in whatever part of Kyiv the government could find for them.

Pripyat was a quiet, desolate place. Almost without exception the buildings were still intact which made it seem even more sinister. I had the feeling that I would only need to turn a corner and find people once again thronging the streets. When I did turn down another avenue I saw a score of people dressed from head to foot in white overalls with hoods, rubber gloves and face masks. A contingent from Greenpeace was in town.

I wasn't too worried about being in Chernobyl: our party was only there for about six hours and some of this time was spent in the canteen where we were given an excellent lunch, starting with borsch. It was impressed upon us that all the food was brought in from outside the zone! Throughout our tour, dosimeters were used to check radiation levels. Before entering the canteen and on leaving the zone we and our vehicle were scanned for radiation. I was hoping to visit one of the villages where there were a few returnees, old people who had found that life wasn't worth living in crowded city apartments; they wanted their gardens and livestock and had no worries about eating the food they produced. Their philosophy was simple: 'we are more likely to die of old age than radiation sickness'.

I have read many books on Chernobyl and the aftermath of the disaster, but I still have no idea how great a human tragedy it really was or what the consequences of it are today. I know that the firemen who stand in the huge metal lookout towers in the Ginger (not Red) Forest are doubly exposed to danger, firstly due to their vulnerable position during the many summer thunderstorms and, secondly, to toxic fumes and radioactive ash, should a fire occur. The forest is said to be the haunt of many large mammals, a nature reserve, with wolves, pigs and deer now that few people inhabit the area. However, during my visit, I heard very few birds singing. The only other signs of natural life I saw were butterflies, a solitary bee and some soldier beetles.

Beekeeping east of Chernobyl

After visiting Chernobyl, Alexander, his seventeen-year-old son Daniel and I set out on a beekeeping adventure which was to last for six days. We took the train east to Kremenchug where two beekeepers were waiting in their car to take us to Piski, an hour's drive away, where our host had arranged an informal meeting for a group of us for two days as a prelude to an important meeting in Hrady'kn later in the week. We arrived in the forecourt of the large house after dark but two of the beekeepers, our host Ivan and his colleague Anatoli, were still at work, dipping beehive boxes into a huge vat of paraffin wax which would preserve them for a dozen years. The pine-scented wood smoke swirling around the yard and the shadowy figures silhouetted by the fire for melting the wax gave it a bizarre atmosphere.

Their wives had prepared supper for us all and waited patiently at the long set table under a pergola. When we sat down for our meal – borsch followed by egg, meat and cheese dishes, we were bombarded by huge cockchafer beetles attracted to the light and falling stunned to the table. To drink, there was fruit compote, a standby in all Ukrainian households, meads of different vintages and strengths and the other important traditional offering, a huge jug of ryazhenka, a type of sour cream with a thick crust on its surface which was consumed with relish by most of the guests.

Most of our group were up by dawn and found Ivan collecting bucketfuls of dead bees from the front of the hives in his garden apiary. Many of the bees still had the tell-tale signs of yellow pollen on their legs which suggested that they had been poisoned by the spraying of a nearby crop of oil seed rape with insecticide. Before breakfast we walked across lush water meadows, grazed by tethered cows and where on telegraph posts storks had built their nests, to visit an enclosed wood where wild boar were reared for hunting, the new litters of striped piglets keeping close to their mothers which were rooting around the oak trees. Many pheasants were housed nearby in huge aviaries to protect them from foxes, their eggs to be collected for incubation. The young pigs and reared pheasants would be released into the wild in autumn for high-ranking government officials and prominent businessmen to hunt.

We were driven to two apiaries that day, I being given pride of place in the front of Anatoli's brother, Alex's UAZ 469 military jeep, a veteran of the Chechen war. We tore across rough, pot-holed tracks and over fields still covered with the previous year's sunflower stalks and maize stubble, throwing up clouds of dry soil. Eventually we reached a clearing, near the edge of a huge tract of woodland, which contained long rows of modern Dadant and traditional one-storey hives. The bees were foraging well on this spring morning, collecting large amounts of pollen as well as water which had been provided for them in five litre upturned glass jars to which bees had access via holes beneath the wooden planks into which the jars had been set. I was able to rest my hand right on the top of the frames of an open colony for some time without any reaction from them. No stings! In one corner of the apiary was a shed which served as a store and sleeping quarters, for the two owners of the bees took it in turns to stay overnight to guard their colonies from thieves.

A row of upturned glass jars were designed to provide the bees with their water mixed with honey

Whilst the rest of the group of beekeepers was transported to Anatoli's apiary, Alexander, Daniel and I said we would join him in walking through the forest – a short cut to his site, he said, which was less than half a kilometre away. We followed a wild boar's track down a steep slope covered with alder, acers and lime trees, but on reaching the bottom found that we couldn't go any further as lots of water had collected in a hollow which the pigs had turned into a deep, muddy wallow. So we went halfway back up the hillside and, as we were unable to find another trail, we walked sideways along the steep slope, stumbling over fallen branches and grabbing at trees to prevent us from sliding downwards, the soil beneath us deep in litter from years of rotted leaves.

We must have been walking for over an hour on what was the first hot day of the year, pestered by flies and mosquitoes, when we heard the distant calls and whistles of our companions who had been searching for us. By then we were more than pleased to get back into our jeep, for we had managed to scramble a couple of kilometres from our intended destination. It was a tight fit, for seven of us managed to squeeze in. 'Don't worry,' Alexander told us. 'There is plenty of room. This jeep was built for five fat Russian Generals!' What he forgot was that he, Anatoli and Alex all fitted that description, leaving very little room for the remaining four of us!

Ukrainian bee farming

A full day spent at Anatoli's apiary gave me a realistic view of Ukrainian bee farming and how much it differed from beekeeping enterprises of a similar size in Western Europe. Apart from the winter months, the beekeepers spent most of the time with their bees, both in the home and out-apiaries. In the main over-wintering apiary, just a few weeks into spring, Anatoli, Alex and a helper for the season had already set up camp at the centre of which was a gigantic, long, old wooden bee house built on a sturdy trailer with huge tractor wheels. Inside the bee house was a sleeping compartment and living space, including a woodburning stove, and an area where honey was extracted and stored, usually in milk churns.

From the roof of the beehouse an awning made from strong polythene stretched across to some trees, under which was a long trestle table with hive boxes on their sides for seats. A lorry battery provided power for lighting and a radio. Half a dozen milk churns contained cool, fresh water from a spring and bottled gas allowed a kettle to be on the boil for most of the day for the innumerable glasses of strong black tea drunk by the beekeepers.

The camp had an ingeniously-made shower: a metal beer keg had been painted black to be heated by the sun. This was pressurised by a

Anatoli's mobile woodland camp/apiary

foot pump, and an outlet to a pipe fixed to a tree ensured that a hot shower could be taken when required. Dotted on trees around the camp, upturned bottles filled with water had been attached for hand washing, the bottle tops modified so that just a slight twist released a jet of water. A fire slumbered at the edge of the camp for cooking, surrounded by several blackened cauldrons and utensils.

Nearby, the friendly guard dog dreamed, its nose and ears twitching from time to time. I asked one of the helpers in the camp, a youngish scrawny man who was always smoking, if he had any of the rough home-grown tobacco, makhorka, commonly used by peasants for centuries. He took some from an old tin, tore a strip of newspaper and rolled a cigarette. The smoke from the strong dark tobacco, with more than three times the usual content of nicotine, had me choking, even though I was sitting across the table.

Plastic pollen traps used in the spring by Anatoli. The grids are inserted every morning to scrape the pollen off the bees' legs

Anatoli had two objectives in early spring: harvesting pollen and building up the colonies so that each had two full boxes of brood ready for the major honey crops, acacia and sunflower. All the hives had plastic pollen traps fitted to their fronts; not the best, Anatoli admitted, especially during wet weather, but they were cheap and gave reasonable results. The plastic vertical screens which scraped the pollen off the bees' legs were only left in place for a few hours each morning; the colonies would need the pollen collected later in the day for brood development. Even so he managed to harvest about 30kg of pollen each day for which there was a growing market and would help to boost his income if honey prices dropped when a glut occurred.

Hybrid Ukrainian Dadant hives

I was interested to see how far forward the colonies were so he opened some up for me. I noticed immediately that he had made two modifications to the standard Ukrainian Dadant hive. The first I had seen years before in Steele and Brodie's heather hives. Instead of the top and bottom edges of the box being flush with each other, they were rebated so that when the hives were being moved they fitted tightly and would not slide apart. I thought this was an excellent idea considering how bumpy the roads were, but I remembered that the chief drawback to this system was that unless well smoked, bees could be crushed when boxes were placed back together after an examination.

A careful beekeeper always gently slides the boxes in place. This was impossible with the rebated modification. Anatoli had also slightly cut down the upper box, thus removing the bee space. This meant that the bottoms of the frames were in direct contact with the frames below. He showed me this had a positive advantage. Drawing out frames from both boxes, he held them one on top of the other and I could see that there was no gap in the brood nest; no barrier of

The strapped hives were lifted onto the lorry with a hoist

pollen or honey to get in the way of nest expansion. Because of this, he said, colonies built up very quickly. He was right. It was only the last week in April and the very cold (-30°C) winter had only recently ended, but his bees in this northern climate were more advanced than some of mine in the south of Greece.

When it was time to move the colonies, they had very little lifting to do. A strong hive-barrow with a single pneumatic tyre could be slid under the hives to carry them to their powerful ex-army lorry. The hives were strapped and tensioned with a strong buckle and lifted into place with the lorry's hoist. A full load of colonies was several tiers high. Most items from the camp would be placed inside the bee house which was attached to the lorry, then once again they were ready for another field, another stretch of woodland; a well-practised system they had followed for years.

Back to the bee camp

In the early evening we were all called together and off we set through the woods, but stopped after a very short time. Anatoli and Alex put on their bee veils, so I assumed we were going to look at more bees. I was wrong. They took milk churns out of the jeep and went down a steep slope to where we could hear the sound of running water. It was from this spring that they had always collected their water, icy cold and clear, but to get it they needed to shield themselves from the thousands of mosquitoes gathered around the nearby muddy pools.

Daniel and I went further into the forest where we saw a huge fallen tree. On closer examination it was obvious what had happened; the tree had been felled by a beaver. The remaining stump and the end of the tree, if fitted together, would have resembled the shape of an egg timer, the beaver having stripped away the wood from the outside to the centre. I filled my deep pockets with the wood chips; they would make excellent fuel for my bee smoker.

The tree had been felled by a beaver. I collected some of the wood chips for my smoker

When we returned to camp, a good-sized carp was being boiled over the fire for a fish soup supper. At dusk, Olga, Sveta and Lisa arrived with their two small Chinese Crested dogs, one completely hairless. The two ladies set to work clearing and washing the table and the many cups and glasses which had accumulated, probably for days. They had brought a jug of ryazhenka (the thick sour cream) with them, some salad from their gardens, and some fruit compote to join the two demijohns of mead and the bottle of vodka already on the table. We had the most delicious fish soup with bread and bunches of spring onions, talking well into the early hours of the morning, fortified by mead and vodka. When hunger struck again there was plenty of pork fat and smoked sausage to eat, Anatoli proud of the fact that it was organically produced. I should have asked him at this point why it was, then, that he treated his bees with chemicals to control a range of pests and diseases, but decided it wasn't the time or place to start a discussion of this sort. I was lucky to have Daniel at my side as he constantly gave me a commentary in English of what was being discussed.

Ukrainian bee conference

The following day we moved on to the very small town of Hradyz'k which was near the Kremenchuk Reservoir, a vast area of water covering two and a quarter thousand square kilometres. Scores of villages along the Dnieper had been flooded so that the dam and Hydro Electric Power station, constructed in 1959 with Russian money, could provide the region with much of its energy. Our beekeeping meeting was held in beautiful parkland with long avenues of trees along the roadsides. Colourful wooden buildings were scattered in clearings amongst the trees. At the centre of the park were two much larger buildings and a covered area sheltering a long double row of sinks for washing. I have read so much about the Russian Pioneer Camps in which most Soviet children had spent the summer months, but I never envisaged that I would see one, for this is what the place had been. It was more obvious when I went into the main hall, for old wall-posters and the stained glass windows all smacked of Russian artwork of the 1950s.

As Daniel was working at his father's table selling his books and journals, I was presented to a young lady named Olga who would act as my interpreter. She was originally from the far east of Russia, but now lived nearby with her beekeeper uncle. As I walked around the stalls she translated everything for me; without her help I would have learned much less that day. For instance, amongst the honey, wax, and propolis tinctures there was a small phial, the contents of which I couldn't recognise.

She found the answer for me. It contained a strained suspension of wax moth larvae which had been steeped in alcohol for some time and which apparently was used to treat people suffering with pneumonia.

Irina told me when we returned to Kyiv that this solution was also used as a general health supplement. A jar, a third of which contained wax moth larvae, approximately just over one centimetre in length, is topped up with alcohol (98% – ethanol) and the contents shaken daily for a couple of weeks. The solution is then strained and 15 drops are added to water and taken orally, each day. I don't think I will be trying it out myself.

I was very surprised to see many beekeepers looking at an old tinplate or zinc honey extractor to which an electric motor had been fitted, running off a car battery. It appeared to be a great novelty, and

Before the lectures began, the Orthodox priest held a short service, then blessed the beekeepers with holy water

I could see that it would help them as most honey was extracted in the apiaries where a car battery would be the beekeepers' only source of power.

I saw just one innovative piece of equipment, a very well-constructed machine, electrically powered, which could remove the wax cappings from a honey comb, though only one side of the comb could be done at a time. At a cost of about seven hundred euros, this was beyond the reach of most beekeepers income so I suggested to the inventor that he might be able to market it abroad. Most of the stalls were selling the mundane things that beekeepers require at the beginning of each season – wax foundation, frames and hive parts, so naturally these were the busiest.

Just before the lectures started there was a short Orthodox service, two old ladies and a man responding in plainsong to a text read by the priest. Before entering the hall, people formed a long line to the side of the priest who dipped a huge paint brush in a bucket of water and sloshed it over their faces, a blessing I had never seen carried out so vigorously.

The meeting began in the hall with the lighting of two candles by the youngest beekeeper, Daniel, and the oldest, the well-respected Vasyl Solomka who shares the editorship of Alexander's journal. He was an interesting character with long white whiskers but no moustache. When he had invited beekeepers to call on him if they were in his neighbourhood, he received hundreds of visitors in the first month alone.

Innovative honey snacks

The first presentation, which lasted for over two and a half hours, was given by a group of beekeepers, but chiefly Alexander and Vasyl, the aim being to show how honey could be obtained in the comb without using beeswax foundation. Alexander had some time ago made very shallow ekes, boxes for honey, divided into many small compartments on which thin strips of wood were placed, so that the bees could build combs full of honey sufficient for one person for one meal. The combs were sold in clear plastic containers for about one euro each.

Alexander's invention had caught on and several stalls outside the hall were selling the ekes and containers, much to his delight, for he wasn't interested in patenting his system. During the presentation a comment was made that it was better not to use 'beeswax' foundation for comb honey as much of the wax was mixed with paraffin wax. A storm of indignation broke out with some of the wax suppliers taking to the floor and shouting at the lecturers. Before long many of the people in the audience joined in the argument and it was a full fifteen minutes before peace was restored.

It was then my turn to make a contribution. I had made a Power Point presentation on Greek beekeeping, its history and current practices, with Alexander commenting on the slides in Russian. Visually, it looked good, but afterwards he told me he wasn't sure if his translation was completely accurate. Nevertheless, it must have been intelligible, for in a break afterwards the Vice-President of the Kazakhstan Beekeepers Association asked me to be a guest at their honey festival in August and give a presentation there.

Daniel and I needed some fresh air, so we found Olga and Lisa and went for a walk around the camp and up to a huge pine-covered bluff overlooking the huge reservoir. We could see clear to the horizon; no sign of land beyond it. Olga said that this was the Pioneer Camp she had come to each summer, enjoying it tremendously.

'What about the propaganda and indoctrination?' I asked.

'Oh that!' she replied. 'We marched and wore our red pioneer scarves like good communists, but it just flowed over us. We were there to have a good time with our friends and enjoy the sports, swimming and other activities'.

I have heard the same reply from many other people who lived during the Soviet era and who regret that those free month-long holidays provided by the state are no longer available.

A phone call summoned us back to the hall as supper was being served; borsch, pork, salad, kasha and later on fish, with plenty of mead and vodka to drink. At the end of the meal the sound of an accordion came from the open doorway and a man in traditional dress walked down the aisle between the tables pumping the bellows for all he was worth. He then turned towards the entrance: three very large, traditionally-dressed women 'dolly-tubbed' down the aisle singing and dancing. All the diners stood up with their glasses and shouting loudly 'Hu, Hu, Hu' downed the contents in one go, a process which was repeated more stirringly each time. This was the strangest and most enjoyable beekeeping meeting I have ever attended, the informal atmosphere, sense of fun and friendliness of the people making it an event that I look back on not only with pleasure, but with gratitude to have had the privilege of being made welcome by so many strangers.

I slept well that night, maybe because of all the vodka toasts. I shared a very comfortable, recently renovated three-bed dormitory with Daniel and Alexander. Regrettably, we had to leave the festival, which was continuing for another day, as we had other places to visit, other beekeepers to meet. In Kremenchuk we were just in time to catch a half-sized bus to Polatava; that is, although there was no firm schedule, the bus was about to depart because it was nearly full. For the length of the journey a DVD was put on for our entertainment, a very badly-produced and directed Russian story of two rival female football teams. Fortunately, the dialogue was a mystery to me but the filming itself showed that the director was most interested in the girls when they were in their football kits, but he made the mistake of zooming in on their footwork during the matches; none of the players had any idea of how to kick a ball, never mind perform a tackle. The countryside which fled by with peasants planting potatoes was far more interesting.

Entrepreneurial beekeeper: honey and breeding queens

Leonid's polystyrene mating hives allow feeding to carried out without opening the hive

Leonid met us in Poltava and drove us to his village home. In the extensive grounds was an old dacha which he and his wife and father had lived in when he took the brave decision of leaving his well-paid job as an aircraft designer. He helped his father with his bees and gradually built up a successful beekeeping business selling firstly honey and then breeding queens. He is now selling 5,000 queens a year at approximately ten euros each. To preserve his strain of bees he gives all the beekeepers in his immediate area free queens each year.

The polystyrene mating hives he uses he designed himself, the three metal moulds for the body, floor and roof cast to his specification. I watched one of the village women as she carefully lined the inside of each section of the mould with silicon and filled the spaces with fine grains of polystyrene. Once each of the moulds had its parts securely clamped together, it was lowered into a tank of boiling water heated by firewood and left for exactly twenty minutes. She used a hoist to pick up the hot mould and swing it into a tank of cold water. Whilst she was waiting for it to cool, other completed hive parts were painted.

Leonid's hives, stacked in spring to be filled with bees, combs and pollen

Leonid's mating hives are unique; unlike others on the market he has designed his so that they do not need to be opened for feeding the bees, for that disturbs the fragile colony and affects the temperature and humidity of the hive. Normally bee breeders use fondant for feeding because syrup can encourage robbers which could easily destroy the small nucleus, but Leonid uses syrup, or honey, managing to get round the robbing problem by fixing neoprene valves to the upturned glass feeders set into the roof so that no leaking occurs, and by having the hive entrance on the underside of the floor. Whilst Leonid sells the hives within Ukraine, he is not interested in exporting them – at ten euros each they would sell well, but as the inventor of the uncapping machine said, the paperwork involved would be too burdensome.

I doubt if Leonid needed the extra work; he was doing extremely well out of his business and had already built a large house with all modern

Andre's hives on a moveable trailer. He lived, slept and did honey extraction in the bee-house on the back of the end of the trailer

190

conveniences under which was a temperature and humidity-controlled cellar in which he kept his bees during the severe winters. He had a well-equipped workshop with woodworking machines for making hives and stands, beside which was a lean-to with a good stack of air dried timber. Before we went inside for supper it was lovely to hear the echoing calls of the cuckoos, a sound I hadn't heard for many years. Whilst we were eating, the family's cat, a Kuril Bobtail, brushed round our legs hoping we would give it a share of our food.

Simple bee-feeding method

On the last day of our travels Leonid took us down a quiet country road where he had arranged a rendezvous with Andre, who would take us to see another large apiary. Andre was waiting in as luxurious a pick-up truck as Leonid's. We took a quick detour to see a village house that he had recently bought for just 8,000 euros in which he manufactured wooden nucleus hives for the bees he sold. His large beehouse was in the garden, the bees busily darting in and out of the many openings. His static apiary was in another village further away, where the hives were standing amongst the trees of a beautiful, secluded orchard already in full blossom.

Beyond the orchard was a huge store room for his honey – as well as small casks of fermented birch sap, mixed with honey, which had a sweet almost spicy taste. The main purpose of the store was for sheltering his colonies during the harsh winters, the hives normally remaining inside from November to March.

We only had a flying visit to the next apiary, in a huge clearing in the woodland which had over one hundred hives in a huge bee house. The inside of the bee house was especially interesting as each of the hives had holes bored into the sides into which plastic right-angle bends of plumbing tubing had been fixed, each housing a glass jar of honey and water making it very easy to feed the bees without opening the hives. A camp meal had already been prepared for us – pickled goose, long, dark, slender forest mushrooms, with the usual salad and bunch of spring onions, with mead if we were thirsty.

Sleeping on hives as therapy

We were all glad of a rest by this time and the long bus ride to Sumi in the north east of Ukraine gave us the opportunity to doze. Once past the industrial edge of the town, Sumi is a beautiful place with parks, gardens and a large pedestrian area in its centre with two magnificent churches. We were here to meet Nikos and his family and the reason for our visit was to experience a new phenomena in Ukrainian beekeeping, initially devised by Nikos himself; sleeping on beehives to improve one's health, a form of therapy intended to solve and partially cure his wife Anna's

Nikos and Anna's rustic dacha

persistent back problem. Alexander's cousin, an ex-army colonel, drove us to the village dacha where we were to experience this therapy for ourselves. He was proud of the car in which we were travelling; a 17-year-old Lada which had done 700,000 kilometres powered by bottled gas.

Anna was waiting for us in the dacha. We sat on a bed, removing any metallic objects. Probes from a machine feeding information into a computer were run over our wrists and the soles of our feet. The Nikitaki diagnostic programme revealed on the computer screen the state of our various organs in the form of bar charts, an important preliminary to our rest on the hives. Amongst the colonies in Nic's apiary were several sheds or bee shelters in which hives had been placed, the entrances for the bees on the exterior.

Nikos' ingenious bed chamber was positioned over the beehives: many have found they can improve their health by doing so

The interior of the almost dark shed in which I lay was bee-proof, but mesh screens beneath a mattress allowed the scents of the colony and the gentle murmuring of the bees to filter through, providing a sensuous and soothing atmosphere. I was asleep in minutes and didn't wake up for three hours. I was loathe to leave the comfort of the shed and decided that I must replicate this system in my garden.

For beekeepers, I couldn't imagine a more perfect way of relaxing. I was monitored once more on my return to the dacha, but I don't think there was any significant change in my metabolism, otherwise I would have been told.

Test for purest beeswax

An overnight train took us back to Kyiv and, apart from helping Alexander for a day or two with his osmia bees and visiting a factory which produced wax foundation, my ten days in Ukraine were, sadly, nearly over. I learned a simple test at the factory to check on the purity of beeswax. Small strips of wax foundation of the same size but from different sources are placed in a row slightly apart from each other. When left in the sun, the waxes which are less pure will soften first, whilst pure beeswax, which has the highest melting point, will be slow to do so.

I had looked forward to visiting Ukraine for years and as I expected I had a lot of interesting experiences and learned a great deal about the beekeepers and how they managed their bees. I knew that I would be returning the following year, for the most important biennial international beekeeping congress was to be held in Kyiv in September 2013. I am hoping to meet Vitaliy whom we last saw in Bulgaria at the event.

I have recently heard from him regarding the 'meteorite' (many of the Russians are suspicious of what the object really was) which exploded over his home city of Chelyabinsk, in the Urals. He said 'I saw a trail like a vapour one from an aeroplane, only ten times brighter. For two minutes there was a loud roaring sound and our workshop shook. The gates in the yard were torn from their hinges and as soon as the telephone system was restored my wife phoned to say that all the windows had been smashed on our balcony. Fortunately, none of our friends and neighbours were injured but emergency repairs were made with plastic sheeting as the temperature was -10°C during the day and -20°C at night.' A month later many windows were still in need of repair in the city and although funds were given for the work, much of it disappeared into the pockets of corrupt officials.

KAZAKHSTAN

I had told Gabit Nuradil, the Vice President of the Kazakhstan Beekeepers Association, that I wouldn't have time to visit the country's honey festival in August. After three emails and a telephone call, I relented. After all, it was only going to be for a few days and my flights, accommodation and all other expenses were to be paid by their government. I managed to get Ilaria Baldi invited as a guest, too.

Ilaria had spent six months learning about beekeeping with me when she was living in a nearby village in Greece. She built her own hive, was excellent at handling bees, and her enthusiasm was unbounded. When she returned to Italy she started beekeeping and now after five years has fifty hives and produces about a ton of acacia and chestnut honey each year. Where I thought Ilaria could make a good contribution to the meeting was her determination to provide beekeepers with clean, unadulterated beeswax, free from harmful residues. To achieve this, she and Bamba, her Senegalese husband, had begun an important beekeeping project in the unpolluted forest regions of Senegal, far away from arable crops. Using their own money, they provided beekeepers with traditional hives, made locally, which could be hung in trees and attract swarms to fill the hives with honey.

Once this was harvested and squeezed out of the combs, the beekeepers normally discarded the wax; they saw no use for it. As part of the agreement, the beekeepers promised to save, melt down and strain the wax and pass it over to Ilaria and Bamba in exchange for the hives and honey. Samples of the wax were sent to Italy and tested for impurities and as the wax was of excellent quality, it was exported to Italy. Each year more beekeepers in Senegal have become involved in the project and the amount of wax sent to Italy continues to increase, much to the delight of beekeepers who are in the market for clean wax which is manufactured into sheets of foundation to fit into the hive frames.

Despite airport delays, as the plane descended to Almaty I was delighted to see outstandingly beautiful countryside below – huge sharp-crested peaks topped with snow formed tooth-like ridges and the foothills had the appearance of scalloped sand on the beach when the tide has ebbed. A short internal flight then took me north to Ust Kamenogorsk, where the honey festival was to be held. At the airport I was met by an attractive, blonde young Russian, Aleksandra, who lectures in English and French

An inexpensive Ukrainian machine for removing wax cappings from honeycombs

at the university, my personal interpreter for three days. Her first task was to try and find out what had happened to my suitcase which hadn't turned up. Unfortunately, I didn't get it until the day before my departure so each night I had to wash my clothes in the hotel bathroom and dry them with a hairdryer.

We were taken by taxi to an apiary where the other guests had already gathered. It was raining and the country roads were deep in mud, but on arrival I was pleased to find not only Ilaria, but also my two friends from Ukraine, Alexander and Vasyl. Despite the weather many beekeepers were watching pallets, each containing four hives, being loaded on to a lorry by a forklift device fitted to the front of a tractor. Others were looking at the uncapping machine that I had already seen at Hradyz'k, a large stainless steel honey extractor, or sampling the mead and the open dishes of sunflower honey to which wasps were helping themselves. Gabit, pleased that I had arrived, introduced me to the President of the Association, and after a short welcoming speech we were driven off to a grassy field where a yurt had been erected. Outside, a group of singers and musicians in traditional costumes entertained us with their songs and dances before we were allowed to enter. There a magnificent feast awaited us. I was very impressed with the yurt; it was roomy yet cosy, and despite the hole in the centre of the roof, for smoke to escape, very little rain came through; if it had, a huge flap would have been stretched across the opening. The framework of the yurt was of thickish but pliable branches, shaped with steam, almost like wicker work but much more open, covered with felted wool. Coverings to other yurts I encountered were made from decorated cloth which gave each one a unique identity.

That evening in the hotel I had time to catch up with Ilaria's news and we were later joined by two Polish men, one the editor of a beekeeping journal, the other having his own beekeeping appliance business, and a Russian Jewish émigré to Israel who has 2,500 hives in orange groves or in areas where the rare Christ thorn bushes grow.

The following morning was devoted to the business part of the meeting. There were far too many participants and too little time for us all to speak, so we mainly heard speeches from government officials and the heads of Kazak and international beekeeping associations. The most informative for me was the report given by Bebykeva Saparbajeva, the Lieutenant Governor of East Kazakhstan, who gave details of their programme to get more people interested in beekeeping. This included the setting up of beekeeping schools and training apiaries, the

Supers with traces of honey were left out in the open for the bees to clean up. However, wasps were soon attracted and eventually displaced the bees

publishing of a website giving information on traditional and modern beekeeping, the distribution of a thousand free DVDs on beekeeping, the passing of a law to allow the setting up of private apiaries, and the provision of 3-4% interest loans to help beekeepers start up or expand their businesses. He also said that it was important to pay more attention to the breeding of carpatica bees, and that he was pleased to announce that he would follow the Japanese example of ensuring that each child up to the end of their junior classes in schools would be provided with 20g of free honey each day.

At the next apiary I didn't glean much from the visit, though I noticed that all the wet supers with traces of honey were left in the open for the bees to clean up. However, most of this honey was lost as wasps were licking the combs instead. Ilaria pointed out to me that the apiary

was completely surrounded by wild cannabis plants. There was one colony of bees in an old fashioned, vertical log hive, the top covered with thatched straw on which had been fixed a horse's skull. Apparently the skulls were commonly used to warn that an apiary was nearby as it has always been thought that bees had a dislike of these animals and would attack them.

Our evening meal was once again in a yurt set up near a river bank. I was told that we would have horse meat on this occasion and it appeared on the serving plates in cold slices, varying in darkness according to which part of the horse

A traditional log hive decorated with a horse's skull

it was from. Some of the slices had yellow fat at their edges which I avoided. I didn't like the idea of eating three-year-old horses, but in the event it was tasty and tender and reminded me of the cold mutton we used to eat at school. I noticed that many people were drinking large glasses of milk and I was finally persuaded to try some. The smell was abominable enough, but the small sip I took was far worse and made me gag. I will never, ever again drink mare's milk which has been fermented for three days in some animal's skin! I downed shot after shot of vodka after every toast but it didn't work. The taste of the milk lingered all night. The Kazakh dancers and singers were joined that night by a trio of beautiful Russians, in long colourful traditional dresses and shawls, whose unaccompanied songs were more to my liking.

The following morning when Ilaria and I were waiting for our interpreters we noticed that many people of all ages were carrying balloons

A stall at a Kazakhstan honey festival. The honey was decanted from milk churns

as they passed our hotel. It wasn't until a short while later when our bus was stopped by a policeman that we discovered that all the inhabitants of Ust Kamenogorsk were making for its centre to celebrate their 'City Day'. From every direction long columns of banner and flag-carrying people converged near the government buildings before taking seats in front of the main stage where officials would address the crowds.

This day had been chosen to coincide with the honey festival and a street over half a kilometre long had a continuous line of stalls selling honey and hive products, many of them five deep in customers waiting to be served. Most of the honey was from sunflower, the bright yellow honey glowing in the sunshine, though some honey from buckwheat and forest trees was available though only in small quantities. Most of the honey in jars was unlabelled, lots of honey was sold in coca cola bottles, and some of the women were scooping honey out of metal milk churns to fill any container they had to hand. Nevertheless, the honey was selling well at about three euros a kilo, and most shoppers had heavy-looking bags when they left the stalls.

On the other side of the street many women were selling tea, and between the tables samovars of all shapes and sizes with dark smoke coming out of the top provided a constant supply of hot water. As in the restaurants the tea was poured out of huge kettles to which milk had already been added.

Three stages had been set up in other parts of the street and for the whole day the city celebrated its diverse culture with dancing and singing, the performers wearing the traditional costumes of their birthplace. And, as it was a honey festival, myriads of young children, dressed in a variety of home-made bee costumes, waited to take the stage and perform the songs and dance routines they had been practising throughout the summer.

I was sad to leave Kazakhstan, sorry to leave almost all of this rapidly developing country unexplored. I wanted to see the huge wild nature reserve in the mountains near Altamy, where golden eagles fly, and the deep valleys from where not only some varieties of tulips and apple trees originated but also a recently-discovered species of honeybee – *Apis mellifera pomonella* – which had developed alongside the apple trees it pollinated. Voluntarily, Aleksandra spent an extra morning to show us more of the wonderful city; the new mosque, the new orthodox church, a new park full of walkways and magnificent plantings, a park with a street with full-sized furnished homes representative of different parts of the Soviet Union; everything looked perfect under the clear blue sky.

But we all knew that despite the new developments due to Kazakhstan's wealth of mineral and oil reserves, something of fundamental importance was lacking. It certainly wasn't the people, for there appeared to be no problems from differences of ethnicity or religion in the country. Indeed, in the nation's new capital, Astana, one building provided every faith in the country with its own place of worship, whose leaders met annually for a conference which benefitted them all. But Aleksandra knew what I was getting at when I asked her what she most wished for. Her answer was short and to the point: 'Clean, unpolluted air!'

If her wish were granted, Kazakhstan would become a paradise, though others might disagree because of the strained political situation. Whilst the long serving Head of State, the Supreme Chancellor Nursultan Nazarbayev is generally liked and has done a lot to improve both the economic situation and infrastructure in his country, he has the right to veto any legislation passed by the government and is known for his fierce intolerance of any opposition.

CHAPTER ELEVEN

Common Problems

WEATHER

In my first 25 years of beekeeping I was devastated when a colony of bees died out, for the simple reason that it was most likely due to lack of care on my part. Normally I would become aware of a dead or dying colony in early spring when few, or no bees at all, were flying from the hive, whilst bees from all the other colonies in the apiary were vigorously collecting pollen or water. A quick hive inspection might show that the colony had died of starvation, for masses of bees would be half-buried, head first into cells where they had succumbed once their food had run out; a truly horrible sight. It is easy to think that a colony provided with adequate stores in autumn would be safe from starvation until well into spring when plentiful forage would be available, but mild weather might promote more activity, or a strain of bee, particularly Italian, might react to an influx of food by continuing with egg laying, both of these scenarios reducing the amount of supplies available for winter.

The converse could also be true. By this I mean a long, hard winter, without a break in the weather, would prevent the bees from moving across to combs filled with honey, so they could die even though stores were plentiful. I have lost colonies two or three times for these reasons, but experience has made me aware of these problems which were usually put right by providing food at the right time and in the right part of the hive, ie, above the bees' cluster.

A more effective measure was my following Beowulf Cooper's advice on frame orientation, ie. having the frames the 'warm way' which helps to prevent bees dying from being isolated from their food stores. Occasionally, a mouse managed to get into a hive if a mouse guard at the entrance became detached – the mouse quietly eating away the stores, unbeknown to the bees which were in a tight cluster. In spring, instead of finding a live colony, I would find that the mouse had made a nest in the combs it had destroyed and in which it was rearing its offspring.

Sometimes I have lost the odd colony due to queen failure (usually because she was too old), or because the bees weren't strong enough to survive the winter. These losses are management problems which I took note of and made efforts to ensure they would not happen again.

American and European Foul Brood

Two diseases which beekeepers are constantly on the alert for are American and European Foul Brood – AFB and EFB. The names describe the foul smell which accompanies the dying and dead brood and the places where the diseases were given their titles. Both diseases are notifiable and the Ministry has officers who check out apiaries for their symptoms – usually visiting beekeepers every three years. However, this can be hit and miss as beekeepers do not have to be registered in the UK and not all of them belong to a beekeeping association, so the officials have no definitive list to work from.

AFB is the most contagious and should it be found then the contents of the hive – bees, frames and stores of honey – have to be burnt and the hives thoroughly sterilised with flame from a blow torch before they can be used again. The Ministry may allow EFB to be treated under their direct supervision. Bees become contaminated with the spores of these bacterial diseases through drifting from other diseased hives or robbing them – or cleaning out the remains of honey in jars discarded by householders – more of a risk if the honey had been imported. Beowulf Cooper said that during his time working for the Ministry he found that AFB was often found in areas around ports through which honey had been imported.

I had a fright once when a neighbour complained that my bees were flying around a pallet of buckets near his house. When I went to look, I saw that the lids had become loose during transport and that honey which had been imported for feeding horses had dribbled down the sides of the tubs giving my bees an easily collected source of food. For weeks I worried about my bees being infected with AFB spores which might have been in the honey, but fortunately, the symptoms never appeared. In some countries beekeepers use antibiotics such as Terramycin as a prophylactic annually to prevent foul brood. However, this can just mask the fact that the colonies have the diseases which can then inadvertently be transmitted to other colonies.

The EU will not allow the use of antibiotics for honeybee diseases as it can leave residues in honey. However, here in Greece, Terramycin can be bought without a prescription and some beekeepers undoubtedly use it. The EU a few years ago also banned the use of Fumidil B, an antibiotic used worldwide for the treatment of *Nosema apis*, a fungal disease which attacks the bee's gut and can seriously debilitate a colony – or even lead to its death. Recently, a newer deadlier strain of the fungus, *Nosema ceranae*, has started causing major problems for the beekeeping industry and there is a call for Fumidil B to be put back on the market. Not long after I started beekeeping, I learned that adding a very small amout of thymol to the bees' winter syrup feed also helped to prevent nosema and since then I have carried out this practice – so far with good effect.

I believe beekeepers would be more alert to disease problems within their hives if MAFF hadn't stopped the free adult bee disease service they used to offer. Every year, I would send about thirty bees from each of my hives to the MAFF laboratory to be checked. Normally, I would receive a report back from the ministry in a few days – always in my case saying the bees were healthy. Now the costs of the service are very expensive so fewer beekeepers send in samples on an annual basis.

Over the last ten years, and even more so recently, the situation regarding honeybee health has changed for the worse and it is common in many parts of the world for beekeepers to lose almost a third of their colonies annually. The difference is that, whereas a decade ago beekeepers wouldn't publicise the numbers of stocks which had died because it reflected on their ability to manage bees, the situation is now so common they are anxious to make the facts known so that something can be done to find out why the colonies are dying and thus prevent further losses. Government organisations, scientific institutes, university departments and many associations worldwide are trying to tackle the problem but so far, predictably, it seems that there is not a single cause that is at work, but a multiplicity of factors are responsible.

CAUSES OF COLONY DEATH

Undoubtedly, one of the chief suspects is varroa, a small brownish mite which parasitises both the developing pupae of the honeybee and the adult. Left untreated, a colony can succumb in three years. It spread rapidly through Europe, partly because in its early stages the mites are not easily detected and by the time their presence is evident in the hive it is often too late to do much about it. Varroa mites and the viruses they carry, have undoubtedly been the main cause of death to millions of bee colonies throughout the world.

Fortunately, one of our writers, Bernhard Mobus, gleaned all the information he could from German publications when the mite appeared in that country, so he was able to give us important information about the creature's *modus operandi*, how it could be detected and how colonies were treated to kill the mites, long before varroa was found in Devon on 14 April 1992. With the help of ministry officials, beekeepers had already started a search for the pest. In my apiary we used the common diagnostic test of smoking the hive with tobacco fumes, closing it for a short time then removing a paper insert to check for mites. MAFFs immediate response to the situation was to close off infested regions of England, prohibiting movement of bees between these and unaffected areas. However, this was a short term measure; the borders between areas kept changing. This had been the experience in other countries too.

Treating varroa

Beekeepers at home and abroad were looking for something to kill the pests and many home remedies were tried, including using the husks of almonds, the smoke from walnut leaves, and vegetable oils. Others tried

Varroa mites on a drone pupa within a closed cell

to import chemicals which were being used with some success abroad, though, on the whole, beekeepers were loathe to use such treatments as they were afraid that residues would end up in honey. Some desperate beekeepers even tried very potent acaricides which killed sheep ticks, or other veterinary medicants which were highly unsuitable for use in beehives.

My correspondent in Uzbekistan used a very lengthy and difficult procedure to kill the mites as he didn't want traces of chemicals in his honey. Once there was no brood in the hive he removed the queen and blew all the bees off the combs into a cylinder with holes big enough for the mites to fall through. The cylinder was put in a cabinet heated to 48°C and revolved for eight to ten minutes (to prevent the bees from clustering) during which time all the mites would fall from the bees and through the cylinder walls. Apparently, this was a common practice in some parts of the Soviet Union.

Like many beekeepers I put a sheet of drone foundation into one frame in every hive. The bees then constructed larger cells into which the queens laid unfertilised eggs that developed into drones. The female mite prefers to lay her eggs in drone cells as the longer pupation time of the drones (three days longer than worker bees) allows more mites to mature by the time the drones emerge. It was easy then to remove the sealed combs from the hive, thus removing many potential pests. The drone pupae did not have to be wasted – they are highly suitable for fishing bait and chickens relish them.

In the same year that varroa was detected, the first drug for treating varroa, Bayvarol, was licenced for use in England, followed by Apistan. Both are synthetic pyrethroid acaricides, compounded into plastic strips which are placed in the hive after honey has been removed. At the time of Bayvarol's launch, Bayer's veterinary representative allayed concerns that residues might remain in the wax or honey, the risk being so low that the analytical equipment currently in use had difficulty in quantifying it. This was a green light for the product and its use was widespread for over a decade until the mites built up resistance to flumethrin, the

Using a fork to uncap drone cells is one way to test for the presence of mites: or the drone comb can be cut out completely

active ingredient; in one experiment only 2% of the mites were knocked down. The same problem occurred with Apistan, the fluvalinate-based acaricide.

By the time mite resistance to Bayvarol had manifested itself, many beekeepers had turned away from relying on 'hard chemicals' and were adopting 'softer' natural control measures, including formic acid, oxalic acid and thymol. The acids, in order to achieve a complete kill, need to be applied in winter when there is no brood in the hive; they are one-shot treatments.

However, thymol crystals evaporate over a long period and therefore kill phoretic (free ranging) mites as well as those which are clinging to newly emerged bees. The precise

Natural thymol crystals (Apiguard here) are used by many beekeepers for varroa control

amount of crystals to use had always been problematic, but over ten years ago Vita-UK's Apiguard came on the market and has become a popular choice for varroa control.

Unlike the crystals, the product doesn't rely on vaporisation alone, for the bees clean out the gel from the trays and by doing so, as they travel through the hive, the mites are killed by contact. I have used Apiguard ever since it came on the market, though I have found that the effectiveness of the product depends on how good the bees are at house cleaning. In colonies of equal strength some trays of gel are completely cleared, in others varying amounts remain. Although Apiguard is available in most of the countries in Eastern Europe that I have visited, the beekeepers were all still using hard chemicals for varroa control, Apiguard being considerably more expensive.

Even 'soft' forms of treatment are not without hazards or are not suitable for all climates. A beekeeper near me who has a thousand colonies uses oxalic acid to eliminate varroa from his hives. At the time of treatment there may be two combs of brood in each hive, but although he knows the brood will be killed by the acidic fumes, he is willing to sacrifice them early in the year if it means his colonies are free from the pest. To ensure that no brood is present when oxalic acid is applied, many beekeepers cage the queen to prevent egg laying for about three weeks.

A cage I saw recently in Ukraine gives the queen the same amount of space to move around in a full-sized frame, but its width is restricted so that the bees cannot build comb within it. I suspect that this doesn't harm the queen much, as she would probably be laying fewer eggs when caged, but it is an extra safeguard in the war against varroa.

Unmated queens

A recent survey of queens sold in the United States showed that a very large proportion of queens were not fully mated and didn't perform as well as those a decade or so before. When a queen goes on a mating flight she seeks out an area where drones abound – a 'drone congregation' area. Unless she is flying in this zone she will be ignored; within it she will be mated several times on her first and subsequent visits until her spermetheca is full, giving her a lifetime's supply of sperm to fertilise her eggs. Chemicals for varroa control have been found to be responsible for reducing both sperm production in drones and the life-span of queens.

Additionally, the elimination of wild honey bees' nests and the loss of colonies due to varroa has lowered the number of drones available, leading to inbreeding and the laying of non-viable eggs by the queen. I have found that in the past three years many of my colonies have become queenless, within only a few months of being given a new young queen.

Other methods of pest control

Most beekeepers practise an integrated form of pest management; using the softer treatments along with other methods. Mesh floors, as opposed to solid ones, allow mites to fall through and if paper is placed beneath them, mite fall can be monitored. All my colonies now have mesh floors.

Floors with mesh screens allow the mites to fall through onto the ground, and being plastic, the floorboards do not rot and they are easy to clean

In summer I sprinkle sugar that has been ground in a coffee grinder between the frames of bees. This helps to dislodge a good number of mites. Finely ground sugar, or icing sugar, can also be used for a speedy check on the status of varroa in a colony. A heaped teaspoonful of it is placed into a glass jar with a mesh top through which mites can fall when it is upended. A sample of about a hundred bees from the middle of the brood nest are brushed into the jar – you have to be quick – and when the top is replaced the jar is shaken for a good two minutes, the dislodged mites falling out through the mesh top. I like this method as it doesn't harm the bees and they can be returned to the hive.

Selecting and breeding queens whose colonies show mechanisms for dealing with varroa is a significant long-term strategy for controlling the mites, and one which is steadily gaining ground. One strand of this work is breeding bees which groom themselves and others, removing the mites which then fall out of the hive if a mesh floor is fitted. Such bees also damage the mites by biting them.

Another characteristic that is being bred for is hygienic behaviour in honeybee colonies. Bees with this trait have the ability to detect problems with pupae and remove the wax cappings and eject them from the hive, thus limiting the numbers of varroa mites which breed in the cells.

Another varroa treatment: fine sugar is brushed on the bees and the mites lose their grip on them and fall through the mesh floor

205

American bee breeders are having considerable success with their Russian bee programme. The bees are from the Primorsky area of Russia where varroa jumped from its original Asian bee host to European bees. They have, over a very long period, been able to tolerate low populations of varroa within their colonies.

Despite all the strategies used against varroa, treatments 'hard' or 'soft', mechanical or management, as well as breeding programmes, their relative success has been unable to do as much as hoped, for an 'after shock' has occurred – the mites have contributed to many colonies being infected with a range of viral diseases which are responsible for many deaths and which have weakened the colonies; the bees ultimately become less resistant to problems they would normally cope with.

This has been exacerbated by factors in the environment, pollution of all types, monoculture (as bees need a variety of food sources to remain healthy), and the widespread use of agrochemicals. The beekeeper is not wholly blameless, for anything that is done which causes significant stress will be an additional strain on a colony.

Colony Collapse Disorder

Six years ago, my beekeeping friends and I lost 80% – 24 out of 30 – of my colonies, the losses coming unexpectedly towards the end of summer. Admittedly, this is probably the time of greatest stress for bees here as there is very little forage, the colony has become reduced in size as fewer eggs are being laid, and it is exceedingly hot. Hives which had been very active a couple of weeks before were completely empty or had just a handful of bees, yet patches of brood still had young bees emerging from them. In each case no queen was present and there was food left in the hive. There was no bad smell or any sign of disease and most surprisingly, the few colonies which were left avoided robbing the remaining stores of honey.

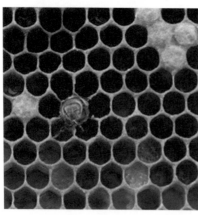

A common sight. Hives, even with food as above, become deserted. Only a few young bees struggle out of their cells

I was devastated. And embarrassed. How would I be able to explain to customers that there would be no honey because there were no bees? The only, but small, consolation was in knowing that this phenomenon was occurring in most parts of Europe and more so in the United States where in some cases beekeepers with hundreds of colonies were losing up to 98% of them. A global 'epidemic' of vast proportions was underway which was not only affecting the beekeeping industry but had a consequential effect on agriculture too, for many crops are dependent on honeybees for pollination. In California, where thousands of colonies are needed each year for the almond orchards, pollination fees offered by growers were increased five-fold to attract those beekeepers who still had good numbers of healthy stocks.

This enormous loss of bee colonies has become known as Colony Collapse Disorder and many resources have been piled into research worldwide to try to solve the problem. A particular virus was considered mainly responsible; then it was blamed on a new form of the fungal disease Nosema, which attacks the bee's digestive system; then agrichemicals were seen as the possible cause, and other forms of pollution. The investigation is on-going.

A clue to the causes may well be in a piece of US research which found that in 749 samples of wax, bee bread (pollen stored in the comb by bees), pollen trapped at the hive entrance, bees, and brood, over a hundred different types of pesticides and metabolites (metabolic derivatives) were found, in many cases the samples containing a cocktail of the chemicals.

Neonicotinoids

One group of insecticides, neonicotinoids, is alarming beekeepers and conservationists.

In the past when crop-spraying was being carried out, it was visible and beekeepers were forewarned. The use of neonicotinoids, however, is normally invisible, as the insecticides are used as a seed dressing. Almost all of the oil seed rape crop grown in the UK has this insidious treatment as does forage maize, which the bees collect pollen from, despite the fact that it is banned in several countries where it is known to have been the cause of the death of thousands of colonies.

Neonicotinoids work systemically; they are translocated to all parts of the plant and are therefore present in nectar and pollen. Studies in the UK on bumblebees show that they have a negative effect on their colonies especially regarding the production of the queens which will overwinter to start new nests the following year. The insecticides affect the nervous system of bees upsetting many of their actions including the interpreting of the dance language of other bees which gives information of the location of nectar and pollen sources. It also affects their ability to orientate and find their way home leading to a depletion in nest populations and storage of sufficient food reserves.

At the beginning of 2013 the European Food Safety Authority proposed a ban on the use of neonicotinoids on crops which were visited by bees, as an urgent precautionary measure, for a period of two years. Sadly, when the motion was put before the Parliament it was not carried, for although fourteen countries supported EFSA, nine countries voted against the measure whilst five others abstained. EFSA lodged an appeal and, on the second vote, much to the delight of beekeepers and conservationists, legislation was put in place to ban the three particularly toxic neonicotinoids which are believed to be harmful. The UK did not support the ban that will come into force in December 2013, although it is subject to the EU ruling. So the autumn-sown crop of oil seed rape will be the last to have its seed dressed with these insecticides. It must be remembered that the problem with neonicotinoids is not confined to bees, but affects *all* the organisms within the soil, and therefore also the higher forms of life, including humans. Once in the soil the pesticides remain there for a very long time poisoning plants and creatures which feed on them – and it was shocking to hear that the purveyors of these chemicals, at a recent Parliamentary Environmental Audit enquiry, were unable to give precise information on the longevity of their products once in the ground.

Other colony pollutants

Insecticides, fungicides and acaricides for the control of varroa are not the only pollutants in colonies. Wax moth caterpillars are responsible for destroying millions of honeycombs in store each year as they feed

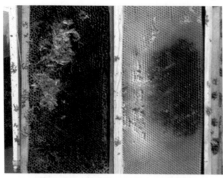

on the cells from which bees have emerged, leaving behind layers of their papery cocoons. The traditional way of dealing with this problem has been the sprinkling of paradichlorobenzine (PDB) on the tops of the frames and wrapping the boxes in newspaper.

However, as wax is absorbent, hence its use in the cosmetic and pharmaceutical industries, PDB residues can be found in the wax, no matter how much airing the combs

Wax moth caterpillars prefer the older, darker combs which have the remains of many empty cocoons

are given in spring. Furthermore, it is carcinogenic. I stopped using PDB over thirty years ago as it gave me violent headaches, and there are other ways of dealing with wax moth.

About five years ago, one of Greece's wholesale honey sellers had to remove vast amounts of its products from supermarket shelves as they were contaminated with PDB. Surprisingly, this year I noticed that an eminent writer in an American bee journal was still recommending this form of control for wax moths, despite the fact that it is dangerous and its use has been discontinued in other countries. The problem of absorption of pesticides and volatile substances like PDB is that it is compounded by the beekeepers' practice of melting down old combs and taking the blocks to wax plants for recycling into new sheets of foundation. A beekeeper supplying colonies with such wax starters is giving the bees already contaminated wax which can be harmful to them.

Honey combs stacked in racks in the light are seldom attacked by wax moths. Combs can also be protected by refrigeration or spraying with B401

Beekeepers are constantly on the alert for new organisms and larger pests which might endanger their colonies, fearing particularly that problems which exist in other parts of the world might turn up in their own apiaries, as did varroa.

Currently, the UK is in line for an invasion of large Asian hornets which are already in Brittany and could easily cross the Channel should a queen hitch a ride on any means of transport. The hornets are extremely aggressive and can quickly destroy a colony of bees it decides to attack. I sympathise with these beekeepers, for I have my own problems with the oriental hornet which is present in great numbers in the south of Greece. From August onwards the hornets will fly constantly around my hives and sieze bees from the front of the hives or try to get inside to get at the stores of honey. Very occasionally, a group of bees will surround a hornet until it is in the middle of the mêlée and either dies of asphyxiation or through the heat generated by the bees' bodies.

I have tried all the usual means of trapping hornets by tempting them with various mixtures of sweet substances or fish (if they require protein for their grubs) with some, but not great success. My efforts now are being put into a special deep hive floor covered with mesh with holes at the sides and back through which the hornets can get in, attracted by the smell of the hive contents. Once inside the trap the hornets cannot get into the hive nor emerge, as the cone-shaped entrances prevent it. I have based this easily-made trap on a more complicated one developed by French and Greek beekeeping scientists in an effort to solve the problem of the Asian hornets in other parts of southern Europe.

A problem which was of great concern to organic farmers, beekeepers and a good proportion of the public, was the sowing of trial plots of genetically-modified crops. The plots soon became the targets of environmental campaigners, or 'eco-warriors'. There was a great fear of the new technology, a Frankenstein future brought about by scientists messing with nature. Two of the GM crops which affected beekeepers were oil seed rape and maize, the former a main source of food for honeybees, the latter providing bees with pollen in summer when there was a dearth of other flowers. One important point of contention was that the distance between trial plots and conventional crops, judged to be safe by scientists to prevent cross pollination, was ridiculously low and could lead to unwanted hybrid plants – and if these happened to be oil seed rape, then 'super weeds' would develop, as the GM rape was Roundup resistant.

Anyone who has lived or travelled in the east of England will know that the main routes to the oil crushing mills are easy to discern, for along the roadsides and between the carriageways of arterial roads, oil seed rape plants grow in abundance, the very fine seed being easily shed from the lorries. The same scenario could occur with GM rape, except it would be difficult to control and it could hybridise with conventional crops over a large area.

Beekeepers were concerned that GM pollen from maize or rape could end up in their honey, a product they valued as being pure and wholesome and would not be welcomed by the public if it contained any GM material. It would also mean that the possibility of the honey having come from a GM source would need to be added to the label, a definite 'put-off' to some shoppers. The government drew a line under this; any GM component, they said, would be so minuscule that it wouldn't warrant such a notice; there was no possibility of hive products being significantly contaminated. However, they were undoubtedly unaware of the fact that many beekeepers harvest and sell pollen which has been scraped off the bees' legs when they pass through a trap placed at the entrance to the hive, which people actually consume in relatively large amounts as a health supplement.

I think most beekeepers were on the side of the activists, and our

BKQ environmental correspondent, Geoff Hopkinson, who was recently awarded a BEM, was to act as an expert witness in the defence of the saboteurs, but the case was dismissed just before the trial was due to open. However, GM technology and its use hasn't just been criticised for its effect on the environment, for it is seen by many as an example of corporate greed and global exploitation, with those who throw in their lot with the conglomerates being tied in to buy their seed and the chemicals needed for plant protection. Many people are tired of the argument that GM crops are needed to feed the world's increasing population for research has shown that almost half of the food produced is spoilt and uneaten – not only that, but a considerable amount of the resources being put into crop production, distribution and preparation of food have therefore been wasted.

Hungary has just destroyed 1,000 hectares of GM maize which was grown illegally. Countries within Europe that allow the cultivation of GM crops have recently been told by the EU that all products with any trace of GM components should carry a label indicating the fact on the food containers. This has come as a big blow to German beekeepers for they are extremely worried about the effect it might have on their honey sales. Developing countries which have tried hard to meet EU standards for honey quality are not exempt from this ruling if they wish to export their honey to EU countries. What was feared over fifteen years ago has come about at last for the UK's Minister for the Environment, Mr Owen Paterson, has stated that he wants his country to be at the forefront of the new technology.

Self-help for beekeepers

Whilst an enormous amount of research is being carried out to solve the problems which are affecting beekeeping, what are beekeepers themselves doing? Quite a lot, in fact. Essentially, many beekeepers are using non-chemical ways of treating their varroa-stricken colonies. Additionally, those who are worried about the quality of beeswax foundation are instead using small starter-strips of wax in the frames for bees to build on, the wax gleaned from the newly-produced cappings of combs which are obtained during honey extraction. Others are willing to pay extra for unpolluted wax foundation from companies like Biecologic Beeswax started by Ilaria (an Italian beekeeping student of mine) and her husband who are importing wax from Africa, their analysis showing that the wax is free from the 200 most likely chemicals that can occur in the environment.

More and more beekeepers like Ilaria Baldi, above, are using top-bar hives which are simple, cheap to make and the bees build their combs naturally

There has also been an upsurge in sustainable beekeeping, where bees are managed with minimum inputs from the beekeeper, the colonies being allowed to produce all the wax that is needed for their own needs even though it might have a slight effect on overall honey production. These colonies are also disturbed less often than in normal beekeeping which causes them far less stress. One particular group of beekeepers use the Warre Hive, or The People's Hive, which was developed in France by Abbé Emile Warré. He claimed that of all the 350 hives he tested, this was the most natural one for the bees. Many others, even some commercial beekeepers in the United States, keep bees in top-bar hives. Functionally, they are similar to the top-bar hives used by Greek beekeepers centuries ago, in that the bees build their combs on laths of wood in a hive that has walls sloping inwards towards the base. Modern top-bar hives usually have room for twenty combs and at the end of the season both the wax and honey are harvested so the bees are always producing new comb each season, which is healthier for the colony.

However, whether beekeepers are falling back on more traditional methods or continuing to work in the conventional way, good husbandry is of paramount importance.

Divining

Recently I was sent a book on beekeeping to review, in which the author claimed that he had found the way to save honeybee colonies from extinction and that it was simple to carry out and wouldn't cost any beekeeper a penny. In fact all the equipment that beekeepers needed was a wire coat-hanger and the shells of two biros to make a pair of divining rods. Bees, he said, chose places to nest where the divining rods crossed, as the earth's vibrations helped the bees to flourish and would even rid the colonies of varroa. All his hives sited in these places were doing well, he wrote, but there was no supportive evidence to back his claims. It was not possible, either, for beekeepers to visit the apiaries for security reasons.

One day, with time on my hands, I made some divining rods to put his theory to the test, with surprising results...

Having an hour or two free one day, I made some divining rods to put his theory to the test. I had another beekeeper with me at the time and, holding the rods, I walked slowly to where two swarms had nested in decoy hives that I had set up around my garden.

Decoy hives need to be dark inside, with a smallish opening and to have a few old combs in them to attract swarms and ideally should be about four metres above the ground. Unlike the other bait hives, the two occupied ones were on stands less than two metres high. In each case, the rods moved from their parallel position and crossed over each other. I was very surprised since no other part of the garden had any effect on the rods. I repeated the experiment in my friend's apiary and as we approached the oak tree onto which the bees had swarmed both that and the previous year, the rods moved rapidly across each other. That this happened, though, is inconclusive as far as the theory is concerned, for bees seldom nest in the place where they first cluster; it is merely a stopping-off point. I am a natural cynic, but I was flabbergasted nevertheless. Whilst so far I had found examples of bees swarming to a particular location I would want to carry out many more experiments to see if it was a common occurrence and, as for finding out if the same locations were ideal for a colony's health and performance, I would need years of testing to validate the author' claims.

Increase in beekeepers

Normally, when major problems beset a sector of agriculture there is a downward trend in people wishing to take it up – or, like the current problems in the dairy industry, some would like to quit it altogether. This has not been the case with beekeeping. The well-publicised decline of bees due to the millions of colony losses globally and its effect on food production has captured the attention of the public, many of whom want to or have already taken up beekeeping 'to save the planet'. The latter refers to the spurious statement purported to have been uttered by Einstein that without bees the world would end in four years. The ranks of beekeeping associations have swollen to such an extent that some are even forced to put would-be beekeepers on waiting lists for courses.

Currently, city beekeeping is becoming the new trend, with its exponents pointing out that bees in the city do better than their country cousins as they have a slightly warmer climate and have a vast range of trees and plants to forage on in the many parks, gardens and along the streets. Honey yields, prospective beekeepers have been told, could be expected to be high and sell at premium prices with London honey selling in some places not long ago for nearly £20 a jar, and not enough to meet the demand.

On the downside, central London's air is very polluted, so much so that the scent of a range of flowers is undetected by bees, which reduces foraging. Furthermore, whilst bees are able to filter out some of the pollutants in the honey, heavy metals are concentrated in the pollen which they feed directly to developing larvae, or indirectly when it is converted by the bees' mouth glands into royal jelly. These pollutants, and any others that the bees pick up, especially pesticides commonly used by gardeners, can upset the fine balance of micro flora and fauna in the bees' gut, with disastrous consequences for the colony.

I am pleased that so many people are interested in the welfare of bees and want to take up the craft, but I want those colonies to thrive. As I know to my cost, with forty years of beekeeping behind me, the task, sometimes, is apparently awesome. If politicians and government officials become more pro-active in caring for its countryside and its wildlife and pay less heed to the lobbying of global agrochemical companies, whose only interest is increased profits, beekeepers would be able to look forward to a more promising future.

Afterword

I would never describe myself as a 'master of bees' but I have enjoyed the good fortune of being able to work in my apiaries for over forty years carrying out the necessary seasonal tasks to the best of my ability, with enthusiasm and pleasure. I will never tire of opening a hive and removing frames to see how a colony is progressing. Unthreatened, given a little smoke and gentle handling, the bees continue working at their various jobs, allowing me to view the intricacies of their social life. Each examination is unique, revealing not only the behaviour of the bees themselves, but also the sensory and aesthetic dimensions: the kaleidoscopic patterns of different coloured pollens packed in their hexagonal cells, the glistening patches of fresh nectar, and the aromatic scents of the colony.

My fascination with bees has also provided me with many avenues which I have been able to pursue as part of my family life, my career as a teacher, my leisure-time as a photographer, writer and traveller. Significantly, too, my involvement with bees has played an important part in times of poor health brought about by my bi-polar problem, for time spent in the tranquillity of the apiary has a beneficial calming effect which alleviates the severity of my moods.

My contact with beekeepers in many parts of the world has confirmed my belief that nationalism and parochialism are unnecessary. Beekeeping is an industry and a hobby in all parts of the world: it transcends all barriers of race, gender, religion, ageism and status, for beekeepers all share the same goals and problems. Only by co-operating with each other are we able to share knowledge and techniques which will help bees and honey production everywhere, especially now when they are facing so many problems.

I gave some thought to the title of this book. Progress is not always linear, diversions can occur and circumstances can knock you backwards. My aims in beekeeping have changed over the years and now I am content just to have a few colonies, produce a sufficient amount of honey, try out new techniques, disseminate the knowledge of our correspondents in our journal, and help other beekeepers either practically or in an advisory way. In fact, in this my 65th year, I am departing, not from writing or beekeeping, but from many of the conventional beekeeping practices that I have carried out during my time as a beekeeper. This Spring I will complete the conversion of Langstroth hives to top bar hives, so goodbye to buying wax foundation and frames, and the tedious job of wiring them ready for use in the hive. Each year my bees will give me honey in the comb – comb built by them alone, fresh each year, so pure and without chemicals. This can be harvested a comb at a time, so that the changing flavour of the honey can be savoured when bees move from one main forage source to another. The honey can be eaten in the comb or pressed out, so it will be goodbye to the honey extractor and the messy and sticky job of uncapping the wax before the honey is spun out. With no combs to store, I will not have to worry about them being destroyed by wax moths; once the bees have cleaned the remaining honey from the remnants of wax left on the top-bars, they can easily be stored away in a moth-proof bag as they take up very little space. In essence then, a return to the simple type of Greek beekeeping that was practised here centuries ago.

My interest in apitherapy has recently been aroused by the treating of our border collie, Meg, with royal jelly. This was advised by our vet, who has a good knowledge of beekeeping, to help the nerve damage in her back which makes it difficult sometimes for her to get up on her hind legs – we have noticed an improvement. He could have prescribed an expensive drug, but he is not motivated by money and he knew we had access to the bee product. I look forward to the increased use of hive products in medicine for they can be effective against many types of illness. There is an urgent need for research in the field of apitherapy so that cheap pharmaceuticals from these naturally occurring substances can be produced to take over from the expensively marketed and aged antibiotics to which so many disease organisms have become resistant.

I will have the chance to travel further afield or entertain in our home writers for the magazine I have never met in person. So many important facets of beekeeping can be picked up during face-to-face conversations, personal views which often throw new light on a local or national situation, which might never be divulged in a written report.

My adventures in the world of beekeeping would have been impossible without the help and support of my wife, Val, who has given me constant encouragement and has joined me in innumerable activities including the running of our honey business and the tedious job of proof reading each issue of the BKQ. Without complaining too much, our children have put up with disruptions to their weekends and holidays when beekeeping events have taken them away from home. I have never actively encouraged them to take up beekeeping, though they are knowledgeable about many aspects of the craft. Perhaps our grandchildren, who show all the signs of being interested in nature, may be tempted to help me here in my apiary in Greece where the bees are very gentle. The world needs a new generation of young beekeepers; young people with a genuine concern for the environment who see their role as putting to right the many mistakes of the past and who have the courage to stand up and fight for what they think, regardless of the effect this may have on their own aspirations. A countryside fit for bees – such a big challenge – but with many rewards.